Protecting Liberty in an Age of Terror

The BCSIA Studies in International Security book series is edited at the Belfer Center for Science and International Affairs (BCSIA) at Harvard University's John F. Kennedy School of Government and is published by The MIT Press. The series publishes books on contemporary issues in international security policy, as well as their conceptual and historical foundations. Topics of particular interest to the series include the spread of weapons of mass destruction, internal conflict, the international effects of democracy and democratization, and U.S. defense policy.

A complete list of BCSIA Studies appears at the back of this volume.

Protecting Liberty in an Age of Terror

Philip B. Heymann
Juliette N. Kayyem

BCSIA Studies in International Security

The MIT Press
Cambridge, Massachusetts
London, England

This book was typeset in Palatino by Sarah B. Buckley at the Belfer
Center for Science and International Affairs and bound in the United
States of America.

MIT Press books may be purchased at special quantity discounts for
business or sales promotional use. For information, please email
special_sales@mitpress.mit.edu or write to Special Sales Department,
The MIT Press, 55 Hayward Street, Cambridge, MA 02142.

Library of Congress Cataloging-in-Publication Data

Heymann, Philip B.
Protecting liberty in an age of terror / Philip B. Heymann,
Juliette N. Kayyem.
p. cm.—(BCSIA studies in international security)
The edited report of the Long-Term Legal Strategy Project for Preserving
Security and Democratic Freedoms in the War on Terrorism.
Includes bibliographical references.
ISBN 0-262-08343-4 (alk. paper)—ISBN 0-262-58257-0 (pbk.: alk. paper)
1. Civil rights—United States. 2. War on Terrorism, 2001–
3. National security—United States 4. Terrorism—Prevention—
Government policy—United States 5. United States—Politics and gov-
ernment—2001– I. Kayyem, Juliette N. II. Title. III. Series.

JC599.U5H43 2005
323.44'0973—dc22

2005047923

10   9   8   7   6   5   4   3   2

Contents

Acknowledgments

It has now been several years since the terrorist attacks of September 11, 2001. At times, it seems the United States has been in one exhausting marathon since that day. In its memory, or to avoid a repetition, wars have been fought, fundamental changes in domestic and international law have occurred, new institutions have been created, and unprecedented practices have been adopted.

Even before 9/11, America often struggled with the tension between security and liberty. The suspension of habeas corpus during the Civil War, the internment of Japanese-Americans during WWII, or domestic spying on anti-war and civil rights protesters during the Vietnam War—and the return to a more typical relationship between government and its citizens after each crisis—suggests that the balance can swing wildly. The point is that it cannot swing permanently.

This book is the culmination of an effort to explore how American democracy can thrive best in a "war on terror." In 2003, it became clear to us that the effort against the terrorist threat could be very long. It also became clear, by that time, that the president had been asserting warlike powers with few checks and little oversight by Congress and the courts. It was then that we decided that bringing together a group of experts in a variety of professional fields related to terrorism, from the left and the right, might provide a good opportunity to establish criteria that should govern a long-term effort against such a new kind of threat.

So, we brought them together. With financial backing from the Memorial Institute for the Prevention of Terrorism, the Long-Term Legal Strategy Project for Preserving Security and Democratic Freedoms in the War on Terrorism came into being. The commission held three two-day meetings over eighteen months with senior counterterrorism experts, most of whom had served in the U.S. government. We invited counterterrorism experts from the United Kingdom who have dealt with their threat, however different, of terrorism and who have learned from successes and failures. In those meetings, we discussed specific substantive topics in a variety of areas, focusing on the details that make so much of this "balancing" difficult.

All members of the Board of Advisors, acknowledged in appendix C, agreed that it was necessary to evaluate the legal terrain governing the "war on terrorism." This book is in many respects a distillation of views and opinions based on honest and difficult discussions during our meetings. The advisors have, from time to time, been offered the opportunity to express views or to make suggestions relating to the matters included in our discussions, but have been under no obligation to do so. We are, ultimately, solely responsible for the final analysis herein. Any faults that remain are the responsibility of the authors. We are, however, grateful for our advisors' tremendous insights and input.

This book is similar to a report by the Long-Term Legal Strategy Project published in November 2004. There are significant editorial changes. We have also tried to update our analysis based on a number of disclosures and court cases in the interim. These are most apparent in the chapters on coercive interrogation and detention standards.

Over the course of this project, we became indebted to a number of people. We sought the advice of colleagues throughout, and we thank them for their input. The team at the Memorial Institute—General Dennis J. Reimer, Donald R. Hamilton, and James "Chip" O. Ellis III—were exceptional partners. Meredith Tunney was a patient project director, able and committed throughout this entire process. Ben Lambert provided indispensable input and organization to this entire effort. Tom Lue and Tom Parker provided exceptional research and assistance; their work is highlighted in the appendixes. Susan Lynch served as our able and willing editor on the report.

We would also like to thank Sean Lynn-Jones and Sarah Buckley for their help with the editing of this book. They turned a report into a polished book and were incredibly helpful throughout. We are indebted to them.

Ann Heymann and David Barron, simply, thank you.

One final note: Our recent experience with the heated debate around the possibility of a legislative solution to the conflicts over highly coercive interrogation convinces us that the gulf is deep and wide between warring views of those most deeply concerned about democratic freedoms and those most fearful of the threat to our safety and security. Our hope has always been to find a place where the two sides can meet, where Congress can finally speak, and where we can preserve our security and our freedoms simultaneously. Our hope is still that we can do that before the next attack when, we fear, government authority will break free of all remaining constraints of democratic processes and laws—the wise constraints that make us free.

—Philip B. Heymann
Cambridge, Massachusetts

—Juliette N. Kayyem
Cambridge, Massachusetts
March 2005

Introduction

"The law spoke too softly to be heard amidst the din of arms."
—Plutarch, Lives: Caius Marius

"At our first public hearing on March 31, 2003, we noted the need for balance as our government responds to the real and ongoing threat of terrorist attacks. The terrorists have used our open society against us. In wartime, government calls for greater powers, and then the need for those powers recedes after the war ends. This struggle will go on. Therefore, while protecting the homeland, Americans should be mindful of threats to vital personal and civil liberties. This balancing is no easy task, but we must constantly strive to keep it right.

"Recommendation: The burden of proof for retaining a particular governmental power should be on the executive, to explain (a) that the power actually materially enhances security and (b) that there is adequate supervision of the executive's use of the powers to ensure protection of civil liberties. If the power is granted, there must be adequate guidelines and oversight to properly confine its use."

—Final Report of the National Commission on Terrorist Attacks upon the United States (*The 9/11 Commission Report*)

What We Have Attempted

It is difficult to remember what the United States of America was like before September 11, 2001. The date itself, now simply referred to as 9/11, represents more than the terrorist attacks on the World Trade Center and the Pentagon and the crashing of a fourth aircraft into a field in Somerset, Pennsylvania. It has come to represent the day that the United States fundamentally changed—when military-scale violence returned to U.S. shores and when distant lands and different religions began to have far greater implications for the safety of those within American borders.

Those changes also altered the powers and authorities that the president would claim and use in the course of protecting the United States and its citizens. A "war on terrorism" was based on the premise that this form of attack on the United States required a different, more aggressive response than had been used in dealing with most of America's historic dangers.

This book examines one particular, yet significant, aspect of the U.S. response to terrorism—the fundamental changes in domestic and international laws and accepted practices that have occurred since 9/11. While agreeing that a rapid response to an urgent problem was required, we now seek to recommend to policymakers the rules and procedures that should govern the U.S. legal system's response to terrorism for decades to come.

We focus on three different but overlapping areas of law and practice that are most relevant today. First, we examine which rules should apply to the "Executive Abroad" in those areas of conduct, such as coercive interrogation, that are often not constrained by domestic constitutional or statutory norms but have been the subject of international law. Second, we examine which rules should apply to the "Executive at Home," assessing the needs and risks accompanying such actions as the collection and analysis of masses of commercial or other nongovernmental data and the surveillance of religious and political groups. Finally, we discuss which rules will establish and ensure "A System of Accountability." In this last section, we examine ways in which oversight and review can be better institutionalized in a legal regime addressing national security threats.

We are, in many ways, not saying anything terribly unique when we argue that the fight against the terrorist threat should not undermine democratic norms. The government and its critics both concur on this point. Governmental and nongovernmental task forces, Government Accountability Office (GAO) reports, and, of course, the 9/11 Commission's important recommendations all concur as well. But the details of what the balance between security, liberty, and democracy should be have too often been left vague. The announcement that American values must be balanced with security is often merely that: a statement of principle that does not provide the specifics needed to resolve the difficult issues that arise in any attempt to strike that delicate balance.

This book seeks to provide those specifics. The recommendations are quite detailed, providing a framework for Congress and executive policymakers to use in an attempt to institutionalize and oversee some of the extraordinary measures required in response to the terror threat. We explicitly note where others have ventured into this area, most specifically the 9/11 Commission, and we try to use their findings as a launching point for new legislative action. The recommendations are followed by commentary that provides legal, policy and comparative context for our findings, a context too often lacking in public discussions today.

Since the project that produced this book first convened, much has happened in the world: the continuing war in Iraq, the events at Abu Ghraib prison, Supreme Court decisions on the status of detainees, the release of *The 9/11 Commission Report*, and a U.S. presidential election. We have purposefully tried to avoid responding to the news of the moment, as our enterprise—both nonpartisan and long-term—is intended to provide guidance for the years to come. Obviously, we were not immune to current events or changing legal standards, but our purpose was to remain relevant and useful, regardless of current events.

Our basic premise is that the practices developed in the first three years of a threat that may be with us for decades have too often given insufficient weight to concerns about democratic freedoms, human rights, lawfulness and international relations. The practices that we are examining—to assess whether the security that they provide justifies their effects on democratic liberties and other critical values—include:

- Asserting a broad power by the executive, on the basis of findings unreviewed by Congress, to kill, detain, imprison and coercively interrogate;

- Claiming new executive powers to increase intrusion into private areas;

- Developing ways unregulated by Congress to collect and then "mine" vast sources of commercial or other privately acquired and held information;

- Investigating in ways that increase the risk of inhibiting free speech or association; and

- Taking certain investigative or security measures on the basis of ethnicity or religion.

In the first three years after the 9/11 attacks, the United States also too often gave insufficient weight to the demands of broader international concerns. The issues here, too, are real and specific:

- If the United States adopts a certain practice, will U.S. citizens be subject to similar treatment in a way that is regarded as unacceptable?

- Will the adopted practices spread more widely to less democratic states, and will U.S. credibility to complain of abuses be reduced, thus lowering international standards undesirably?

•Or will the practices, rather, result in a new, better and more realistic form of international understanding?

•As a result of the reaction to U.S. actions, will it be more difficult— or even impossible—to achieve what the United States intended to achieve because others will not cooperate, either by flatly refusing cooperation or by merely going through the motions of cooperation?

•Will U.S. actions result in a negative reaction by others that may have a longer term, more general, deleterious effect on U.S. foreign relations?

•Will U.S. actions hinder long-term foreign policy aims of encouraging political and economic freedom abroad?[1]

Our approach is to demonstrate that it is possible to consider and shape new rules and practices that simultaneously address national security, democratic liberties at home, legality and human rights abroad, and broader foreign policy interests. That goal should not be beyond the capacity of the governing institutions of the United States. We are thus proposing a rejection of both of the extremes that have characterized the debate since 9/11. We agree that U.S. practices at home and abroad had to, and have to, change to reflect the threats of far more dangerous terrorism than previously seen. We reject, however, the notion that those dangers warrant a major shift in the country's historical balance among legislative authority, judicial powers, individual rights and executive authority. It is not possible to have minimal risk from terrorism and absolutely maximally protected freedoms, but it is possible to preserve 90 percent of what concerns each camp. It is also possible for legislation to strike a detailed and thoughtful balance between these unattainable absolutes that will endure over the decades ahead. That is what we hope to demonstrate.

The threat that the United States faces and options for dealing with it have analogies. America's closest ally, the United Kingdom, has wrestled with somewhat similar issues for thirty-five years. Recognizing that there was much to learn from this experience, we made British counterterrorism experts a critical part of the task force. Their insights are reflected throughout the commentary, as well as in the appendices. Recognizing differences is as important as seeing analogies. In every age in which a balance between security and freedom has been struck in the United States—and in every age some such balance has been struck—the particular context in which the debate occurred has also mattered. It should be no different now; the United States cannot simply adopt the practices of

---

1. The authors are indebted to Paul Lettow (Harvard Law School, '05) for his work in this area.

the Civil War, of World War II, or of the United Kingdom's struggle against Irish Republican Army (IRA) terrorism.

The public would be better served if those leading the fights on one side or the other acknowledged this more than they presently do. Terrorism after 9/11 is not "just" in the mold of Oklahoma City bomber Timothy McVeigh, given its transnational character and the potential for a single terrorist act to kill many thousands of people. On the other hand, this is not the era of anarchist bombings. This is neither the Cold War nor a time of war involving a powerful and hostile state. Our debate over the balance that needs to be struck is occurring in light of a peculiar and dangerous threat, emanating largely from a particular region and involving specific tactics, and the U.S. response has the potential to significantly alter the rights of individuals abroad and here at home—particularly of nationalities or ethnic and religious groups within the United States.

Furthermore, the comprehensive USA PATRIOT Act, which immediately gave the government broad, new authorities, was passed in response to a largely undefined threat from a poorly understood source. The sunset stipulation of a number of the act's provisions in 2005 calls for a broad re-examination of what are and what are not defensible practices in light of the experience of the intervening years.

The Structure of Our Proposals

Our recommendations are designed to address systematically a set of six questions that have always been considered fundamental to U.S. democracy:

1. To what extent should particular executive powers depend on legislative authorization?

2. What should those standards be for each of the very dangerous powers claimed in the effort to prevent very dangerous forms of terrorism?

3. Who should apply those standards?

4. Who should review the application of the standards—congressional committees, specialized or ordinary federal courts, or administrative review bodies such as inspectors general or the Department of Justice?

5. Should the standards applied by the executive branch be made known to the public?

6. How long should new powers last?

Whether one calls U.S. efforts a war or not, the nature of the threat now faced will inevitably call for more aggressive actions by the president and executive agencies. Policing, intelligence gathering, diplomacy and military action will all be necessary components to disrupt potential attacks in the United States and abroad. The recognition that the president will often be in charge is, however, neither a conclusion that the other branches of the government should remain silent nor an acknowledgement that standards, procedures, and institutional accountability should be left to the sole discretion of the president.

Each of these questions ought to be, and can be, answered. As we framed our answers to these questions, we remained cognizant of three very important criteria: accountability, transparency, and accurate reassessments.

First, throughout, we address the issue of accountability, a matter particularly relevant for a long-term legal strategy. We have sought to develop some form of review over executive judgment on all occasions, though the content of that review differs depending on the context. Sometimes, a familiar federal court is most appropriate, whether issuing a warrant or reviewing detention under habeas corpus jurisdiction. In other contexts, a specialized court may be better suited to address questions of national security and confidentiality. In some instances, congressional oversight may be most appropriate. In one way or another, a system of accountability to other institutions must be developed if the country is to fully honor a system of divided, shared powers.

Sharing executive responsibilities and powers with the Congress and courts has long been a contentious issue in the area of national security. Whichever party has been in power, the president has often insisted that his powers are either inherent or explicitly granted by the U.S. Constitution and therefore cannot be regulated or even monitored. One successful way of resolving the dispute among the branches of the federal government has been for Congress to legislate and for the president to state his continued claim of inherent power while still signing the legislation and adopting its procedures (the War Powers Resolution is an example). This may be a wise way to resolve disputes over constitutional powers when there is general agreement on the substantive content of our recommendations.

Second, the core principle of the U.S. government is that ultimate accountability is and must remain in the hands of an informed citizenry. We, the authors, recognize that secrecy and confidentiality are sometimes necessary components of specific steps to combat a terrorist threat. We believe that the United States cannot, however, allow new legal powers or extralegal practices to exist in total secrecy. Whatever the rules or practices are that govern or define the exercise of a particular power, they should be available for debate by Congress and the public, unless a very convincing reason requires otherwise. Authorization of new investigatory powers demands serious debate, and attempts to pass such proposals hidden in large omnibus spending bills with little or no public debate and little or no time for reflection by the country does a disservice to citizens. At the same time, however, transparency does not necessarily include knowing the details of a particular mission or the application of those rules to specific individuals. The specific operations can not always be transparent, but the system that the United States is operating under should be.

The most dangerous secrecy may be a form that has become far too common after 9/11. For some of the issues that we highlight, we exist in a legal state where a certain practice is occurring, but where there are no rules or guidance other than internal, often secret, and sometimes incomplete rules within the executive branch. Specifically, the traditional ban against the use of assassination by U.S. personnel or persons acting as agents of the United States appears now to have greatly reduced legal or geographic constraints and with essentially no congressional oversight in the context of counterterrorism activity. A serious review of whether the assassination ban is still relevant is an appropriate discussion to have. More important, however, is a serious review of what kind of controls and standards the United States should institutionalize to ensure that there is a system of oversight and accountability regarding this most permanent of options.

We have been willing to recommend granting and then regulating powers that are new and that sometimes infringe on traditional notions of the rights of citizens, aliens and states. The passage of time could show that the United States can safely return to tradition. It could also show that the proposals have been unacceptably stretched or abused—or have added too little to the effectiveness of counterterrorism to warrant their continuation.

Thus, third and finally, inherent in our final recommendation is the notion that there should be some mechanism for determining whether, in fact, extraordinary powers granted to deal with the aftermath of 9/11 are indeed working. In the USA PATRIOT Act, a number of provisions have sunset stipulations, set to expire very soon. Given the nature of the threat that the United States faces today, for all additional extraordinary measures delineated in this book, a five-year sunset provision gives ample opportunity for the government to assess the danger and, if it continues, to show that the new authorities recommended are still necessary. Broad new executive powers should not be allowed to survive any longer than the extraordinary danger that justifies them. In the United Kingdom, a number of extraordinary provisions will lapse in the next few years. Independent assessors of counterterrorism legislation are expected to provide guidance to the legislature and the public to determine whether a measure is still appropriate. Public commentary is welcome and read, as the United Kingdom attempts to determine what balance is most appropriate given their unique democratic structure. The United States ought to adopt similar measures and should not gamble unnecessarily with the balance of powers and the respect for individual rights that have shaped U.S. democracy for more than two hundred years.

Important Choices Defining the Scope of Our Recommendations

The importance of defining rules for a "war on terror" is that such a "war" is limitless in duration and place. Thus choices must be made in order to confine the nature of authorities allowed. As part of a mandate to create a long-term legal strategy, it is essential that lines be drawn rationally and with some sensitivity to the nature of the threat the United States faces.

THE INDIVIDUALS AND LOCATION OF ACTIVITIES COVERED
Throughout U.S. national security law, as well as rules with regard to law enforcement powers, the coverage of any set of protections has depended principally on two factors: whether the targeted individual is a U.S. person (a citizen or resident alien) and whether the governmental activity occurs within the United States. Granting greater protection to U.S. persons wherever they may be and to all persons regardless of their citizenship within the United States is more than parochial or political. Great executive powers always bear the grave political risk of being used to punish either mainstream or fringe opposition. But this particular risk—a very serious one in the minds of those writing the U.S. Constitution—only applies if the governmental power can be brought to bear on those with strong U.S. connections by nationality or residence.

In a number of recommendations, we have permitted broader governmental authority if it is directed at non-U.S. persons who are not within the United States. These limitations will fully protect political liberties within the United States. We recognize that this approach is not without costs. It may raise a serious likelihood that the United States would permit doing to other nationals what the American public would not tolerate if applied to citizens. reciprocity (bad sense)

We have strived to ensure that, despite the occasional use of exemptions for U.S. persons, our recommendations do consider their likely effect on both U.S. allies and foes. The United States has traditionally seen its policies and actions as an example for the rest of the world—a "city on a hill." It is worth returning to the source of that phrase, which was used by John Winthrop, first governor of the Massachusetts Bay Colony, en route to Massachusetts in 1630.

"We must consider that we shall be as a City upon a Hill, the eyes of all people are upon us; so that if we shall deal falsely with our God in this work we have undertaken, and so cause Him to withdraw His present help from us, we shall be made a story and a by-word through the world."[2]

Significantly, Winthrop used the simile as a warning, not as a point of self-congratulation. In the modern era, the United States has not merely seen itself as a model for others but also as an active source of positive change in the world. That tradition must continue.

EXCLUSION FROM OUR RECOMMENDATIONS OF ZONES OF ACTIVE COMBAT

The question "is this war?" proves too often to be both controversial and not amenable to a simple yes or no answer. A declaration of war against a nation, a "solemn war," is easy because it is so constitutionally simple. Congress declares war against a nation, and the executive branch conducts it. In reality, of course, it has rarely in U.S. history been that simple, and it is even less so today.

After September 11, 2001, Congress authorized the president to use all necessary and appropriate forces against those nations, organizations, or persons he determines planned, authorized, committed, or aided the terrorists attacks of 9/11, or harbored such organizations, or persons, in order to prevent any future acts of international terrorism against the United States by such nations, organizations, or persons.

The content of that delegation of authority was to be implemented by the president in a variety of ways, with very little congressional debate or oversight. The present U.S. struggle with terrorists has no established or predictable geographic or time limitations, and no clear end point. Thus, the concept of war in the classic sense provides incomplete guidance about the content of specific procedures. Moreover, the special necessities that are implied in the notion of "war"— where killing within a set of rules established by the laws of war is legal and encouraged—apply in their full scope only in locations of active combat. Those are the locations where the special powers available to the executive branch in times of war are generally needed; elsewhere, the need is exceptional.

We attempt to address the question "is this war?" by finding guidance in court cases that differentiate, albeit quite formally, between the authorities of the president "in a zone of active combat" or "in a foreign theater

---

2. Richard S. Dunn and Laetitia Yeandle, eds., *The Journal of John Winthrop, 1630–1649* (Cambridge, Mass.: Belknap Press, 1996), p. 10, from Matthew (5:14).

of conflict," as recognized in the Supreme Court's June 2004 detention cases, and authorities of the president outside those contexts. Thus, it is beyond the scope of this book to set guidelines or restrictions on the commander-in-chief's traditional broad war powers where there is a clear zone of active combat outside the United States. Afghanistan, and certainly Iraq, satisfy those standards. Elsewhere, and certainly in the United States, these additional powers available in time of war should be greatly lessened or even absent.

More significantly, we would require that the president designate "zones of active combat" every six months, so that Congress and the nation as a whole would know where in fact war is being fought. We do not believe that this standard is onerous. It is also consistent with the needs of our foreign relations. Some of the authorities that the president may seek to use should be authorities of last resort in situations where the United States simply has no other practical alternative. These authorities should exist only when the country where action is to be taken is unwilling or unable to act on behalf of the United States. When operating in allied countries such as the United Kingdom or Germany, then, which are not legitimately "zones of active combat," the United States should not exercise wartime powers without the consent of the country concerned. In countries that are more difficult to classify, such as Yemen, the president should be authorized to use more aggressive procedures, but only if he had already declared—so that the recognition is subject to debate and consideration by the Congress (and in all but rare instances the public)—that the country or territory was either part of a zone of active combat or an area unwilling or unable to cooperate in fighting terrorists planning to attack the United States or its allies.

Thus, our recommendations do not generally restrict the president's extensive powers where the conditions for active combat or a foreign theater of conflict are satisfied, though our recommendations on interrogation make no such distinctions. It is with regard to actions outside that zone that we recommend that Congress enact rules and standards for the exercise of executive authority.

Years after 9/11, it is time to reassess whether the changes that have occurred were wise and appropriate and, if so, whether they are still needed. Politics is irrelevant to this determination. We are, instead, concerned with a system of laws that would govern us not simply today, but through the course of a threat that is likely to be a problem for decades to come. The following recommendations provide such guidance.

Summary of Recommendations

Chapter One: Coercive Interrogations

TREATY AND STATUTORY COMMITMENTS

•**Without exception, the United States shall abide by its statutory and treaty obligations that prohibit torture.**

•**Consistent with the provisions under "Emergency Exception," the United States shall abide by its statutory and treaty obligations that prohibit cruel, inhuman, or degrading treatment.** Lawfulness under the U.S. reservation to Article 16 of the Convention Against Torture ("cruel, inhuman, or degrading treatment") requires at least compliance with the due process prohibition against actions that U.S. courts find "shock the conscience." Nothing in the following effort to define compliance with these obligations is intended to supplant our additional obligations when particular circumstances make applicable the Third and Fourth Geneva Conventions.

TRANSFER OF INDIVIDUALS

•**The United States shall abide by its treaty obligations not to transfer an individual to a country if it has probable cause to believe that the individual will be tortured there.** If past conduct suggests that a country has engaged in torture of suspects, the United States shall not transfer a person to that country unless (1) the secretary of state has received assurances from that country that he or she determines to be trustworthy that the individual will not be tortured and has forwarded such assurances and determination to the attorney general; and (2) the attorney general determines that such assurances are "sufficiently reliable" to allow deportation or other forms of rendition.

•The United States shall not direct or request information from an interrogation or provide assistance to foreign governments in obtaining such information if it has substantial grounds for believing that torture will be utilized to obtain the information.

•The United States shall not encourage another nation to make transfers in violation of the prohibitions of the Convention Against Torture.

OVERSIGHT OF THE USE OF ANY HIGHLY COERCIVE INTERROGATION (HCI) TECHNIQUES

•The attorney general shall recommend and the president shall promulgate and provide to the Senate and House Intelligence, Judiciary, and Armed Services Committees, guidelines stating which specific HCI techniques are authorized.[1] To be authorized, a technique must be consistent with U.S. law and U.S. obligations under international treaties including Article 16 of the Convention against Torture, which under "Treaty and Statutory Commitments" above, prohibits actions that the courts find "shock the conscience." These guidelines shall address the duration and repetition of use of a particular technique and the effect of combining several different techniques together. The attorney general shall brief appropriate committees of both houses of Congress upon request, and no less frequently than every six months, as to which HCIs are presently being utilized by federal officials or those acting on their behalf.

•No person shall be subject even to authorized HCI techniques unless (1) authorized interrogators have probable cause to believe that he is in possession of significant information, and there is no reasonable alternative to obtain that information, about either a specific plan that threatens U.S. lives or a group or organization making such plans whose capacity could be significantly reduced by exploiting the information; (2) the determination of whether probable cause is met has been made by senior government officials in writing and on the basis of sworn affidavits; or (3) the determination and its factual basis will be made available to congressional intelligence committees, the attorney general and the inspectors general of the pertinent departments (i.e., Department of Justice, Department of Defense, etc.).

---

1. Highly coercive interrogation methods are all those techniques that fall in the category between those forbidden as torture by treaty or statute and those traditionally allowed in seeking a voluntary confession under the due process clauses of the U.S. Constitution.

EMERGENCY EXCEPTION

• **No U.S. official or employee, and no other individual acting on behalf of the United States, may use an interrogation technique not specifically authorized in this way** except with the express written approval of the president on the basis of a finding of an urgent and extraordinary need. The finding, which must be submitted within a reasonable period to appropriate committees from both houses of Congress, must state the reason to believe that the information sought to be obtained concerns a specific plan that threatens U.S. lives, the information is in possession of the individual to be interrogated, and there are no other reasonable alternatives to save the lives in question. No presidential approval may authorize any form of interrogation that would be prohibited by the Fifth, Eighth, or Fourteenth Amendments of the U.S. Constitution if applied to a U.S. citizen in similar circumstances within the United States.

• **The president shall publicly report the number of uses of his special necessity power biannually to Congress.**

INDIVIDUAL REMEDIES AND APPLICABILITY

• **An individual subjected to HCI in circumstances where the conditions prescribed above have not been met shall be entitled to damages in a civil action against the United States.**

• **No information obtained by highly coercive interrogation techniques may be used at a U.S. trial, including military trials, against the individual detained.**

Chapter Two: Indefinite Detention

PERSONS SEIZED WITHIN THE UNITED STATES AND THE SEIZURE OF U.S. PERSONS
ANYWHERE IN THE WORLD EXCEPT IN A ZONE OF ACTIVE COMBAT

•**Any U.S. person and any person within the United States who is seized or arrested outside a zone of active combat shall be detained only on criminal charges.** If the present array of statutes is considered inadequate, additional criminal laws should be passed, including, for example, incorporation in Title 18 of the U.S. Code (18 U.S.C.) of the principles of command responsibility in cases where the conduct for which the individual is to be tried constitutes a grave breach of the provisions of the Geneva Conventions of 1949. No such person shall be detained without probable cause to believe that he has committed or is planning to commit an act previously criminalized by statutes. Such persons captured by personnel of military or intelligence agencies must be transferred without delay to the custody of civilian authorities.

•**Any such person seized with probable cause that he is planning, assisting or executing an act of terrorism can and should be charged with conspiring to violate one of the many U.S. statutes criminalizing acts of terrorism.**

•**A judicial officer shall order the pre-trial detention (under 18 U.S.C. § 3142(e)) of the individual arrested upon a showing that there is reason to suspect that the individual arrested** (1) has committed a terrorist act; or (2) is planning or supporting a planned terrorist act; and (3) cannot be prevented from assisting in that effort by any other reasonable means.

•**The detainee shall be allowed access to an attorney of his choice.** If the government intends to rely on classified information at any stage of the detention proceedings, it will make every effort to provide security clearance as quickly as possible to that attorney and will make available, in the meantime, a list of cleared defense attorneys. If the detainee cannot be represented by a cleared defense attorney of his choice at a critical stage of detention proceedings, the court shall promptly appoint a "special advocate" who is cleared to see all evidence and whose role is to argue the case against detention. This special advocate shall not thereby form an attorney-client relationship with the detainee.

•**The judicial officer may deny the detainee, but not his cleared attorney or "special advocate," access to parts of the detention hear-**

ing if, on the basis of a governmental petition, the officer concludes this step is necessary to protect national security secrets.

•On showing to a court that, despite the Classified Information Procedures Act, an immediate trial would be impossible without significant loss of national security secrets, and evidence that cannot be revealed in public demonstrates that release of the detainee would significantly endanger the lives of others, a federal judge may delay the trial date for a period of ninety days and renew the delay for a period of up to two years while the government pursues evidence that can be used at a public trial without compromising national security. During this period, the government must seek orders extending pre-trial detention for every ninety-day period. The first such order must be issued within ninety days of initial detention. Each order shall be subject to prompt appeal whether or not it is considered a final judgment.

•A person so detained who is not thereafter brought to trial shall be entitled to fair compensation from the United States for the period of detention. Whenever the executive detains a non-U.S. person who is in violation of his immigration status or his permission to enter the United States, he shall not be detained for a period longer than that required for his deportation unless pursuant to the procedures of this Section. No person shall be detained as a material witness, rather than under the provisions of this Act, unless a federal judge specifically determines that the risk of non-appearance, the importance of the witness to the proceeding, and the importance of the proceeding justify that detention as a matter of law.

NON-U.S. PERSONS SEIZED OUTSIDE THE UNITED STATES AND NOT IN A ZONE OF ACTIVE COMBAT

•A non-U.S. person cannot be seized by a U.S. intelligence or military agency acting within any state in which the U.S. secretary of state has certified that the state is willing and able (practically and legally) to assist the United States in all legal ways to prevent attacks on U.S. territory, persons or property, unless such seizure is with the permission or concurrence of appropriate authorities of that state. If the secretary of state has not so certified or if the individual is delivered to U.S. officials by officials of the place where he is found, he may be detained.

•No individual will be seized abroad outside a zone of active combat by U.S. forces, civilian personnel, or others acting on behalf of the United States unless a senior legal officer of the agency responsible for the seizure has made a written and documented finding that there is probable cause that the individual is planning a terrorist attack against the United States.

•**A competent military or specialized civilian tribunal defined by statute shall substitute for a federal court abroad, and may perform the functions otherwise assigned in the previous section of our recommendations on indefinite detention to a federal judge or magistrate and under the same restrictions and conditions, determine whether detention by an intelligence or military agency or other U.S. authorities is legal and appropriate.** A decision to detain and each renewal and denial of personal legal assistance shall be subject to judicial review. The above procedures, relating to ex parte hearings and the designation of a "special advocate" if a personal attorney is not available or not permitted access to classified information, shall apply during this judicial review. In any case to be tried within the United States (as described in chapter 3) the period of pre-trial detention prior to transfer to the United States for trial shall not exceed thirty days.

•**Access of the detainee to an attorney of his choice may be delayed up to seven days by order of the judicial officer on a showing that the individual arrested has information which may prevent an imminent terrorist attack and that any interrogation will be conducted in a way consistent with the U.S. Constitution and U.S. statutory and treaty obligations.** No statement obtained by custodial interrogation in the absence of a lawyer representing the detainee or any evidence derived from any such statement will be admissible at any criminal prosecution of the detainee.

•**The federal district court in the geographic jurisdiction to which the person seized and detained is first transferred shall have jurisdiction to try the charges.** Our preceding provisions for persons seized within the United States and for U.S. persons seized abroad apply to the trial.

PERSONS SEIZED WITHIN A ZONE OF ACTIVE COMBAT

•**A "designated zone of active combat" is territory declared by the president, either publicly or in a classified presidential determination made available to the appropriate oversight committees of Congress, as constituting a theater of military operations** (1) in connection with a declared war or other armed conflict between the United States and a foreign state, organization, or defined class of individuals; or (2) the territory occupied and administered, consistent with the Geneva Conventions, by the U.S. military following such a conflict; or (3) within the territory of a state that the United States has been asked to assist in connection with the suppression of an armed insurrection or other uprising within that state.

• **The rules set forth in the first two sections do not apply to the detention of persons captured during hostilities in a designated zone of active combat.** Whatever rights and liabilities now exist for such persons are not affected in any way by those sections.

• **The U.S. Constitution, the decisions interpreting it, the Third and Fourth Geneva Conventions (to the extent applicable) and relevant Department of Defense directives consistent with these sources and any other U.S. treaty obligations shall be fully honored.**

• **At a minimum, the following protections shall be available:**

1. An individual captured in a zone of active combat is entitled to an initial determination, after a hearing before a competent tribunal to be held as soon as practicable under the circumstances, of whether he was engaged in or actively supporting those engaged in hostilities against the United States and whether he is entitled to prisoner of war (POW) or other protected status under the Geneva Conventions of 1949.

2. During the continuation of hostilities but outside the zone of active combat designated by the president, the detainee shall be accorded a periodic review to determine whether his continued detention is warranted because he continues his support for the hostile force to which he belonged.

• **Detainees held in a facility under U.S. control and outside a zone of active combat shall** (1) be accorded the right to challenge their detention through habeas corpus in U.S. federal court, under 28 U.S.C. §2241; and (2) be accorded such fundamental due process rights under the Fifth Amendment as the federal courts determine are appropriate in light of the factors set forth in *Mathews v. Eldridge*: the private interest of the person asserting the lack of due process; the risk of erroneous deprivation of that interest through the use of existing procedures and the probable value of additional or substitute procedural safeguards; and the competing national security interests of the government.

• **After the president or Congress has determined that the hostilities in connection with which he was detained have terminated, the detainee shall without undue delay be released and repatriated to** his country of citizenship or prosecuted for violations of the laws of war or other applicable penal provisions before a federal court or other appropriate tribunal.

DETENTION ON THE BASIS OF A JUDICIAL WARRANT

•Notwithstanding any other provisions in this section, the Foreign Intelligence Surveillance Court may issue and renew a warrant for thirty days of detention for an individual who is not a U.S. person, whether seized inside or outside the territory of the United States. A warrant shall be issued only in the following circumstances:

1. The attorney general must personally approve the application.

2. The application must satisfy the court, on the basis of affidavits or sworn testimony, that the individual to be detained either (1) must be prevented by detention from assisting in an imminent terrorist attack, or possesses information critical to the safety of U.S. persons or citizens of other democratic nations from imminent terrorist attack and will be subjected to lawful interrogations for a period authorized by the court; or (2) is a high-level leader in the planning or financing of an extended plan of terrorist attacks and either will be subjected to lawful interrogations for a period authorized by the court or is not yet known by his associates to have been captured, creating important possibilities of tactical surprise for a limited period.

•The application for the warrant and its justification must be made available promptly, under conditions of assured secrecy, to the appropriate committees of Congress. The number of such warrants and renewals of warrants issued each year shall be made public annually. The warrant issued by the Foreign Intelligence Surveillance Court shall specify (1) the location, duration, and conditions of detention authorized by the warrant; and (2) any necessary conditions of judicial monitoring of interrogations for legality under U.S. law and treaties.

Chapter Three: Military Commissions

ADDITIONS TO THE CLASSIFIED INFORMATION PROCEDURES ACT (CIPA)

•The U.S. Congress should consider the need for adding to the terms of the Classified Information Procedures Act. The U.S. Congress should include such provisions as are thought necessary to permit the trial of terrorists and others for violations of federal terrorist statutes or the rules of war. As in the case of CIPA, there must be adequate guarantees that any modifications of familiar court or court-martial procedures do not significantly undermine the fairness of a trial. Subject to that constraint, any modifications adopted should protect national security secrets from revelation either to the defendant or to a wider public during a trial. If the constraint of fair trial cannot be met and if any trial would disclose critical national security secrets, only temporary detention can be used, not as a punishment but as a form of needed, but temporary, incapacitation.

JURISDICTION OVER VIOLATIONS OF THE LAWS OF WAR

•Any case of military trial for violation of the laws of war of a person seized as a combatant within a zone of active combat will be tried before a court-martial under the jurisdiction granted by 10 U.S.C. § 818.

•Persons seized within a zone of active combat will be tried only by such court-martial, whether the individual is deemed a lawful combatant, and therefore entitled to the protections of the Geneva Conventions, or an unlawful combatant.

•Except for U.S. military personnel, all prosecutions for violations of the laws of war committed by U.S. persons captured outside a zone of active combat or of individuals found within the United States shall be carried out in a federal district court.

•If seized outside a zone of active combat and outside the United States, a non-U.S. person detained for violating the laws of war is subject to court-martial only if the attorney general certifies to the appropriate military authorities that (1) there cannot be a fair and secure civilian trial before a U.S. district court; and (2) either there is no reliable prospect of a fair and vigorous trial before a court of the state where the criminal acts of planning a terrorist attack on the United States took place, or any such trial in a foreign court would require the revelation of national security secrets that would otherwise be protected by a U.S. district court.

Chapter Four: Targeted Killing

TARGETED KILLING IN A DESIGNATED ZONE OF ACTIVE COMBAT

•**The following rules do not apply to targeting those engaged in active hostilities in a zone of active combat.** A "designated zone of active combat" is territory designated by the president, either publicly or in a classified presidential determination made available to the appropriate oversight committees of the Congress, as constituting a theater of military operations (1) in connection with a declared war or other armed conflict between the United States and a foreign state, organization, or defined class of individuals; (2) in the territory occupied and administered, consistent with the Geneva Conventions, by the U.S. military following such a conflict; or (3) within the territory of a state that the United States has been asked to assist in connection with the suppression of an armed insurrection or other uprising within that state.

TARGETED KILLING OUTSIDE A DESIGNATED ZONE OF ACTIVE COMBAT

•**In all situations and locations outside designated zones of active combat, any targeted killing must be pursuant to procedures outlined in legislation detailing the conditions for such an action.**

STANDARDS FOR THE USE OF TARGETED KILLING

•**Any such authorization of targeting a particular individual outside a zone of active combat must be justified as necessary to prevent, or in defense against, a reasonably imminent threat to the life of one or more persons.** To be "necessary" there must be no reasonable alternative such as arrest or capture followed by detention. To be "reasonably imminent" there must be a real risk that any delay in the hope of developing an alternative would result in a significantly increased risk of the lethal attack. Retribution for past events, as opposed to prevention of future attacks, cannot justify a targeted killing.

•**Under familiar rules applicable to military action under the laws of war, the action taken must be proportionate to the objective to be obtained, and the selection of the time, place, and means employed must avoid to the extent reasonably possible harm to innocent persons.**

•Even when these conditions are met, there shall be no targeted killing of: a U.S. person; any person found in the United States; or an individual found in any foreign state that has previously agreed to, and displayed a willingness to try, extradite, or otherwise incapacitate those reasonably suspected of planning terrorist attacks on U.S. citizens and facilities.

•Any decision to target an identified individual for killing must be approved by the president of the United States in a finding, provided to appropriate committees of the Congress, and setting forth (1) the evidence on which the necessary conclusion of imminent danger has been made; (2) the alternatives considered and the basis for rejecting them; and (3) the reasons for concluding that the previous conditions have been met.

•The president shall promulgate detailed procedures for making these findings reliably and for maintaining a permanent record, available to appropriate committees of Congress, of any such decision.

•The rules described in the previous section shall be made public. Particular findings in any individual case and the fact that such targeting was approved by the president need not be made public, but must be provided to appropriate committees of the Congress.

Chapter Five: Communications of U.S. Persons or Others within the United States Intercepted During the Targeting of Foreign Persons Abroad

ACQUIRING CONTENTS OF FOREIGN COMMUNICATIONS

•**Targeting the content of communications of persons within the United States or of U.S. persons abroad should be governed by the following rules:**

1. No U.S. agency may target for interception the content of any domestic communications of a person known to be within the United States or of any international communications of a U.S. person within the United States without satisfying the legal requirements of Title III (regarding electronic surveillance for criminal purposes) or FISA (regarding electronic surveillance for foreign intelligence purposes).

2. To target for interception the content of communications of a U.S. person located outside the United States, the attorney general must find probable cause to believe that the communications may reveal evidence of a crime, or that the U.S. person is an agent of a foreign power and the purpose of the collection is to acquire foreign intelligence or information about the person's involvement in espionage, international terrorism, or foreign-directed covert operations against the United States.

3. There shall be a presumption that a pattern of repeated acquisition of communications to or from a U.S. person is the result of activity targeted on that person, and thus requires compliance with the above rules respectively.

•**Targeting the content of communications of non-U.S. persons abroad shall be governed by the following rules:**

1. The content of communications of non-U.S. persons located outside the United States ("foreign communications") may be the target of interception so long as the purpose is to gather foreign intelligence or evidence of a violation of U.S. law. This rule applies whether or not another party to the targeted communication is known to be a U.S. person; whether or not the content of the communication is expected to involve the activities of a U.S. person; and wherever the interception is accomplished, as long as the person whose communications are sought is outside the United States.

2. When the communications targeted for interception are of a person mistakenly—but reasonably—believed to be neither a U.S. person nor in the United States, the communications have not been targeted as the communications of a U.S. person or of anyone within the United States.

3. Communications to or from a U.S. person intercepted unexpectedly during a content-based collection reasonably directed at communications of non-U.S. persons outside the United States for intelligence purposes are not deemed targeted on U.S. persons or territory.

THE CONSEQUENCES OF UNINTENTIONAL ACQUISITION

•**The retention, dissemination, and use of the content of communications of U.S. persons or of communications of persons in the United States which have been unintentionally acquired while targeting non-U.S. persons abroad shall be governed by rules determined by regulations of the attorney general.** These regulations shall, as closely as possible, duplicate the provisions for information obtained under the Foreign Intelligence Surveillance Act under 50 U.S.C. 1801(e) and (h) and 50 U.S.C. 1804(a)(5). The basis for concluding that information identifying a U.S. person is necessary to the conduct of foreign affairs or the national defense as well as to understand its content or importance must be set forth in writing along with the names of those to whom that information will be furnished. The record of this request will be maintained by the agency furnishing the information and will be available to the intelligence committees of Congress.

ACQUIRING INFORMATION OTHER THAN THE CONTENTS OF FOREIGN COMMUNICATIONS

•**Neither a U.S. person abroad nor anyone within the United States is constitutionally entitled to a finding of some factual basis for suspicion of terrorist activity or of being an agent of a foreign power before the government reviews to whom an electronic communication was sent or when and how it was sent.**

•**An agency responsible for gathering foreign intelligence may gather such information (other than the content of the communication) by targeting the messages of U.S. persons or individuals within the United States only if it is acting as an agent of, and under the control of, the attorney general, and it is subject to all the departmental regulations of the attorney general.**

Chapter Six: Information Collection

GENERAL DATA-MINING PROCEDURES

•A federal district court or a specialized court, such as the Foreign Intelligence Surveillance Act (FISA) court, should be authorized by Congress to issue a warrant making available to the federal government access to extensive systems of commercial and other third-party records when there is clear and convincing evidence that (1) the systems of records to which the government is given access will, when combined, be no broader than necessary to permit a determination of whether there is a high risk of terrorist activity; (2) anonymization techniques will initially prevent the identification of any individuals with any particular record unless and until the court authorizes the release to the government of the individual's identity, as discussed in the section below; (3) the systems of records and any copies of them will not be retained by the federal government but will remain at all times under the control of their owners; (4) systems will be in place that guarantee an adequate audit trail of who has had access to what information and for how long; and (5) the access will not be unduly disruptive of the activities of the custodian of the records.

•The court shall authorize the federal government to demand or obtain the identities of individuals whose activities are revealed by analysis of commercial or other private systems of records if the government establishes to the court's satisfaction that a pattern of activities revealed by the systems of records has a significant probability of being a part of a plan for terrorism; and the individuals whose identities are to be revealed are so related to the pattern of activity as to have a significant probability of being engaged in terrorism.

•Once an individual has been identified in this or in any other legal way, based on reasonable factual inferences that the individual is likely to be planning terrorism or is part of an organization or group planning terrorism, the federal government shall have access to commercial records and to records of other third parties relevant to determining the identity of his or her associates and discovering other activities in connection with this plan.

ACCESS TO INDIVIDUALIZED DATA

•Records of activity of identified individuals should not be subject to compelled government access for prevention of terrorist activities unless they are sought pursuant to the investigation of an individual or organization already reasonably suspected of terrorism.

REQUIRED SECRECY CONCERNING DELIVERY OF RECORDS

•**The court ordering the revelation of records may forbid the non-governmental custodian of documents to reveal that the government has demanded them,** but only upon a showing of cause and for a limited, renewable period.

•**Any requirement that a nonjudicial demand, such as a National Security Letter, be kept secret shall be valid for only sixty days** but can be renewed by a court on a particularized showing of the need for continued secrecy.

Chapter Seven: Identification of Individuals and Collection of Information for Federal Files

PERMISSIBLE DEMANDS FOR BIOMETRIC INFORMATION

•**Biometric or other systems of identification are necessary and appropriate for reliably matching federal "files" of accumulated information on an individual with the current activities of that individual** (1) whenever the federal government, a state or local government, or a private facility can appropriately check all or part of a file maintained by the federal government before deciding whether to give an individual access to a sensitive resource or target of a terrorist attack; (2) in order to keep a reliable federal record of requests for access to sensitive resources and targets, whether such a record is developed by obtaining information from another organization or governmental unit or by electronically or otherwise recording requests for access to federal facilities; and (3) whenever an individual is either visiting or returning to the United States.

IMPERMISSIBLE DEMANDS FOR BIOMETRIC INFORMATION

•**Biometric or other systems of identification are neither necessary nor appropriate for matching federal "files" of accumulated information on an individual with the current activities of that individual during random requests for identification when an individual is neither seeking access to sensitive resources or targets nor seeking to enter the country.** In these circumstances (where demanding identification is not appropriate), no federal records of individual activity should be created or maintained.

Chapter Eight: Surveillance of Religious and Political Meetings

MONITORING RELIGIOUS AND POLITICAL ORGANIZATIONS

• **An investigation of a religious or political organization pursuant to the rules regarding domestic intelligence investigations may be authorized where there is a reasonable and articulable basis for suspecting that a group, or leaders of a group, are** (1) planning terrorist activity; (2) recruiting participation in an organization involved in such activity; (3) actively advocating political violence; or (4) actively advocating hatred against another group.

• **The authorization shall be governed by the following conditions:**

1. The request for authorization shall be made, in writing, to be approved by a senior official at FBI Headquarters.

2. It shall last for only sixty days, renewable upon written evidence that the information acquired during the authorization continues to satisfy the conditions in the above section.

3. The number of such authorizations shall be furnished publicly to the members of the House and Senate Judiciary committees.

RECORDS OF RELIGIOUS AND POLITICAL GROUP MONITORING

• **In instances where federal agents are permitted to attend religious and political meetings under the above section, the keeping of records is appropriate so long as it is limited to persons engaged in the activities of the above section or who support and encourage these activities.**

Chapter Nine: Distinctions Based on Group Membership

DISTINCTIONS REGARDING U.S. CITIZENS

•**Broad profiles based on national origin of a U.S. citizen, or on the race or religion of any individual, are never permissible.** Affiliation with a religious or political group may be considered if there is reason to suspect that group of either advocating violent or illegal activities (pursuant to our recommendation on "Surveillance of Religious and Political Meetings") or being an agent of a foreign power.

•**Lawful permanent resident aliens should be afforded the protections of U.S. citizens for purposes of this recommendation,** unless they have been in the United States less than the required time (presently five years) for becoming naturalized citizens.

•**Distinctions based on the fact that an individual is not a U.S. citizen, such as in employment at sensitive sites or locations, are legitimate.** It is customary and rational to limit certain privileges to U.S. citizens.

DISTINCTIONS REGARDING GROUPS OF NONCITIZENS WITHIN THE UNITED STATES

•**As a trigger for further review, distinctions among aliens based on their nationalities, such as those from the United Kingdom as compared to those from Iran, are permissible in situations in the United States where there already exists a discretionary level of review before access or entry is permitted,** such as at an airport or a sensitive facility.

•**While enough to trigger more careful review, the fact that someone is a national from a particular country associated with a terrorist threat will generally hold little weight in determining whether that specific individual should be denied access.** Thus, the fact that a high proportion of terrorists come from a particular country may make its citizens subject to additional review, even though only a minuscule portion of that population will generally be a threat.

•**Despite the high risk of error, when the facts of a particular terrorist incident suggest the culpability of a state or its citizens, it is appropriate to give disproportionate attention in the initial stages of investigation to the citizens of that state.**

Chapter Ten: Oversight of Extraordinary Measures

CONGRESSIONAL OVERSIGHT OF NEW COUNTERTERRORISM LAWS AND PRACTICES
HAVING SIGNIFICANT EFFECTS ON TRADITIONAL RIGHTS OF INDIVIDUALS

•As ongoing extraordinary measures are retained by legislation or acquiescence, the congressional leadership should establish a five-year nonpartisan commission to make findings and recommendations regarding the continuing need for these measures for consideration by the Congress and the relevant committees of each House.

•With regard to any extraordinary measure for addressing the dangers of terrorism that the Congress determines to have or have had significant effects on the liberties of citizens, the commission should establish a system of continuing review.

1. The list of extraordinary measures to be reviewed should include measures undertaken by the president with or without congressional authority.

2. The frequency of review should be at least annual.

3. The members of the commission should be subject to security clearance procedures and then provided access to classified information on terms similar to those now applicable to the Intelligence Committees.

4. At an absolute minimum, such assessments should examine the case for and against the efficacy of an extraordinary measure in light of:

-The use, or lack thereof, of the measure;

-The likelihood of the assumptions under which the extraordinary measure would be effective;

-The likelihood of the rival assumptions under which it would fail;

-The history and experience that may throw light on these relative probabilities;

-The experience of other democracies in utilizing similar measures; and

-The adequacy of oversight of these extraordinary measures.

5. The published results of the review should not contain classified information that was made available to the commission acting on

behalf of the relevant congressional committees. While as much detail as possible should be furnished, even a review that merely reaches unclassified conclusions, if carried out by a credible body, would be valuable.

EXECUTIVE OVERSIGHT OF SUBSTANTIVE LEGAL REFORMS

•**Congress shall enact legislation that provides that each inspector general (IG) shall conduct a systemic review of the use made of each of a list of provisions granting extraordinary powers to the IG's agency.** The review shall include their effectiveness and their costs (intangible as well as tangible) to those affected as well as to the agency, on an annual basis, for no less than five years. This list shall include, but not be limited to, any provisions with sunset clauses in past legislation. While present statutory authority would not preclude reviews of the civil liberties impact of an agency's counterterrorism activities by an inspector general, specific statutory authority and responsibility should be explicitly granted to all relevant IGs as it has already been to the inspector general of the Department of Justice. In both the reviews of effectiveness and of the impact on civil liberties, the IG's authority should extend to reviews of private sector and state and local government conduct, when done pursuant to a mandate from or agreement with the Department.

•**Any new legislation granting extraordinary authorities should include requirements that the relevant inspector general conduct annual reviews, in a classified and unclassified form, of the efficacy of any measure.**

•**To provide a coherent review of (1) extraordinary power vested in more than one agency; and (2) the effect of using different extraordinary powers of different agencies for a shared purpose, the Congress should authorize and fund an interagency committee of IGs that would establish criteria** for any investigation that would involve more than one department or agency and create structures to allow joint-OIG reviews and recommendations.

Chapter 1

Coercive Interrogations

Rules proscribing the use of torture and other cruel and inhuman treatment by the United States provide little guidance as to the legitimacy of specific interrogation techniques and when they can be used. The exact coverage of the international torture prohibition (UN Convention Against Torture) is far from clear. The same is true of the U.S. reservations and understandings on ratifying it, which narrow the definitions of torture and cruel, inhuman, or degrading treatment. Whether it binds the president is disputed, as are the conditions, if any, on which the lesser prohibition (Article 16) of cruel and inhuman treatment can be waived. No other set of specific rules and procedures regarding highly coercive interrogation, not forbidden by the UN Convention Against Torture or the Geneva Conventions, exists. In this context of uncertainty, the use of particular coercive techniques remains and has been subject to serious abuse. On the other hand, the controversy surrounding interrogation tactics in Iraq and elsewhere, and the resulting criminal charges against military personnel, has resulted in a dramatic swing of the pendulum that may discourage legitimate interrogation tactics. That is not a beneficial response either. Our recommendations seek to provide guidance on which standards ought, and ought not, to be utilized.

Explanation and Background

Inadequately monitored and regulated coercion against prisoners has the potential to prove a setback for U.S. foreign and military policies and goals. The Bush administration has portrayed the problem as one of failed management, in the field, of a few bad apples. An internal Army inspector general's report and an independent Department of Defense report came to the same conclusion. To prevent a repetition, however, a full U.S. governmental investigation of the management of detention and interrogation in

Afghanistan, Iraq, and elsewhere is needed, as well as a broad examination of the policies and systems that the United States needs for the future.

There are six major questions that have to be addressed in setting up any system dealing with interrogation for intelligence purposes. They are:

1. What coercive steps are permissible under U.S. treaty and statutory obligations and in light of U.S. moral and policy concerns?

2. Under what circumstances may highly coercive but legal and duly authorized steps of interrogation be used?

3. Who should decide each of the first two questions?

4. How should the process be managed by the Department of Defense or other executive agencies to assure that the rules are complied with and not ignored in the field?

5. Under what, if any, circumstances should the president have the power to waive either of the first two determinations?

6. What form of oversight by non-executive entities should be put in place for each of these situations?

It is revealing to consider how these questions were answered prior to the public revelations about Abu Ghraib. Department of Justice attorneys appear to have spent considerable time trying to defend maximum flexibility for interrogation tactics, but the Bush administration subsequently distanced itself from that analysis. A list of permissible and impermissible methods seems to have been promulgated, with a few exceptions, at the general officer or cabinet level, in documents kept secret from the public. We cannot tell how the list of tactics was thought to relate to judgments about either applicable treaty law or domestic constitutional law (for example, the contention of the administration that, because of its reservation, Article 16 had no application to prisoners held outside the United States).

Under which circumstances the approved coercive steps could actually be used is a decision that often seems to have been made, without any statement of standards, by intelligence or prison personnel at a quite junior level in the military. A startling absence of management controls also allowed the rules to be ignored at operating levels. There was no oversight by legislative or judicial bodies; indeed, executive secrecy was pervasive, and no audit requirements were there to ensure documentation.

With no public rules or accounting, the president's discretion has been absolute and wholly delegable to any level. This means, of course, that the president is not formally accountable for the decisions actually made.

The question that the Congress must now address is how the answers to these six questions should change in the future. Nothing less is at stake than the claim of the United States as a nation to self-respect and to a needed level of the respect of others.

Treaty and Statutory Commitments

•**Without exception, the United States shall abide by its statutory and treaty obligations that prohibit torture.**

•**Consistent with the provisions under "Emergency Exception," the United States shall abide by its statutory and treaty obligations that prohibit cruel, inhuman, or degrading treatment.** Lawfulness under the U.S. reservation to Article 16 of the Convention Against Torture ("cruel, inhuman, or degrading treatment") requires at least compliance with the due process prohibition against actions that U.S. courts find "shock the conscience." Nothing in the following effort to define compliance with these obligations is intended to supplant our additional obligations when particular circumstances make applicable the Third and Fourth Geneva Conventions.

At the outset, there must be—without exception—a commitment to U.S. treaty obligations under Article 1 against torture. The Congress and the president have already resolved a number of questions by submitting and ratifying, with reservations, the UN Convention Against Torture. The president cannot legitimately violate a treaty or a statute which was passed and is in effect. No exception to the prohibition of torture in Article 1 is permitted by the treaty.

Unfortunately the language of both Article 1 (defining torture) and Article 16 (prohibiting cruel, inhuman, or degrading treatment) of the treaty is far from clear; the lack of clarity was only exacerbated by a Senate Reservation limiting the U.S. definition of torture and interpreting "cruel, inhuman, or degrading treatment" to mean the treatment prohibited by the Fifth, Eighth, and Fourteenth amendments to the U.S. Constitution— amendments which do not generally deal with efforts to prevent grave future harms). Moreover, the question of when and where the full protections of the Geneva Conventions apply has been the subject of intense debate and further muddles the extent of U.S. legal obligations toward individuals captured and detained overseas.

Regardless of these ambiguities, the United States has a firm commitment to uphold a reasonable interpretation of treaty and statutory obligations against torture and related conduct. As will be noted in the sections below, we recommend no exceptions to U.S. statutory and treaty prohibitions under Article 1 against torture. Moreover, we recommend a regulated system of interrogation that will be consistent with U.S. obligations under Article 16 of the Convention Against Torture to "undertake to prevent" cruel, inhuman, or degrading treatment, with only one narrowly limited exception—an exception that could only be used in extreme circumstances and would require presidential authorization.

Having carefully reviewed the very limited legislative history of the Senate reservation to Article 16, we can find no substantial indication that the Senate, which plainly accepted the fact that the Article 1 prohibition of torture had worldwide application to U.S. officials, had an opposite understanding of Article 16. Indeed, if interpreted to merely repeat protections that already fully existed within the United States, the country's agreement to Article 16 would have had no effect at all on U.S. obligations, although the act of ratifying that article with reservations would have been intended to lead other signatories to believe that the U.S. had accepted some serious obligation. We do not believe the Senate would have thus intended to mislead the other signatory nations. The far more likely, and only expressed, purpose of the reservation to Article 16 was to limit what the United States would accept as "degrading" to a type of activity like that prohibited by the Fifth, Eighth, or Fourteenth amendments of the U.S. Constitution, not to limit the territorial reach of the obligations the United States accepted solely to the area where they would be redundant.

Transfer of Individuals

•**The United States shall abide by its treaty obligations not to transfer an individual to a country if it has probable cause to believe that the individual will be tortured there.** If past conduct suggests that a country has engaged in torture of suspects, the United States shall not transfer a person to that country unless (1) the secretary of state has received assurances from that country that he or she determines to be trustworthy that the individual will not be tortured and has forwarded such assurances and determination to the attorney general; and (2) the attorney general determines that such assurances are "sufficiently reliable" to allow deportation or other forms of rendition.

•**The United States shall not direct or request information from an interrogation or provide assistance to foreign governments in obtaining such information if it has substantial grounds for believing that torture will be utilized to obtain the information.**

•**The United States shall not encourage another nation to make transfers in violation of the prohibitions of the Convention Against Torture.**

Before addressing a regulated system of coercive interrogation, we propose a firm and all-encompassing commitment prohibiting the rendition of individuals to other countries where they will be tortured. U.S. obligations should require the secretary of state to vouch for the trustworthiness of required assurances from the receiving country that the person will not be tortured and the attorney general to find such assurances reliable before undertaking any deportation or informed rendition decision.

In addition, the United States can neither condone such torture by other countries nor promote it by another country. Thus, the United States cannot direct or request information from an interrogation or provide any assistance if there are substantial grounds for believing that torture has been, or will be, utilized by that country. In order to recognize its prohibitions against torture, the United States should also not encourage another nation to make any transfers in violation of such prohibitions.

Oversight of the Use of Any Highly Coercive Interrogation Techniques

•**The attorney general shall recommend and the president shall promulgate and provide to the Senate and House Intelligence, Judiciary and Armed Services Committees, guidelines stating which specific HCI techniques are authorized.**[1] To be authorized, a technique must be consistent with U.S. law and U.S. obligations under international treaties including Article 16 of the Convention against Torture, which under "Treaty and Statutory Commitments" above, prohibits actions that the courts find "shock the conscience." These guidelines shall address the duration and repetition of use of a particular technique and the effect of combining several different techniques together. The attorney general shall brief appropriate committees of both houses of Congress upon request, and no less frequently than every six months, as to which HCIs are presently being utilized by federal officials or those acting on their behalf.

•**No person shall be subject even to authorized HCI techniques** unless (1) authorized interrogators have probable cause to believe that he is in possession of significant information, and there is no reasonable alternative to obtain that information, about either a specific plan that threatens U.S. lives or a group or organization making such plans whose capacity could be significantly reduced by exploiting the

---

1. Highly coercive interrogation methods are all those techniques that fall in the category between those forbidden as torture by treaty or statute and those traditionally allowed in seeking a voluntary confession under the due process clauses of the U.S. Constitution.

information; (2) the determination of whether probable cause is met has been made by senior government officials in writing and on the basis of sworn affidavits; or (3) the determination and its factual basis will be made available to congressional intelligence committees, the attorney general and the inspectors general of the pertinent departments (i.e., Department of Justice, Department of Defense, etc.).

Within the uncertain limits imposed by international agreements, the United States could rely on a presidential list of permissible techniques or on a statutory prohibition defined in general terms. The difficulty of making a statute precise enough in what it allows and forbids leads us to prefer a carefully defined presidential list. The result to be avoided in either case is a rule so vague that it can be secretly interpreted to permit what the American people would otherwise reject.

The substance of our recommendation is relatively clear-cut. These rules are intended to supersede any covert action authority in law, and thus we would recommend the equivalent of a national security act for coercive interrogation purposes.[2] Highly coercive interrogation methods are methods falling between those forbidden as torture by our statutory and treaty obligations and those that would be otherwise acceptable to obtain a confession under the due process clause of the U.S. Constitution. There is, of course, a long list of possible techniques that fall into this category, but we would require the attorney general to recommend to the president a specific listing of permitted techniques; the language of Article 16 is simply too unclear to be helpful to U.S. interrogators on the ground. In addition, the listing must address questions of duration, repetition, and the effect of combining several different techniques, for these make a certain tactic more or less objectionable.

These standards would be promulgated and distributed to relevant congressional oversight committees. Making the presidential list of permissible techniques public may provide the best form of oversight, but there are legitimate worries that knowing which interrogation techniques are available may assist terrorists. Furnishing a list of approved techniques to the relevant committees of both Houses of Congress is a near-substitute without that cost. This briefing might also include how many times HCIs were used in a given period; whether the use of HCIs yielded useful information; what acts of terrorism were prevented or limited as a result of obtaining the information; whether there was a breach of any guideline; and whether any deaths or serious injuries occurred during or as a result of the use of HCIs.

---

2. At the time of writing, several legislative proposals based on these recommendations were being discussed.

The standards to be applied before a highly coercive technique could be used in any individual case could be highly restrictive (requiring some reason to believe that the information sought would save lives and thus satisfying a common standard for a criminal law "necessity" defense) or more permissive (allowing the use of specifically authorized coercive techniques whenever the individual is believed to have information that would be helpful in defeating a terrorist group). Our standard, somewhat in the middle of this range, is supplemented by a requirement that alternative means of gathering information (other than highly coercive interrogation) would not be likely to accomplish the same purpose. Far too much of the present "war on terror" has come to rely on a single weapon—interrogation—from what should be an array of intelligence techniques.

There is no particular reason to call on the same decisionmaker for deciding 1) which techniques are permissible, and 2) when those techniques may be used. The decision as to which techniques are authorized and found to be legal under U.S. statutory and treaty obligations is one that will have to be made only occasionally. In light of its extreme sensitivity, we have analogized it to decisions about covert action that require a presidential, if not a legislative, decision.

The application of duly promulgated standards for when authorized techniques may be used in individual cases could be made in a far more decentralized way. The alternatives are either relatively senior officials in the field or judges. Since the decision would be made in many cases abroad and often under urgent conditions of combat or military occupation, judicial decisionmaking will often be impracticable. An additional weakness of that option is that it makes it difficult to determine who is really accountable. A judge may well believe that he should give very broad discretion to intelligence agents who provide the judge with the necessary information, while the intelligence agents may believe that they need not exercise real judgment because the decision is being made by the judge. Thus, we recommend that senior officials in the field must find probable cause that a specific plan threatens U.S. lives or that the capacity of a group or organization making such plans could be significantly reduced by exploiting the information, that there is no reasonable alternative to obtain the information, and that the person being interrogated under HCI tactics is in possession of the significant information. The determination must be in writing on the basis of sworn affidavits.

The management of the process to be sure that highly coercive interrogation techniques are not used contrary to the standards required by Congress and the president has to fall to the Department of Defense, the Central Intelligence Agency (CIA) and, to whatever extent it is involved, the Federal Bureau of Investigation (FBI). Congressional hearings should fully explore the failings and remedies in this area. The fact that there have already been major failings suggests the need for oversight to be systematic, not just occasioned by scandal. Oversight in any event is essential to ensure that there is a more public check on the president's determination as to what is legal and permissible in the way of coercive interrogation and, on lower level decisions applying statutory standards, as to when coercive techniques can be used on prisoners. There is a requirement to disclose both the general authorizations, as well the more specific factual determinations, to Congress.

Emergency Exception

•No U.S. official or employee, and no other individual acting on behalf of the United States, may use an interrogation technique not specifically authorized in this way except with the express written approval of the president on the basis of a finding of an urgent and extraordinary need. The finding, which must be submitted within a reasonable period to appropriate committees from both houses of Congress, must state the reason to believe that the information sought to be obtained concerns a specific plan that threatens U.S. lives, the information is in possession of the individual to be interrogated, and there are no other reasonable alternatives to save the lives in question. No presidential approval may authorize any form of interrogation that would be prohibited by the Fifth, Eighth, or Fourteenth Amendments of the U.S. Constitution if applied to a U.S. citizen in similar circumstances within the United States.

•The president shall publicly report the number of uses of his special necessity power biannually to Congress.

The establishment of a quite rigorous set of processes and standards for the use of highly coercive techniques that themselves fall short of torture has its own cost. Much of the public will worry—and any administration will argue—that the system will interfere with handling a highly unusual case of extraordinary danger. An example would be the capture of a terrorist who knew where a nuclear weapon or other weapon of mass destruction had been placed. To deal with this remote but still worrisome possibility, the president would be authorized to waive the proposed rules except for the prohibition of "torture" as defined by statute and treaty, in a finding of extraordinary danger in highly unusual circumstances—a finding which he or she would be required to submit promptly to the appropriate committees of the Congress. But this power must not be an excuse for devaluing the lives of non-Americans. Thus, it can only be used when its exercise would be consistent with the U.S. Constitution if applied to U.S. citizens in the United States under similar circumstances.

In addition, the president would be required to disclose publicly to Congress, on a biannual basis, the number of uses of his power. Like the required disclosure of the quantity of foreign intelligence wiretaps, this disclosure provides an oversight mechanism without disclosing specific cases.

Individual Remedies and Applicability

•An individual subjected to HCI in circumstances where the conditions prescribed above have not been met shall be entitled to damages in a civil action against the United States.

•No information obtained by highly coercive interrogation techniques may be used at a U.S. trial, including military trials, against the individual detained.

An additional and perhaps essential form of oversight extends the provisions of Article 14 of the UN Convention Against Torture (which requires states to provide legal remedies to victims of torture) by adding a judicial damage action against the United States if any highly coercive interrogation techniques have been used illegally. This would set aside any special defenses the government may enjoy in other settings but would not affect present law with regard to criminal or civil liability of individual perpetrators. This form of oversight has the immense advantage of not only compensating people wrongfully subjected to severe coercion but also of providing judicial review, after the fact, of the legality of the techniques under our international and domestic legal obligations and of the procedures used before applying them.

In addition, in recognition of the demands of the Fifth Amendment and given the differences between the uncertain product of interrogation tactics and information that is sufficiently credible to be allowed in criminal proceedings, no information obtained by HCI techniques may be used at a U.S. trial (including military trials) against the individual detained.

Chapter 2

Indefinite Detention

In a series of opinions in June 2004, the Supreme Court ruled on the constitutionality and validity of long-term detentions of persons who were believed to be engaged in an armed conflict against the United States. The opinion in *Hamdi v. Rumsfeld*—dealing with the detention of an enemy combatant—held that the U.S. citizen, who was alleged to have been engaged in supporting forces hostile to the United States, must be given some adjudication, before a neutral tribunal, as to the validity of his designation as an enemy combatant. In the Guantanamo Bay detainee case, *Rasul v. Bush*, the Court held that both citizens and aliens are entitled to invoke the federal courts' authority under the U.S. habeas corpus statute, 28 U.S.C. § 2241, at least if they are being detained where the United States exercises as much jurisdiction and control as it does in Guantanamo Bay. In response and with very few specifics as to the nature of the content of the habeas appeal, the Department of Defense announced that it was creating a Combatant Status Review Tribunal in which detainees may challenge their designation as enemy combatants. The legal adequacy of that response was promptly contested in federal district courts, with differing assessments on the nature of the process due.

The Supreme Court carefully limited its holdings in these cases to their specific facts. *Hamdi v. Rumsfeld* is limited to the detention of enemy combatants pursuant to the congressional "Authorization for Use of Military Force" (AUMF) against those responsible for the 9/11 terrorist attacks. Thus, the Court's rulings provide little guidance on the issues presented by new groups and individuals who are determined to attack the United States but were not involved in the attack that took place in 2001. In *Rasul v. Bush*, the Court never reaches the merits of the habeas claim; thus, it is still unclear whether due process rights for foreign-born, foreign-captured detainees (e.g., Guantanamo Bay detainees) are the same (or less) than the due process rights of U.S. citizen detainees captured abroad (as in

Hamdi v. Rumsfeld) or within the United States (as in *Padilla v. Rumsfeld*, which was decided on jurisdictional grounds, rather than on its merits).

The significance of this series of Supreme Court decisions—*Hamdi v. Rumsfeld* in particular—goes beyond these narrow holdings. In a situation of armed conflict deemed applicable by the Court, persons including, but not limited to, active combatants, may be detained as long as necessary—neither as a penal sanction nor for purposes of interrogation, but rather simply to ensure that they do not rejoin the conflict.

These decisions have created a situation where significant parts of the laws of war, which had been largely developed in the context of international armed conflict between and among states, may constitutionally be applied by Congress and the president in response to situations and persons that have previously been viewed as within the exclusive ambit of criminal law. This has resulted in a tremendous tension between the constitutional and statutory procedures and protections enjoyed by those accused of violating the criminal law and the sweeping powers available to the executive branch, at least when granted by Congress, under the U.S. Constitution during an armed conflict.

Reflecting the principles of judicial restraint and prudence, the Court decided these cases as narrowly as possible. The lower courts have been varied in their responses to the cases in individual claims. Resolution of the host of other issues that may arise from governmental actions in the undefined area between traditional interstate war and law enforcement should not be left to the unilateral determinations of either the executive branch or the ad hoc rulings of the courts.

The recommendations that follow present a series of principles and approaches that we believe Congress should follow in creating a statutory framework.

Explanation and Background

We recommend that separate rules be applied to each of three categories of detainees. At one extreme the executive must plainly be able to detain, for reasonable periods of time and under fair and legal conditions, those seized in a zone of active combat fighting against U.S. forces. The primary purpose of this kind of seizure is to take the detainee out of combat, although where the Geneva Conventions permit, interview or interrogation may also be a purpose.

At the opposite pole is the seizure and detention of U.S. persons anywhere or any other person seized within the United States. Here the protections should be greatest, and to the extent it is possible, the United

States should seek to avoid creating a tradition of administrative detention that has been troublesome wherever it has been used and has played no part in the U.S. legal tradition.

In the middle is the third category of people who are not U.S. persons (i.e., neither a citizen nor a resident alien) and who are seized outside the United States but not in a zone of active combat. Such persons—and the countries from which they are seized—deserve protections similar to those enjoyed by U.S. persons or others in the United States, but cannot be accorded any pre-trial protections which depend upon immediate access to U.S. courts. There we provide, as a substitute, a competent military or civilian tribunal.

We will discuss, first, the treatment of U.S. persons and any persons seized within the United States; second, the modifications necessary for those not within these categories but not captured in a zone of active combat; and, finally, the protections for those seized within a zone of active combat.

PERSONS SEIZED WITHIN THE UNITED STATES AND THE SEIZURE OF U.S. PERSONS ANYWHERE IN THE WORLD EXCEPT IN A ZONE OF ACTIVE COMBAT

- **Any U.S. person and any person within the United States who is seized or arrested outside a zone of active combat shall be detained only on criminal charges.** If the present array of statutes is considered inadequate, additional criminal laws should be passed, including, for example, incorporation in Title 18 of the U.S. Code (18 U.S.C.) of the principles of command responsibility in cases where the conduct for which the individual is to be tried constitutes a grave breach of the provisions of the Geneva Conventions of 1949. No such person shall be detained without probable cause to believe that he has committed or is planning to commit an act previously criminalized by statutes. Such persons captured by personnel of military or intelligence agencies must be transferred without delay to the custody of civilian authorities.

- **Any such person seized with probable cause that he is planning, assisting, or executing an act of terrorism can and should be charged with conspiring to violate one of the many U.S. statutes criminalizing acts of terrorism.**

- **A judicial officer shall order the pre-trial detention (under 18 U.S.C. § 3142(e)) of the individual arrested upon a showing that there is reason to suspect that the individual arrested** (1) has committed a terrorist act; or (2) is planning or supporting a planned terrorist act; and (3) cannot be prevented from assisting in that effort by any other reasonable means.

•The detainee shall be allowed access to an attorney of his choice. If the government intends to rely on classified information at any stage of the detention proceedings, it will make every effort to provide security clearance as quickly as possible to that attorney and will make available, in the meantime, a list of cleared defense attorneys. If the detainee cannot be represented by a cleared defense attorney of his choice at a critical stage of detention proceedings, the court shall promptly appoint a "special advocate" who is cleared to see all evidence and whose role is to argue the case against detention. This special advocate shall not thereby form an attorney-client relationship with the detainee.

•The judicial officer may deny the detainee, but not his cleared attorney or "special advocate," access to parts of the detention hearing if, on the basis of a governmental petition, the officer concludes this step is necessary to protect national security secrets.

•On showing to a court that, despite the Classified Information Procedures Act, an immediate trial would be impossible without significant loss of national security secrets, and evidence that cannot be revealed in public demonstrates that release of the detainee would significantly endanger the lives of others, a federal judge may delay the trial date for a period of ninety days and renew the delay for a period of up to two years while the government pursues evidence that can be used at a public trial without compromising national security. During this period, the government must seek orders extending pre-trial detention for every ninety-day period. The first such order must be issued within ninety days of initial detention. Each order shall be subject to prompt appeal whether or not it is considered a final judgment.

•A person so detained who is not thereafter brought to trial shall be entitled to fair compensation from the United States for the period of detention. Whenever the executive detains a non-U.S. person who is in violation of his immigration status or his permission to enter the United States, he shall not be detained for a period longer than that required for his deportation unless pursuant to the procedures of this Section. No person shall be detained as a material witness, rather than under the provisions of this Act, unless a federal judge specifically determines that the risk of non-appearance, the importance of the witness to the proceeding, and the importance of the proceeding justify that detention as a matter of law.

Here we insist on the application of familiar criminal law rules with relatively minor modifications for a simple but powerful reason: except for the most dire of necessities (discussed in the final section of our recommendations on indefinite detention), the United States should not create a new category of administrative detention without criminal trial. This has proved to be a dangerous executive power wherever in the world it has been exercised. It is a threat to freedom and democracy. Our objective has been to use the normal and traditional American way of handling dangerous people—the criminal law with its extensive judicial protections—to deal with almost anyone found in the United States and with every U.S. person found anywhere in the world outside a zone of active combat. That decision means that persons in either of these categories cannot be detained without probable cause of having committed a crime and arrest for prosecution of that criminal charge.

In considering our recommendations for this category, it is useful to have in mind the situation where the United States would most want and need some form of detention. In the not-unlikely event that a friendly foreign government were to provide information on the condition that the United States not reveal its source (perhaps because of the danger to its sources and methods) and that the information suggested the planned participation of an individual within the United States (or by a U.S. person anywhere else in the world) in a domestic terrorist attack, preventing that attack might require the prompt detention of that individual. How can that be accomplished, consistent with U.S. traditions, without revealing to the public or the defendant the source of what may be highly specific information about the danger? Equally important, how can this be done without creating a tradition of detention either without judicial protections or without proof of having violated a federal statute? This is the core problem we considered.

If preventive detention of terrorists should be limited to those that the United States has probable cause to believe are planning terrorist acts, and for a period of time no longer than necessary to bring such suspects to trial, then a very high percentage of American national security and civil liberties concerns can be reconciled by carefully extending the present statutory requirements for a speedy trial in cases where sources and methods of intelligence gathering must be protected.

We believe that nobody within the United States and no U.S. person abroad should be detained with less than probable cause to believe he is engaged in terrorism. On that basis he or she can routinely be held pending trial for committing a U.S. terrorist offense. Without probable cause, careful surveillance of any individual suspected of plotting terrorist acts should be used; the line would simply be drawn at detention with probable cause, and nothing less. If a person is arrested and held for trial, he or she should and would be detained pending trial under ordinary federal statutes (18 USC 3142 (e)).

In seeking a judicial decision to detain an individual, the government need not today reveal the name of the informant to the defendant or his counsel, and often not even to the court. The same would be true of arrest or detention based on any other intelligence sources and methods that might be compromised for the future by revelation. The judge, who must simply be satisfied by government evidence that the source is reliable and trustworthy, can decide how much information he or she requires to satisfy that standard.

We would grant the arrested suspect prompt access to an attorney of his choice who shall be granted security clearance if possible and as quickly as possible. Pending his attorney's security clearance, the suspect shall be assisted, at any stage requiring access to classified material, by a "special advocate" whose role it is to argue on his behalf—for example, against the continued detention. This is a protection that is not generally available in the case of those involved in organized crimes who were arrested on the basis of confidential information.

The only special step for the category of persons seized within the United States or for U.S. persons seized elsewhere is a somewhat extended opportunity for the U.S. government to ready its case. Under our American traditions and Constitution, the trial must be public and all evidence used for conviction must be available to the defendant and his counsel. Thus, in the hypothetical we are considering, the evidence for conviction must be provided openly and not secretly, as in the case of evidence for arrest and detention, to the court. At the same time, the evidence from foreign or other sources that must be protected cannot, in our example, be made public at trial.

The government must therefore be given a reasonable period of time in which to pursue usable evidence from other sources. For that purpose, we allow the trial court to delay the trial date for a period of ninety days renewable for a total period of up to two years while the government pursues evidence that can be used at a public trial without compromising national security. This can only happen if the court makes two critical findings—that despite the Classified Information Procedures Act a trial would currently be impossible without a severe loss of national security secrets; and that the evidence that cannot be revealed in public demonstrates that the release of the detainee would significantly endanger the lives of others. Any such decision to delay the trial for ninety days is subject to prompt appeal. At the end of two years, if no trial has begun, the detainee must be released and shall be provided with fair compensation from the United States for the period of detention.

Detentions based on immigration status or the material witness statute should not be used as subterfuges for a carefully delineated criminal justice system. We would carefully confine any such cases to their intended purposes.

NON-U.S. PERSONS SEIZED OUTSIDE THE UNITED STATES AND NOT IN A ZONE OF ACTIVE COMBAT

• **A non-U.S. person cannot be seized by a U.S. intelligence or military agency acting within any state in which the U.S. secretary of state has certified that the state is willing and able (practically and legally) to assist the United States in all legal ways to prevent attacks on U.S. territory, persons, or property, unless such seizure is with the permission or concurrence of appropriate authorities of that state.** If the secretary of state has not so certified or if the individual is delivered to U.S. officials by officials of the place where he is found, he may be detained.

• **No individual will be seized abroad outside a zone of active combat by U.S. forces, civilian personnel, or others acting on behalf of the United States unless a senior legal officer of the agency responsible for the seizure has made a written and documented finding that there is probable cause that the individual is planning a terrorist attack against the United States.**

• **A competent military or specialized civilian tribunal defined by statute shall substitute for a federal court abroad, and may perform the functions otherwise assigned in the previous section of our recommendations on indefinite detention to a federal judge or magistrate and under the same restrictions and conditions, determine whether detention by an intelligence or military agency or other U.S. authorities is legal and appropriate.** A decision to detain and each renewal and denial of personal legal assistance shall be subject to judicial review. The above procedures, relating to ex parte hearings and the designation of a "special advocate" if a personal attorney is not available or not permitted access to classified information, shall apply during this judicial review. In any case to be tried within the United States (as described in chapter 3), the period of pre-trial detention prior to transfer to the United States for trial shall not exceed thirty days.

• **Access of the detainee to an attorney of his choice may be delayed up to seven days by order of the judicial officer on a showing that the individual arrested has information which may prevent an imminent terrorist attack and that any interrogation will be conducted in a way consistent with the U.S. Constitution and U.S. statutory and treaty obligations.** No statement obtained by custodial interrogation in the absence of a lawyer representing the detainee or any evidence derived from any such statement will be admissible at any criminal prosecution of the detainee.

•**The federal district court in the geographic jurisdiction to which the person seized and detained is first transferred shall have jurisdiction to try the charges.** Our preceding provisions for persons seized within the United States and for U.S. persons seized abroad apply to the trial.

We would treat this category of persons as similarly as possible to U.S. persons or others seized within the United States. Several differences are, however, essential.

First, the issue of a non-U.S. person abroad presents questions of international law and sovereignty that are not presented when the seizure is within the United States. While a seizure abroad may be necessary when it occurs within a state that is not cooperating in efforts to prevent attacks on the United States, it is not justified when it is carried out within a state that is willing and able to help prevent attacks on U.S. territory, persons, or property. We therefore forbid seizures within the latter category unless the seizure is with the permission or concurrence of the appropriate authorities in the state where the individual is found.

Because the seizure abroad would be made by those not necessarily familiar with the standards of probable cause that are well known to law enforcement personnel within the United States, we require that a senior legal officer at the agency responsible for the seizure approve the arrest on the basis of probable cause to believe that the individual is planning a terrorist attack against the United States. The detainee should have a right to an attorney thereafter, but only so far as this is practicable in the place where he or she is held abroad. In any event, we allow a military judicial officer or the judge of a specially created civilian court to delay the appointment of an attorney for a non-U.S. person seized abroad for up to seven days, so long as any interrogation during that time is conducted in a way that is consistent with the U.S. Constitution and U.S. statutory and treaty obligations. Where there is no attorney present, no statements obtained during custodial interrogation are to be admissible in any criminal prosecution.

The decision to detain the individual pending transfer to the United States for trial is to be made by a competent military or specialized civilian tribunal if the individual is outside the jurisdiction of the United States courts. As in the case of arrests within the United States, the decision to detain is subject to prompt judicial review either within the military system or, by habeas corpus, within the United States. In any event, the period of pre-trial detention prior to transfer to the United States may not exceed thirty days.

Trial must generally be within the United States under the procedures established for those arrested within the United States or for U.S. persons arrested elsewhere.

PERSONS SEIZED WITHIN A ZONE OF ACTIVE COMBAT

•**A "designated zone of active combat" is territory declared by the president, either publicly or in a classified presidential determination made available to the appropriate oversight committees of Congress, as constituting a theater of military operations** (1) in connection with a declared war or other armed conflict between the United States and a foreign state, organization, or defined class of individuals; or (2) the territory occupied and administered, consistent with the Geneva Conventions, by the U.S. military following such a conflict; or (3) within the territory of a state that the United States has been asked to assist in connection with the suppression of an armed insurrection or other uprising within that state.

•**The rules set forth in the first two sections do not apply to the detention of persons captured during hostilities in a designated zone of active combat.** Whatever rights and liabilities now exist for such persons are not affected in any way by those sections.

•**The U.S. Constitution, the decisions interpreting it, the Third and Fourth Geneva Conventions (to the extent applicable), and relevant Department of Defense directives consistent with these sources and any other U.S. treaty obligations shall be fully honored.**

•**At a minimum, the following protections shall be available:**

1. An individual captured in a zone of active combat is entitled to an initial determination, after a hearing before a competent tribunal to be held as soon as practicable under the circumstances, of whether he was engaged in or actively supporting those engaged in hostilities against the United States and whether he is entitled to prisoner of war (POW) or other protected status under the Geneva Conventions of 1949.

2. During the continuation of hostilities but outside the zone of active combat designated by the president, the detainee shall be accorded a periodic review to determine whether his continued detention is warranted because he continues his support for the hostile force to which he belonged.

•**Detainees held in a facility under U.S. control and outside a zone of active combat shall** (1) be accorded the right to challenge their detention through habeas corpus in U.S. federal court, under 28

U.S.C. §2241; and (2) be accorded such fundamental due process rights under the Fifth Amendment as the federal courts determine are appropriate in light of the factors set forth in *Mathews v. Eldridge*: the private interest of the person asserting the lack of due process; the risk of erroneous deprivation of that interest through the use of existing procedures and the probable value of additional or substitute procedural safeguards; and the competing national security interests of the government.

• After the president or Congress has determined that the hostilities in connection with which he was detained have terminated, the detainee shall without undue delay be released and repatriated to his country of citizenship or prosecuted for violations of the laws of war or other applicable penal provisions before a federal court or other appropriate tribunal.

We define the category of a "designated zone of active combat" as one formally determined and publicly (when possible) announced by the president as a theater of military operations in connection with an armed conflict, or an occupation following such a conflict, or territory in which the United States is operating at the request of a government to suppress an armed insurrection or other uprising. Individuals seized within that area do not enjoy the special protections described above. Their protections flow from the obligations that are imposed by the U.S. Constitution, ratified treaties, or Defense Department directives applicable to such situations. The Geneva Conventions are an important source of such protections where they apply. What we seek to provide is a floor of protections that is available even if there are no other such sources.

Every individual captured in a zone of active combat is entitled to an initial determination of whether he or she was engaged in or actively supporting hostilities against the United States, and, if he or she was, whether he or she is entitled to POW or other protected status under the 1949 Geneva Conventions.

If in light of these determinations, if the individual is detained outside the zone of active combat designated by the president, he or she is entitled to periodic review to determine whether his or her continued detention is warranted because he or she continues his or her support of the hostile force to which he or she belongs. During that time the individual is entitled to judicial review by habeas corpus in accordance with the recent Supreme Court decisions. The procedures for the purpose of that review will be determined by courts under the Fifth Amendment requirement of due process and in light of the by now well-established standards of *Matthew v. Eldridge*.

When the hostilities in connection with which the individual was detained have terminated, the detainee must be promptly released and repatriated to his or her country of citizenship, unless he or she is prosecuted for violations of the laws of war or other applicable penal provisions.

DETENTION ON THE BASIS OF A JUDICIAL WARRANT *exception*

•**Notwithstanding any other provisions in this section, the Foreign Intelligence Surveillance Court may issue and renew a warrant for thirty days of detention for an individual who is not a U.S. person whether seized within or outside the territory of the United States. A warrant shall be issued only in the following circumstances:**

1. The attorney general must personally approve the application.

2. The application must satisfy the court, on the basis of affidavits or sworn testimony, that the individual to be detained either (1) must be prevented by detention from assisting in an imminent terrorist attack, or possesses information critical to the safety of U.S. persons or citizens of other democratic nations from imminent terrorist attack and will be subjected to lawful interrogations for a period authorized by the court; or (2) is a high-level leader in the planning or financing of an extended plan of terrorist attacks and either will be subjected to lawful interrogations for a period authorized by the court or is not yet known by his associates to have been captured, creating important possibilities of tactical surprise for a limited period.

•**The application for the warrant and its justification must be made available promptly, under conditions of assured secrecy, to the appropriate committees of Congress.** The number of such warrants and renewals of warrants issued each year shall be made public annually. The warrant issued by the Foreign Intelligence Surveillance Court shall specify (1) the location, duration, and conditions of detention authorized by the warrant; and (2) any necessary conditions of judicial monitoring of interrogations for legality under U.S. law and treaties.

For much the same extraordinary situation that, we believe, warrants presidential power to create a limited exception to the regulation of highly coercive interrogation (but not to the prohibition of torture), we recommend an extraordinary exception to the requirement of our system that detention be based on familiar principles of pre-trial detention. To permit lawful and limited interrogation in a case of urgent necessity, or to allow secrecy about the capture of individuals critical to a terrorist scheme, we would allow the Foreign Intelligence Surveillance Court to authorize a detention of up to thirty days, renewable if the conditions of initial detention remain in place.

A warrant would be issued only if the attorney general personally certifies and provides sworn evidence that the individual's extraordinary role in an imminent attack or in overall planning of many attacks justifies either temporary secrecy about his capture or interrogation without the familiar protections surrounding interrogation after arrest on criminal charges. The warrant shall specify the location, duration, and conditions of detention. The warrant and the factual support justifying detention must be promptly sent to appropriate Congressional committees.

Chapter 3

Military Commissions

Military commissions are intended to impose punishment for violations of the laws of war. They are neither meant as a form of detention nor are they justified as a form of deterrence or punishment, except on the basis of a fair determination of guilt. They are, in other words, not justified as a device for allowing severe punishment to be imposed on foreign citizens without a fair opportunity to contest the evidence and without the same level of certainty required for other criminal convictions under U.S. authority.

There are thus only two justifications for the use of military commissions as the appropriate tribunals to judge accusations of war crimes against members of hostile forces. First, the requirements of familiar rules of evidence in trials within the United States, including the constitutional right to confrontation, may be inconsistent with maintaining critically important secrecy about matters of national security. Second, the difficulties, costs, and inconvenience of moving a trial from a remote battlefield to the United States may require some form of tribunal other than a federal court within the United States.

The specific (and for our purposes most relevant) use of military commissions, on display now at Guantanamo Bay, raises significant concerns about their viability and fairness. The administration has spent several years justifying a tribunal system that appears to be unmoored from any justifications for its use.

We believe that the desire to use secret evidence at trial should be dealt with by a transparent legislative procedure, making such additions to the Classified Information Procedures Act as are thought to be both necessary to protect national security and consistent with the fairness that is traditional in the United States before imposing punishment, particularly with severe penalties. Any such additions should presumably apply not only to trials of foreign combatants, but also to trials of U.S. civilians and of members of the U.S. armed services.

As to the second reason for military commissions—the great administrative inconvenience of trials within the United States of individuals seized on remote battlefields—it applies primarily to those seized in a zone of active combat. There, the availability of courts-martial, with their accumulated traditions and understood rules of procedure, should provide the needed convenience and feasibility without most of the political and moral costs of using military commissions. For those seized outside zones of active combat, trial for violation of the laws of war should, whenever possible, be in a civilian court either within the United States or where the acts of planning or executing terrorism took place.

Explanation and Background

In February 2004, the Department of Defense (DoD) announced that it would utilize new military commissions against alleged terrorists who were captured in Afghanistan and had been detained at Guantanamo Bay. These commissions would be pursuant to President George W. Bush's Military Order of November 13, 2001, authorizing the use of military commissions to try non-U.S. citizens who are or were members of al-Qaida, who engaged in acts of international terrorism or who knowingly harbored such persons. Subsequently, the Department of Defense issued detailed instructions on when military commissions could be used, the procedures that would apply to such trials and the form of appellate review.

The United States has utilized military commissions in the past, most recently a half-century ago. There is thus nothing unprecedented about the administration's proposed alternative to traditional courts-martial for those captured and detained in the course of armed conflict. We make no assessment on their past necessity. Previous military commissions were limited in time and place. What is at stake here today, however, is the existence of an alternative tribunal—the military commission tribunal—that may for the indefinite future serve as an easy alternative to the more rigorous demands of criminal or court-martial tribunals, based merely on a presidential finding that the person had some relationship to the war on terror.

Even if a plea of guilty makes a trial unnecessary, the issue of unfairness is stark. The extent to which the existence of military commissions has altered the historic equilibrium between the government and defense can not be ignored. The case of Zacharias Moussaoui, the alleged twentieth 9/11 hijacker, stalled on what some would argue were "procedural" debates, but what others believe cut to the core of a defendant's right to exculpatory evidence. The trial judge in the case required the government to make available to the defense captured high-level al-Qaida members who might state that Moussaoui had nothing to do with the planning of the 9/11 terrorist attacks. The government refused, believing the precedent dangerous. This should be resolved by adjudication, but, in the background, clearly, lay the threat that if the government did not win on appeal, it could easily seek to dismiss the criminal case and immediately take Moussaoui to a closed military tribunal where different rules would apply. Moussaoui eventually pled guilty.

Any tribunal imposing punishment should have, and appear to have, five characteristics.

1. It should have clear substantive prohibitions that predate the actions of the defendant.

2. It should have fair procedures, including fair rules of evidence.

3. Decisions must be in the hands of fair-minded fact finders.

4. The law must be addressed by unbiased and competent judges on questions of both substance and procedure.

5. The tribunal must provide for a competent and dedicated defense.

Both federal courts for the civilian population of the United States and courts-martial for the military population and for prisoners of war have, and are seen to have, those characteristics.

In contrast, the military commissions in their present form face grave difficulties in being, and especially in appearing to be, unbiased, because they deal only with enemy soldiers, not with U.S. military personnel or civilians. Their procedures and rules of evidence were decided ex parte and for the particular defendants and not on the basis of legislation, open administrative process or precedent. The new commissions involve unusual restrictions on the actions of defense counsel. Among other things, their provisions for appeals from conviction are far less formal and go to officials less trusted than the appellate judges who review convictions from federal courts or courts-martial. Procedural changes to the specifics of military commissions are not needed, since their legitimate functions can be handled by courts-martial.

ADDITIONS TO THE CLASSIFIED INFORMATION PROCEDURES ACT (CIPA)

•The U.S. Congress should consider the need for adding to the terms of the Classified Information Procedures Act. The U.S. Congress should include such provisions as are thought necessary to permit the trial of terrorists and others for violations of federal terrorist statutes or the rules of war. As in the case of CIPA, there must be adequate guarantees that any modifications of familiar court or court martial procedures do not significantly undermine the fairness of a trial. Subject to that constraint any modifications adopted should protect national security secrets from revelation either to the defendant or to a wider public during a trial. If the constraint of fair trial cannot be met and if any trial would disclose critical national security secrets, only temporary detention can be used, not as a punishment but as a form of needed, but temporary, incapacitation.

This recommendation seeks to link the use of military commissions with justifications for their use. Regarding the concerns about whether national security secrets would be disclosed, the same issue—to what extent fairness in imposing punishment depends upon revealing national security secrets and, in those circumstances, what the reconciliation should be—is true not only in trying foreign "illegal combatants," but also in trying prisoners of war or U.S. soldiers or U.S. civilians for violations of the laws of war or plotting terrorism or espionage for a foreign enemy. Based on this justification, there is no sound reason why the resolution should be different and harsher for foreign citizens who were captured abroad and are not entitled to POW status than for those who are. There is no reason why the resolution should be different for either of these categories of non-U.S. persons than it is for U.S. persons, whether in the military or not.

We therefore first propose that the Congress address directly, thoughtfully, and transparently what, if any, additions must be made to the protections of classified information from trial disclosure now found in the Classified Information Procedures Act. That this is an extremely difficult issue and likely to be very contentious is not a reason to hide it in the creation of ad hoc tribunals capable of imposing punishments up to execution for foreign combatants.

JURISDICTION OVER VIOLATIONS OF THE LAWS OF WAR

• **Any case of military trial for violation of the laws of war of a person seized as a combatant within a zone of active combat will be tried before a court-martial under the jurisdiction granted by 10 U.S.C. § 818.**

• **Persons seized within a zone of active combat will be tried only by such court-martial,** whether the individual is deemed a lawful combatant, and therefore entitled to the protections of the Geneva Conventions, or an unlawful combatant.

• **Except for U.S. military personnel, all prosecutions for violations of laws of war committed by U.S. persons captured outside a zone of active combat or of individuals found within the United States shall be carried out in a federal district court.**

•If seized outside a zone of active combat and outside the United States, a non-U.S. person detained for violating the laws of war is subject to court-martial only if the attorney general certifies to the appropriate military authorities that (1) there cannot be a fair and secure civilian trial before a United States district court; and (2) either there is no reliable prospect of a fair and vigorous trial before a court of the state where the criminal acts of planning a terrorist attack on the United States took place, or any such trial in a foreign court would require the revelation of national security secrets that would otherwise be protected by a U.S. district court.

Given the need to confine military jurisdiction to traditional areas, to protect fundamental rights of citizens, and the potential abuse of the threat of military trial, we have addressed the appropriate tribunal question based on the status of the detainee and where he was captured. Throughout, we have sought to tie the use of any non-civilian court to the explicit need.

Thus, one purpose of military commissions—the convenience of operating anywhere in the world, including under battlefield conditions—can be fully accommodated by substituting the military courts-martial with their established procedures and tradition of seeking fair resolution of issues of guilt in dealing with the U.S. military for the military commissions now being established by the Department of Defense for any person captured within a zone of active combat. Indeed, military courts-martial are specifically authorized by statute (10 U.S.C. § 818) "to try any person who by the law of war is subject to trial by a military tribunal and may adjudge any punishment permitted by the law of war." For persons captured within a zone of active combat, there is no sound reason to avoid court-martial. (Prosecuting authorities may always, of course, choose to bypass court-martial and have cases tried in federal court.)

It may be that some changes in procedures to protect national security secrets are fair, and therefore permissible in courts-martial under the power granted the president by 10 U.S.C. § 836 (to alter for courts-martial any rules of evidence used in the trial of criminal cases in the U.S. district courts that the president finds impracticable). It is unresolved whether some such changes in procedure might nevertheless be precluded in federal district courts by the Supreme Court's 2004 interpretation of the Sixth Amendment Confrontation Clause in *Crawford v. Washington*, 124 S. Ct. 1354 (2004). This would only mean, however, that trials in federal district courts in the United States would have to be conducted under conditions less protective of national security.

Outside an active zone of combat, for all prosecutions for violations of the laws of war, civilian trials should apply to nonmilitary U.S. persons or to individuals found within the United States. In those circumstances, they should be tried in federal district court. There is simply no basis for the use of military tribunals in those circumstances.

Finally, civilian trials should also be the preferred option for non-U.S. persons captured outside a zone of active combat (and not in the United States), except in special circumstances certified by the attorney general. In those circumstances, the attorney general would need to satisfy the appropriate military authorities that a civilian trial in the United States is impossible, and that the country where his unlawful acts took place either would not adequately prosecute him or could not without disclosing national security secrets that would otherwise be prosecuted in a U.S. trial. In these limited circumstances, a court-martial would be permitted.

Chapter 4

Targeted Killing

The United States should adopt new rules and oversight for the use of targeted killings to combat terrorism. The existing assassination ban in the United States is vague and of uncertain applicability in the context of counterterrorism waged in part by overt and covert military action. As a result, the United States has failed to adequately define the appropriate use, if any, of targeted killings.

During times of active combat, killing is an obvious result of, and often the specific object of, military action. It is unclear now to what extent targeted killing is being used in our efforts against terrorism. What is clear is that the new context requires a set of clear rules and standards for this kind of action in order to avoid the abuse that may occur, and may already have occurred, in the absence of such rules and standards.

In the gray area between war in the traditional sense and law enforcement in the ordinary sense in which counterterrorism actions are now being conducted, neither the general authority to attack personnel who may be lawfully engaged in combat roles under the law of war nor the strict law enforcement prohibition against targeted killing is appropriate.

The following detailed set of recommendations is intended to supplement previous executive orders, any criminal statutes regarding murders abroad, and the more general statutory provisions governing covert actions. In other words, these recommendations detail additional and specific standards for this one type of action—targeted killing outside zones of active combat.

Explanation and Background

America's long-standing prohibition against the use of targeted killings, commonly referred to as assassination if occurring outside of war, has been challenged in new ways by current counterterrorism actions. Whatever one's view on the degree to which the laws of war and the wartime powers of the president do or do not apply in various contexts to our current actions, it is generally accepted that the deaths of Osama bin Laden and other prominent members of al-Qaida would be a legitimate and desired outcome of those actions. The justification given by many inside and outside of government for the acceptability of such an outcome is that the military is engaged in active combat against leaders who are, under domestic, military, and international norms, lawful targets for death. The campaign to kill bin Laden and his senior associates, admitted openly and discussed publicly, has committed the United States for the first time to public targeting of specific, named individuals whether or not they are within a zone of active combat.

Our effort here is to develop rules. In what contexts, under which conditions, and following which procedures should a system of killing suspected terrorists be used?

The primary source of domestic law governing assassination is Executive Order 12333, which reads, "No person employed by or acting on behalf of the United States Government shall engage in, or conspire to engage in, assassination." For several reasons the coverage of the Executive Order has become less clear over the years. First, the president may secretly create exceptions to it or suspend the order. In addition, it would not be considered assassination under the Executive Order to target the leader of a hostile state's military force during an armed conflict. Second, the president may invoke the nation's right to self-defense, recognized in Article 51 of the UN Charter, in order to justify a killing. Third, the president may interpret the ban narrowly. For example, after the bombing raid on Libya in 1986, President Ronald Reagan's White House legal counsel argued that Colonel Muammar Qaddafi's possible death during the bombing of his compound would not have violated the Executive Order because the compound was a valid military target.

Indeed, many believe that the Executive Order is basically no standard at all, mostly because of the series of exceptions that have, in the end, greatly narrowed the scope of the prohibition. In conversations with people who have worked within the CIA in senior positions, the ban proved, in the words of one, "sort of a reminder that we shouldn't go after guys like Castro again, but in the real world, we knew that there were ways to get around it."

If a targeted killing were to be carried out in the form of a covert action by an intelligence agency, the president would have to comply with specific procedures under federal statutes. In order to authorize a covert action, the president must make a finding that the action (1) is necessary to support identifiable foreign policy objectives of the United States and (2) is important to the national security of the United States. Such a finding must be in writing and must generally precede the launch of the covert action, but may be issued forty-eight hours after the action if circumstances demand it. These findings must be sent to the congressional intelligence committees, but, in extraordinary circumstances, they may be sent only to the congressional leadership. (if = same political party ....)

The application of either the Executive Order or the federal statute to covert military operations against terrorists is less than clear. Congress has, however, discussed requiring a presidential finding before special operations units may be used secretly. Lethal military operations and targeting have been justified as being part of the "preparation of the battlefield" in the global war against terror and are therefore viewed as being routine support of traditional military activities. In legislative debates regarding the use of military covert activity, it was recognized that while the operation as a whole may be publicly acknowledged, such support could be kept secret but still be subject to rules governing military conduct. Under this view, if the war on terror is considered a publicly acknowledged operation, then such covert targeted killings may be routine support and, if so, are exempt from the assassination prohibition or the requirement of a presidential finding.

During war in the traditional sense, the military is proscribed from using assassination or any other lethal targeting of persons other than legitimate targets. Legitimate targets include, among others, "individual soldiers or officers of the enemy whether in the zone of hostilities, occupied territory, or elsewhere." In time of war, it is as a general proposition lawful for the military to target and kill any non-surrendering enemy combatant, in any place and at any time, regardless of what that combatant had done or was doing and regardless of whether that combatant posed an imminent threat or any individualized threat at all.

The application of the assassination ban to military special operations and the scope of the national security justification were tested before the war on terrorism. In Mark Bowden's book about the death of Pablo Escobar, *Killing Pablo*, he details the extensive history of U.S. Special Forces units engaged in an effort to kill the Colombian drug lord. Without presidential approval, at the very least, the units were actively involved with Escobar's death, though many disagree with Bowden's assessment that U.S. military personnel actually pulled the trigger. Nonetheless, few deny that the military provided valuable assistance in the targeted killing of a man not clearly a direct or imminent threat to U.S. national security.

A complicated series of laws govern the use of assassinations within international law. For present purposes, in times of peace, the prohibitions on assassination are codified in international law, specifically in the International Covenant on Civil and Political Rights (ratified by the United States). Any killing that is carried out beyond a zone of active combat and within a different state without its permission is also, absent a right of self-defense triggered by that state's malfeasance or nonfeasance, a flagrant violation of that state's sovereignty. Thus, Israel's use of assassination in other countries—most notably, the 1988 killing of Palestinian terrorist Abu Jihad in Tunisia—has been condemned for violating Tunisia's territorial integrity protected by Article 2(4) of the UN Charter.

The problem with applying this body of law—Executive Orders, statutes, and treaty commitments—to targeted killing of terrorists is that while the rules governing a traditional war may justify lethal action against both soldiers and senior command-and-control leaders in a combat zone and perhaps beyond, the war on terrorism has no explicit geographic or temporal limits. Afghanistan is, from this perspective, an easy example of a zone of combat, but the use of a Predator drone to kill a senior al-Qaida leader in Yemen in November 2002 (along with his entourage, including a U.S. citizen) seems different. The military was not engaged in active combat in Yemen; it was, in that regard, like any other state in the world. The war on terrorism that the United States is pursuing is, moreover, likely to last for decades.

TARGETED KILLING IN A DESIGNATED ZONE OF ACTIVE COMBAT

•**The following rules do not apply to targeting those engaged in active hostilities in a zone of active combat.** A "designated zone of active combat" is territory designated by the president, either publicly or in a classified presidential determination made available to the appropriate oversight committees of the Congress, as constituting a theater of military operations (1) in connection with a declared war or other armed conflict between the United States and a foreign state, organization, or defined class of individuals; (2) in the territory occupied and administered, consistent with the Geneva Conventions, by the U.S. military following such a conflict; or (3) within the territory of a state that the United States has been asked to assist in connection with the suppression of an armed insurrection or other uprising within that state.

The campaign against terrorists does not easily fall into the category of either war or not war. On the other hand, a policy that views targeted killings, with no standards, as acceptable cannot be justified either to the world or to U.S. citizens. Countries that have used targeted killings, such as Argentina and Chile, have done so with tremendous and detrimental consequences to their own populations. Israel, which has explicitly and openly used a program of targeted killings aimed at senior Palestinian terrorists, has a very detailed procedure used by the government to authorize a killing. The Israeli population, however, as well as senior government leaders there, are torn about the benefits—let alone the morality—of such a policy.

Recognizing that setting up additional rules for zones of active combat (including situations of occupation by military means as in the case of Iraq) is neither wise nor practical, we have instead sought to give real content to a structure of rules and standards governing targeted killing outside the zones of active combat.

TARGETED KILLING OUTSIDE A DESIGNATED ZONE OF ACTIVE COMBAT

•In all situations and locations outside designated zones of active combat, any targeted killing must be pursuant to procedures outlined in legislation detailing the conditions for such an action.

The future of the terrorist threat is not only worldwide, but also of indefinite duration. People involved in terror against the United States often operate out of foreign countries. Because these foreign countries are independent sovereign states, the United States is normally obligated to rely on their governments to incapacitate or kill the terrorists. Many foreign governments are, however, either unable or unwilling to help the United States for a variety of reasons. The nation itself may have a government hostile to the United States, such as Syria or Iran. Nations may have friendly governments but populations or governmental elements that are hostile to the United States, thus making it difficult for the governments to combat terrorists on our behalf. Some nations may have no effective control over parts of their own territory, such as Yemen, Pakistan, or Sudan. Others may lack extradition treaties with the United States or, in some instances, may not have harsh enough penalties against terrorists. Nations may even have nonexistent or ineffective governments, such as Somalia or the Palestinian Authority.

In any of these contexts, unable to rely on the cooperation of a foreign government, U.S. options regarding how it may deal with the terrorists on its own are quite limited. There is always, of course, the option to do nothing and hope that the terrorists go to another country where they could be apprehended or killed. Alternatively, the United States could invade the country with a military force large enough and willing to stay long enough to destroy the terrorists or change the regime, an option used in Afghanistan. Realistically, this option is quite limited. Militarily, it costs lives and is quite expensive. Abroad, it is extremely risky both politically and diplomatically. Legally, it creates the kinds of problems under international law that were present in debates leading up to the war in Iraq.

Because of these limitations, targeted killings against known terrorists have become a real and accepted option within the United States as the only reasonably effective way of reaching a hostile target. The targeted killing of a terrorist could prevent a planned attack and could serve as a deterrent to terrorist groups or to individuals who may be inclined to join them. Targeted killing, in some contexts, would also improve domestic morale because it shows progress against a specific terrorist enemy. One can readily imagine the impact of the known death of Osama bin Laden on the sense of security in the United States. Still, the most basic purpose is trying to stop the next attack. The targeted killing of a leader or a critical member of a terrorist group may temporarily incapacitate the organization and at least delay terrorist activity. Given the other options available, killing a terrorist receiving shelter in a hostile state would be far less costly in terms of lives and money than invading that state. Where a threat is imminent, targeted killing—which does not require extensive evidence gathering for trial or preparation for full-scale invasion—also provides needed speed.

The costs of targeted killing are, however, imposing. Osama bin Laden is the easy example, but the practice of targeted killings against specific individuals will lead the United States down a path of both legal and moral ambiguity. Its legality under international law, outside of a zone of active combat, is extremely doubtful. Its morality for domestic or foreign audiences depends upon a set of conditions and procedures that are not generally specified by its supporters. In many, perhaps most, cases it will alienate allies and discourage forms of cooperation that we badly need. It predictably creates a vicious cycle of attack and counterattack.

While some have argued that the U.S. ban on assassination has proved to be as well known for its exceptions as for its prohibition, it has likely symbolically served as a way to discourage other states from using targeted killing and at least has given the United States some moral authority to condemn excessive killing by other nations, such as Guatemala or Argentina. Targeted killings may in fact radicalize elements within the opposition group, inspiring new recruits. Several studies of the Phoenix Program in Vietnam, which targeted the Viet Cong infrastructure for killing, state that the process of deciding who will be killed can be subject to all sorts of self-interested manipulations; without adequate intelligence, a strategy of targeted killing is fatally flawed.

This is clearly what animated the disunity among members of the task force regarding this subject. What created passionate debate was not so much targeted killings in Iraq, or even a particular individual like bin Laden, but the November 2002 death of terrorist Qaed Salim sinan al-Harethi, who was killed by an unmanned Predator reconnaissance aircraft while in his car in Yemen. Five other passengers were killed, including a U.S. citizen. The aftermath of the attack—congressional inquiries and "infighting" among U.S. Defense Department officials about how much actionable intelligence is required before targeting future terrorists—led to the acknowledgement that two other Predator missions had been called off. Rightfully so, as it was later learned that the cars were filled with Bedouins—not al-Qaida members.

STANDARDS FOR THE USE OF TARGETED KILLING

- **Any such authorization of targeting a particular individual outside a zone of active combat must be justified as necessary to prevent, or in defense against, a reasonably imminent threat to the life of one or more persons.** To be "necessary" there must be no reasonable alternative such as arrest or capture followed by detention. To be "reasonably imminent" there must be a real risk that any delay in the hope of developing an alternative would result in a significantly increased risk of the lethal attack. Retribution for past events, as opposed to prevention of future attacks, cannot justify a targeted killing.

- **Under familiar rules applicable to military action under the laws of war, the action taken must be proportionate to the objective to be obtained, and the selection of the time, place, and means employed must avoid to the extent reasonably possible harm to innocent persons.**

- **Even when these conditions are met, there shall be no targeted killing of: a U.S. person; any person found in the United States; or an individual found in any foreign state that has previously agreed to, and displayed a willingness to try, extradite, or otherwise incapacitate those reasonably suspected of planning terrorist attacks on U.S. citizens and facilities.**

- **Any decision to target an identified individual for killing must be approved by the president of the United States in a finding, provided to appropriate committees of the Congress, and setting forth** (1) the evidence on which the necessary conclusion of imminent danger has been made; (2) the alternatives considered and the basis for rejecting them; and (3) the reasons for concluding that the previous conditions have been met.

- **The president shall promulgate detailed procedures for making these findings reliably and for maintaining a permanent record, available to appropriate committees of Congress, of any such decision.**

- **The rules described in the previous section shall be made public.** Particular findings in any individual case and the fact that such targeting was approved by the president need not be made public, but must be provided to appropriate committees of the Congress.

The recommendation focuses on what circumstances, short of a general state of ongoing armed conflict, would permit a targeted killing. Given that the military is engaged in many covert operations, the concern here is also to create common rules for our military and intelligence agencies.

We would limit targeted killings to situations in which it is necessary to prevent a greater, reasonably imminent harm or in defense against a reasonably imminent threat to the lives of the targets of the planned terrorist attack. This is, in effect, a three-prong test: to be "necessary" means that there is no other reasonable alternative, that targeted killing is a practice of last resort; to be "reasonably imminent" means that the development of an alternative (capture, arrest, etc.) would not eliminate a real likelihood of imminently threatened lethal attack or would be inordinately dangerous to U.S. or allied personnel; and, finally, to be preventive, the targeted killing can only be for prospective purposes, rather than as retribution for previous bad acts under those standards. Since it is based in some measure on traditional criminal law notions of justification for private use of lethal force and also in some measure on international law's acknowledgment of a state's power to act in anticipatory self-defense, this viewpoint may engender more support both at home and from allies and the international community. It also sets the bar very high.

Under our recommendations, we would permit targeted killing outside of armed conflict, but sharply limit its permissibility. In a system based upon this defense, targeted killing could occur when the harm posed by the continued life of the target is greater than the harm that would result from violating the sovereignty of another nation, killing without due process and the possibility of killing innocents. In addition, the targeted killing must not involve danger to innocent individuals that is disproportionate to the harm to be prevented.

Because of the inherent risks of a targeted killing policy and because it should only be used as a procedure of last resort, we believe that per se rules should prohibit its use in the following contexts. First, it is impossible to justify its use against a U.S. person or any person found in the United States; not only is it against federal and state law, there are simply too many alternatives available for the United States to ever permit a targeted killing in those circumstances. Second, it is also impossible to justify its use against persons who are found in countries that have previously agreed to, and displayed a willingness to, make those reasonably suspected of planning terrorism available for trial. We are likely to engender too much international condemnation and to start down a path where targeted killings are used too lightly, if we too easily ignore the host state's willingness to try the individual or to render him or her to us for trial.

By applying a well-defined and existing framework to targeted killing, the discretion of the executive branch is decreased, and its accountability is increased. Targeted killing would be constrained to urgent situations in which the benefits outweigh the costs and to terrorists who are actually going to carry out future attacks imminently. The framework would also apply equally to intelligence operatives and the military. Indeed, such constraints on the military are consistent with accepted military norms as to what is a lawful targeting mechanism: military utility, necessity, proportionality, and discrimination (or minimal collateral damage).

But even this approach must be constrained in some fashion. A focus on the process, as was true for conditions regarding highly coercive interrogation, is necessary as well. Indeed, ensuring that the targeting has been subject to political and administrative review will protect troops and operatives engaged in targeted killing. As one participant explained, "You could develop careful rules of engagement or rules on the use of force that would, from a political and policy perspective, make sure that you were only using this very rarely; there are costs involved every time you use lethal force in a context like Yemen so you have to make sure that the target is worth the cost." There are detailed rules covering, for example, covert operations; similar rules should apply in this regard outside of zones of active combat requiring a decision by the president on the basis of a detailed procedure justifying the attack on the named individual.

The "process" question has two distinct issues. The first is the authorization issue: who decides who can be killed. Targeted killing would be based on a presidential finding meeting legislative standards. The findings would be furnished promptly to the appropriate committees of Congress. The president would be required to promulgate detailed procedures for making these findings reliably and for maintaining a permanent record, available, once again, to appropriate committees of Congress about any particular decision. These findings would include evidence satisfying the three-prong requirement above. Thus, there would have to be solid evidence of a high likelihood of prospective terrorists attacks that could well be prevented by targeted killing. Evidence would have to show that any alternatives were tried or examined and rejected. For example, there may have to be an attempt at a capture or some kind of record that makes it clear why the target could not be captured with reasonably available means. Finally, the president would have to certify that the person targeted is not a U.S. person, is not within the United States and is in a state that has failed to make the suspect available or has consented to the action.

This desire for constraints leads to the second process issue: the question of the duty to disclose to the public that this is in fact U.S. policy. We believe that any targeted killing, outside the zones of active combat, should be pursuant to procedures outlined in legislation. In addition, the rules that are eventually adopted, such as the rules described in the recommendation, should also be made public. The public would be better served by an open and enunciated policy than the secret and ambiguous policy that the United States seems to now embrace. Specific authorizations, however, need not be disclosed.

Chapter 5

Communications of U.S. Persons or Others within the United States Intercepted During the Targeting of Foreign Persons Abroad

The Fourth Amendment and statutory law regarding physical and electronic searches have long distinguished between searches abroad and searches in the United States, as well as between searches involving those with substantial connections to the United States and others. It has been widely assumed that U.S. citizens retain their protection against U.S. searches while abroad and that everyone legally within the United States, from citizens to temporarily visiting aliens, enjoys the protection of the Fourth Amendment and U.S. statutes—although U.S. persons (i.e. citizens and aliens with substantial and lasting contacts with the United States) also enjoy additional statutory protections under the Foreign Intelligence Surveillance Act (FISA). Thus, FISA and law enforcement rules, including the statutes regulating electronic surveillance at home or abroad, cover the field. On the other hand, because neither the Fourth Amendment nor any statute protects against U.S. searches abroad of persons who are without substantial connections to the United States, this form of intelligence gathering is largely unrestrained by U.S. law.

With two such diametrically opposed structures of rules, problems inevitably arise when communications of U.S. persons are acquired while permissibly targeting foreign citizens abroad. This can occur in any of several ways. The foreign citizen may either receive an electronic communication from a U.S. person or send an electronic communication to a U.S. person and receive a reply. When an intelligence agency is searching abroad on the basis of the content of electronic messages without knowing either the recipient or sender, a U.S. person may turn out to be the recipient or sender. A U.S. person's activities may be the subject of a communication between two foreign citizens abroad. Finally, the operation of cellular telephones and electronic relay mechanisms may mean that a communication that seems to be taking place wholly abroad may have actually originated or terminated within the United States.

Our recommendation is neither modeled nor based upon the present regulations, largely classified, that govern the use of information related to

U.S. persons or other persons within the United States that is acquired while engaged in searches of communications targeted upon non-U.S. persons abroad. Our effort has been, rather, to build a new structure on familiar and accepted principles regarding the scope of a citizen's privacy in the United States while remaining consistent with rules of constitutional law.

Explanation and Background

The danger to privacy and political freedom is greatest when the government purposefully pursues the communications of its citizens and others within the United States. Thus, the U.S. government may not target the content of private communications of any individual within the United States or, even if already abroad, of a U.S. person without having adequate basis for expecting to find either evidence of a crime or material relevant to intelligence or counterintelligence concerns.

There is far less danger to the privacy of an individual ("W")—particularly of someone who fears that his privacy may be invaded because of his political opposition to an administration—from the revelation of private conversations discovered by government agents incidental to a search of a third party ("V") than from a search targeted on W himself. (By "targeted" on W, we mean that the search would not have taken place had there been no anticipation of discovering W's conversations.) For this reason, the general rule for searches and electronic surveillance within the United States is that the government is free to keep and use any information it acquires about W when engaging in a search of V, even if the search of V lacked probable cause or some other required predicate.

As a general rule, the predicate—usually "probable cause" that evidence or intelligence will be discovered—must be found by a judge. This last requirement has not been followed, however, when the search is of communications of a U.S. person abroad. Here a finding by the attorney general has been considered adequate, and we do not propose any changes in that practice.

ACQUIRING CONTENTS OF FOREIGN COMMUNICATIONS
   •**Targeting the content of communications of persons within the United States or of U.S. persons abroad should be governed by the following rules:**

   1. No U.S. agency may target for interception the content of any domestic communications of a person known to be within the United States or of any international communications of a U.S. person within the United States without satisfying the legal require-

ments of Title III (regarding electronic surveillance for criminal purposes) or FISA (regarding electronic surveillance for foreign intelligence purposes).

2. To target for interception the content of communications of a U.S. person located outside the United States, the attorney general must find probable cause to believe that the communications may reveal evidence of a crime, or that the U.S. person is an agent of a foreign power and the purpose of the collection is to acquire foreign intelligence or information about the person's involvement in espionage, international terrorism, or foreign-directed covert operations against the United States.

3. There shall be a presumption that a pattern of repeated acquisition of communications to or from a U.S. person is the result of activity targeted on that person, and thus requires compliance with the above rules respectively.

•**Targeting the content of communications of non-U.S. persons abroad shall be governed by the following rules:**

1. The content of communications of non-U.S. persons located outside the United States ("foreign communications") may be the target of interception so long as the purpose is to gather foreign intelligence or evidence of a violation of U.S. law. This rule applies whether or not another party to the targeted communication is known to be a U.S. person; whether or not the content of the communication is expected to involve the activities of a U.S. person; and wherever the interception is accomplished, as long as the person whose communications are sought is outside the United States.

2. When the communications targeted for interception are of a person mistakenly—but reasonably—believed to be neither a U.S. person nor in the United States, the communications have not been targeted as the communications of a U.S. person or of anyone within the United States.

3. Communications to or from a U.S. person intercepted unexpectedly during a content-based collection reasonably directed at communications of non-U.S. persons outside the United States for intelligence purposes are not deemed targeted on U.S. persons or territory.

The troublesome cases arise where the government targets the communications of aliens abroad but incidentally picks up the communication of people within the United States or of U.S. persons abroad. There are at least five ways that the content of communications of U.S. persons or of persons in the United States ("A") can become involved in intelligence gathering that targets the contents of communications of non-U.S. persons abroad ("F"):

1. Targeting F abroad, F calls (i.e., initiates a communication with) A and content is intercepted.

2. Targeting F abroad, A calls F and content is intercepted.

3. Targeting someone believed to be a non-U.S. person abroad, a mistake is made and the targeted individual is really a U.S. person or someone within the United States.

4. Targeting F abroad, a mistake is made and F's communication is really made (or relayed) from the United States.

5. Targeting particular words or phrases in messages largely abroad (the sender and recipient are unknown), A's message is picked up.

For the retention, dissemination, and use of material acquired in one of these situations, we recommend that the attorney general develop a set of rules consistent with the well-established constitutional propositions now applicable in the domestic intelligence context of the Foreign Intelligence Surveillance Act (FISA). They correspond, roughly, to the law enforcement rules regarding (1) incidental acquisition of untargeted communication, and (2) reasonable and good faith mistakes as to facts critical to the determination of the legality of a search.

In so recommending, we have assumed that whatever would be constitutionally permissible if affecting a U.S. person in the United States as a result of an investigation for prosecution purposes should be permitted if affecting a U.S. person abroad as a result of an investigation for intelligence purposes. We assume that, if there is less protection anywhere, it is abroad and that intelligence powers are generally at least as broad as law enforcement powers.

These assumptions are not incontestable. We rejected a rival contention that there must be greater protection of U.S. persons whose communications were not targeted but collected while targeting a non-U.S. person abroad (than of third parties whose communications are picked up in a criminal investigation of a suspect) because in the latter case there is at least the limit of needing probable cause as to the targeted suspect. We believe that this purported distinction in relying on some finding of probable cause is undermined by decisions holding that evidence against X discovered even in an illegal search of Y's private property without probable cause may be used against X.

As to communications within the United States, we see no reason why the communications of an individual should be protected unless he is himself located within the United States. Nothing should turn on how or where a communication of a non-U.S. person outside the United States is intercepted, particularly in light of the difficulty of defining and determining where a search of communications has taken place in the modern world of cellular telephones and the Internet.

THE CONSEQUENCES OF UNINTENTIONAL ACQUISITION

• **The retention, dissemination, and use of the content of communications of U.S. persons or of communications of persons in the United States which have been unintentionally acquired while targeting non-U.S. persons abroad shall be governed by rules determined by regulations of the attorney general.** These regulations shall, as closely as possible, duplicate the provisions for information obtained under the Foreign Intelligence Surveillance Act under 50 U.S.C. 1801(e) and (h) and 50 U.S.C. 1804(a)(5). The basis for concluding that information identifying a U.S. person is necessary to the conduct of foreign affairs or the national defense as well as to understand its content or importance must be set forth in writing along with the names of those to whom that information will be furnished. The record of this request will be maintained by the agency furnishing the information and will be available to the intelligence committees of Congress.

To determine the legal consequences of the untargeted, unintentional acquisition of the content of communications of U.S. persons, or of communications taking place in the United States, we believe that regulations, promulgated by the attorney general, are appropriate. These regulations should, however, be guided by well-established rules regarding either interception of untargeted communications during domestic law enforcement or good faith mistakes and the disclosure of information under FISA. In that case, the law requires that minimization procedures be in place to ensure that no unnecessary disclosure occurs. These would include a written assessment of the necessity of the disclosure and to whom (person and agency) the disclosure was furnished. Developed quite specifically by Supreme Court precedent and lower court rulings, these standards, as supplemented by the additional minimization requirements of FISA, are the appropriate model for handling any unintentional acquisition in the field of U.S. foreign intelligence as well.

ACQUIRING INFORMATION OTHER THAN THE CONTENTS OF FOREIGN COMMUNICATIONS

• **Neither a U.S. person abroad nor anyone within the United States is constitutionally entitled to a finding of some factual basis for suspicion of terrorist activity or of being an agent of a foreign** power before the government reviews to whom an electronic communication was sent or when and how it was sent.

• An agency responsible for gathering foreign intelligence may gather such information (other than the content of the communication) by targeting the messages of U.S. persons or individuals within the United States only if it is acting as an agent of, and under the control of, the attorney general, and it is subject to all the departmental regulations of the attorney general.

One final recommendation deals with executive powers to gather sharply limited non-content information about the external characteristics of the communications of U.S. persons or others within the United States and the role that our foreign intelligence agencies should play in the process.

Normally, there is no constitutional protection of this type of information because such "externals" are freely revealed to such third parties as the telephone company. But here the potential volume of revealing information leads us to rely on another of our recommendations regarding the collection of third-party information for purposes of data-mining. Our recommendation here would permit such intelligence gathering, but only under the strict guidelines established in the recommendations on information collection (chapter 6).

Moreover, the dangers inherent in using, for domestic intelligence purposes, foreign intelligence agencies with their vast resources and capacities and their traditions of minimal obligation to respect the privacy of those targeted abroad lead us to require any such use to satisfy two conditions. The foreign intelligence capacities must be under the complete control and responsibility of the attorney general and their use must comply with all the laws and regulations that constrain domestic intelligence.[1]

---

1. In making these recommendations we have regarded one issue as beyond our immediate task. Our commitment to not targeting U.S. persons or anyone within the United States without the factual bases we have described depends upon an assumed level of a relatively high, but not uniquely dangerous and urgent, threat of attack on the United States or its citizens. If, instead, an attack was reliably determined to be so imminent that the secretary of homeland security raised the threat level to the highest level, it might well be reasonable to allow the pursuit of the additional information required to prevent the attack with a reduced level of suspicion as to any single individual.

Chapter 6

Information Collection

Controversies surrounding the use of public and commercial information have resulted in a failure to define and regulate adequately the appropriate standards for the federal government when seeking access to relevant and valuable information in order to detect and interdict terrorist activity. This is particularly the case for government access to, and searching of, databases containing information about common transactions engaged in by private individuals, where the government is not investigating a particular individual but is seeking to identify suspicious patterns of activity that are potentially indicative of terrorism and warranting closer scrutiny. The issue here is not about changing the rules regarding access to a small part of one system of records but, rather, access to much of multiple databases, enabled by new technology. This change in scope requires us to move from the existing framework—which is based on the privacy implications of accessing a single set of records in a single database—to a framework that recognizes the privacy implications of enabling the government to, in essence, review extensive records about each and every one of us searching for "suspicious" activity. There is no federal standard for such efforts, resulting in disorganized procedures and little transparency.

Explanation and Background

The continuing growth in technology has increased the amount of data that is collected about individual persons by governmental agencies and commercial entities. Specifically, computer capacities vastly expand the possibilities for the government to gather information about common transactions in which people engage, such as buying an airplane ticket, renting a hotel room, visiting a doctor, buying a handgun, etc. The range of possibilities regarding increased surveillance has created new challenges regarding individual expectations of privacy. Much public controversy has surrounded new government projects, most specifically the now defunct program of the Defense Advanced Research Projects Agency (DARPA), which sought to develop mining techniques by which the government could collect and search such transactional information from governmental and commercial databases in order to identify suspicious patterns indicative of terrorist activity. The basic question is under which conditions and to what extent the government should have access to what has become a huge database of information collected, in the course of people's normal activities, by credit card companies, schools, banks, medical facilities, and many others.

There is no novel problem when the government starts with a suspect and uses its traditional access to records of a particular individual to determine what the suspect has done, with whom he has been dealing, where he has been, and what he has been doing with his money. In that case, there is a law enforcement tradition of considerable access at the request of a prosecutor by means of subpoena or various other types of court order. While the USA PATRIOT Act permitted much greater use of administrative subpoenas and National Security Letters to collect information, this area of the law is relatively established.

The more difficult case is when the government starts without a suspect, relying instead on a template of potential activities in which a terrorist may engage. The government then would go through large volumes of information that would require very powerful computing, looking for the person or persons whose activities match the template. The government may find people who do satisfy the template, but the government would also have reviewed great volumes of information about large numbers of other people.

Our focus is mostly on this second scenario where there is no suspect initially. On any given day, an individual may visit a doctor (making insurance claims that are recorded), use his credit cards (again, engaging in a transaction that is recorded and stored), rent something of sufficient value that would warrant keeping records of the renter or borrower (including video tapes, library books, and cars) and much else. That individual may also, on the same day, write checks revealing his activities and make telephone calls and send email messages whose numbers and addresses would reveal his associates.

If the government has the capacity to gather and then process these records to look for suspicious patterns without legal restriction or oversight, the only limitation on the government's ability to scrutinize innocent people's daily lives is the computational cost of engaging in the data search, but that is rapidly declining. To date, the Congress has failed to define and impose appropriate standards for the federal government when seeking access to such information.

In many ways, our recommendation mirrors the guidance given by the Report of the Technology and Privacy Advisory Committee, a working group which had been asked by the secretary of defense to review the then-existing Defense Department programs (in light of the DARPA controversy) on data-mining. We concur that information technology may provide tremendous opportunities to focus on national security threats; we also believe, however, that without a system-wide, federal standard, there is likely to be too much ad hoc assessment and too little transparency. Here, we seek to provide the appropriate legislative framework that is necessary to achieve an appropriate balance.

GENERAL DATA-MINING PROCEDURES

- **A federal district court or a specialized court, such as the Foreign Intelligence Surveillance Act (FISA) court, should be authorized by Congress to issue a warrant making available to the federal government access to extensive systems of commercial and other third-party records when there is clear and convincing evidence that** (1) the systems of records to which the government is given access will, when combined, be no broader than necessary to permit a determination of whether there is a high risk of terrorist activity; (2) anonymization techniques will initially prevent the identification of any individuals with any particular record unless and until the court authorizes the release to the government of the individual's identity, as discussed in the section below; (3) the systems of records and any copies of them will not be retained by the federal government but will remain at all times under the control of their owners; (4) systems will be in place that guarantee an adequate audit trail of who has had access to what information and for how long; and (5) the access will not be unduly disruptive of the activities of the custodian of the records.

- **The court shall authorize the federal government to demand or obtain the identities of individuals whose activities are revealed by analysis of commercial or other private systems of records** if the government establishes to the court's satisfaction that a pattern of activities revealed by the systems of records has a significant probability of being a part of a plan for terrorism; and the individuals whose identities are to be revealed are so related to the pattern of activity as to have a significant probability of being engaged in terrorism.

- **Once an individual has been identified in this or in any other legal way, based on reasonable factual inferences that the individual is likely to be planning terrorism or is part of an organization**

or group planning terrorism, the federal government shall have access to commercial records and to records of other third parties relevant to determining the identity of his or her associates and discovering other activities in connection with this plan.

The Privacy Act of 1974 regulates and limits the access that other federal agencies and other public and private entities have to information that is identified with a particular individual from files of a federal agency. It does not deal with the access of the federal government to the files of state and local governments or of private businesses within the United States. The Privacy Act shows considerable sensitivity to the risks of matching programs designed to discover fraud; but it specifically excludes regulation of matching programs among federal agencies for counterintelligence purposes, which would include terrorism (at least with a foreign-based sponsor).

There is no legislation forbidding or granting federal access to state and local records or to the records of private businesses for pattern recognition purposes. This is surprising because making available information that had been collected and has heretofore been used only for limited commercial, educational, or other purposes for an additional set of federal governmental purposes greatly expands the potential impact of those records on the individual.

While the great mass of such data would have no relevance to terrorism and may well involve quite private matters, access to these records may still be useful to detect terrorist plans. The government may be able to develop patterns of activities ("templates") that would be either necessary for or likely to accompany terrorist attacks, at least warranting further scrutiny, and unlikely to accompany innocent activity. If the government can develop programs that can check for such a revealing pattern by using access to a variety of records systems, it can discover plans previously hidden from view.

The mining of records systems to look for patterns of activity that would be unusual outside of terrorist activity could be done on the basis of a template of a single terrorist's activity or, with greater difficulty but more utility, on the basis of a template combining the activities of several members of small groups. The latter approach would deal with the fact that a terrorist group would be likely to use different people to carry out different tasks both for efficiency and so as to avoid identification of a suspicious pattern.

The efficacy of pattern detection in discovering fraud is well established. Whether it could be used effectively to detect the less identifiable signs of terrorism has yet to be established. Although the number of false positives in pursuing terrorism could be reduced to a very small number by increasing the number of items in the pattern until the pattern suggested nothing other than terrorism, the price of doing this would be to increase the false negatives (the "missed" terrorists) greatly. Keeping the false negatives at an acceptable level, the matching would also have to accept enough false positives. Its usefulness, then, would generally be in providing the basis for further investigation and not in taking action directly against the individual or even in denying access to a location or resource.

Thus, the overall efficacy of combining systems of data in search of suspicious patterns would depend on:

1. Whether it is possible to develop a template or pattern of suspicious activities that would identify for further investigative attention persons who may well be terrorists and would not produce, for each true suspect, a sizeable number of people who would later be shown to be innocent of any involvement with terrorism; and

2. Whether the available records systems would provide the information needed to apply any such template to the selected population.

Data mining for suspects has some real policy drawbacks. If the technique is used to focus investigative attention on one small portion of a much larger group, terrorists who are able to place their activities outside the area of heightened attention would be able to reduce surveillance by exposing themselves only to the lesser attention left for the larger, less-suspected class. Even if the conditions of heightened surveillance are kept secret, a terrorist group may be able to experiment to determine which of its members would not trigger special attention when boarding a plane or buying explosives. Then, it could use only those members that the screening did not detect to carry out a terrorist action. Thus, the risks of strategic jujitsu are real unless the technique is used merely to supplement, rather than to partially replace, other forms of surveillance.

With true pattern recognition, the government would be using secret algorithms to find suspicious patterns of activity in order to determine whether someone warrants closer investigation—about which the terrorist may not even be aware. It would thus be harder to manipulate that system through testing. It is conceivable that terrorists could use large numbers of operatives to travel to suspicious places, buy airplane tickets with cash, buy fertilizer, and engage in all sorts of other activites and then see whether any governmental investigation of any of these operatives is discernable. That would be far harder, however, than defeating a straight watchlist screen by testing to see which individuals are determined to be "clean" when they go through an airport checkpoint or when they seek to purchase explosives.

As a legal matter, an attempt to regulate this area raises important questions. The Privacy Act does not apply at all to commercial records; it applies only to federal records, and it has, even there, a broad exemption for both law enforcement and an all-inclusive exemption for counterintelligence. It may very well be that the collection and manipulation of commercially available or other organizational records are not protected by the Fourth Amendment—although some might argue that government access to masses of such information is akin to a sweep search, which would raise some constitutional issues of lack of particularity. In either case, regulating government authority in this new realm—as has been done historically in a variety of contexts when new technology invaded areas that had been previously considered private, such as electronic and oral communication—would be adding a new protection for individuals against what appears to be the unrestricted authority of the government to collect and mine such information.

The stakes involved in deciding how much data-based surveillance should be permitted and under which conditions include, on the side of privacy: the right of individuals to preserve, free of social pressures, spheres of conduct without significant effects on others; the fear of governmental or private misuse of information gathered for legitimate purposes; the preservation of choice about appropriate levels of intimacy and exposure in the complicated world of our social and work relationships; and preserving the conditions of safely exploring unpopular views. In addition, the risk of mistake by the government does exist, as do the burdens that would be created for individuals who are mistakenly subjected to investigation or denied access to certain resources or facilities because of pattern recognition. On the opposite side, governmental investigations do need to prevent and punish dangerous activities, and nongovernmental actors do have a legitimate interest in having sufficient information about those with whom they have come into contact and may deal.

The Supreme Court has sometimes argued that information made freely available to a third party for one purpose enjoys no privacy protection against use by the government for other purposes. But this notion precipitously narrows the privacy that most U.S. citizens expect. Others argue that since government agents can generally go wherever private individuals can go, they should be able to purchase any data that private companies can purchase, based simply on the proposition that the government should not be denied access to information available to private individuals or companies. The government is, however, more threatening in its potential uses of personal data; it can act against a person in ways that other private individuals or organizations cannot readily duplicate. Moreover, in pattern detection, the ability of the government to discover private patterns of activity undetectable by others is far greater. No private party would likely be motivated to seek patterns going well beyond individual transactions or types of transaction. As a result, the aggregate combination of data sources, each of which private parties could buy, may make information available to the government that otherwise would not be available to anyone other than the suspect. These concerns will remain in competition despite a history of judicial attempts to reconcile the competing demands.

In the end, concerns must be weighed against each other. The importance of making data available for counterterrorism investigations also depends, in the case of surveilling a known suspect, on the degree and reliability of the initial suspicion of that suspect and, in the case of searching for patterns in masses of collected data, on the likelihood that matching the data sources will both produce a manageably small number of suspects and that our efforts, once discovered, cannot be used by terrorist opponents to avoid detection of their operatives. The balance must also reflect the proportion of sensitive but irrelevant information that would be revealed by access to particular sensitive types of data collection. Medical records, for example, may be more sensitive than supermarket records. Thus, the Congress has enacted legislation protecting a variety of specific collections of data from revelation to the government or others except under specific circumstances. Finally, the balance must also consider the availability of alternatives to the government.

These crucial determinations about what data-based surveillance should be allowed are legislative in the first instance. Recognizing that the executive branch generally has a pro-investigative bias, the Congress has frequently assumed this responsibility on prior occasions. Moreover, the novelty of the technology that raises the issue and the need for a wider range of procedures and remedies for intrusions on privacy makes it unwise to solely defer to the courts and constitutional interpretation.

The lack of standards in the present legal framework requires some oversight by both the political and judicial branches. The two broad options are either to limit the federal government's access to any of the information recorded by private parties and state and local governments, or to limit the government's access to only that part of the information that provides the identity of the individual whose activities have been revealed by the record search as likely terrorist activities. Given the benefits that a system of data collection may have on terrorism-related investigations, curbing all access is too draconian a policy.

Instead, we seek to give structure to an area of law that has little. There are five important themes animating this recommendation. First is the question of congressional authorization. The political branches ought to be involved in establishing a process by which the collection of vast amounts of data will be authorized. Second is the type of authorization that would permit (or prohibit) the collection of information based on whether the government has satisfied congressional standards. This could be an executive decision, but we recommend a judicial determination, either by a federal district court or a specialized court, such as the FISA court. Third, a judicial determination is necessary when the government seeks to unveil the identity of the names of persons that it has accessed through data collection. Fourth is oversight of the whole process to ensure that it is functioning appropriately and adequately. This is largely a political and legislative function. The important issue regarding accountability when people are harmed by the government intrusion is last. For this, access to courts by injured plaintiffs is appropriate.

The recommendation addresses the standard that Congress ought to establish in order to permit the data collection. It would require a court to find, by clear and convincing evidence, that the systems of records to which the government is given access will be no broader than necessary to permit a determination of whether there is a high risk of a certain type of terrorist activity. It would place a burden on government to show that it will not unduly disrupt the activities of the custodian of the records. In addition, judicial authorization is required for the government to learn the identity of any individual. This will prevent the government from collecting vast amounts of information on large numbers of specified persons.

The standard that we propose—that the individual is so related to a pattern of activities revealed by the records systems that there is a significant probability of him being a part of a plan for terrorism—creates a serious hurdle for the government. That being said, once an individual has been identified in such a manner, then the gates should be open to allow access to his records or to the records of others that may expose a plot or others connected with the plan, pursuant to the normal, existing rules governing criminal and national security investigations of suspected terrorists.

ACCESS TO INDIVIDUALIZED DATA

> **•Records of activity of identified individuals should not be subject to compelled government access for prevention of terrorist activities unless they are sought pursuant to the investigation of an individual or organization already reasonably suspected of terrorism.**

Long before the increased authority of National Security Letters—to reach a growing list of businesses and commercial entities—a series of statutory provisions already governed the collection of records of activities that were generally innocent. A miscellany of federal rules, with a different set applicable to different subject matter areas, regulate whether:

> 1. Certain categories of information may be furnished voluntarily to the federal government with neither governmental nor court order.

2. Certain records can be obtained under a National Security Letter or instead require either a subpoena or even a search warrant. (See, e.g., 18 U.S.C. § 2710)

3. Revealing that the government has requested and has been furnished such information is prohibited.

For subject matter areas that are not specifically regulated by one of these provisions, the default legislative rules permit voluntary compliance with the government's request, and permit the government to subpoena records as part of an open investigation, subject only to the objection that the request is overly broad and too unnecessarily burdensome to satisfy the Fourth Amendment.

No investigative steps—from gathering information from governmental or commercial files to following a suspect physically to use of an informant—can be taken by an FBI agent without compliance with the Attorney General's Guidelines for criminal or national security investigations. The criminal investigative guidelines require a "reasonable indication" of a crime or a plan to engage in illegal political violence before an investigation can be opened, and forbid investigative steps when no investigation is open unless the FBI is merely checking leads or pursuing a more limited, in scope and duration, preliminary inquiry.

Uninhibited federal access to immense collections of private records of identified individuals without a reasonable indication of illegal or dangerous activity would vastly increase the amount of information that the federal government has about citizens whom there is no reason to suspect of terrorist involvement. The information could, of course, be misused by the government to punish the administration's enemies, as the experience of the Watergate scandal reminds us. In that case, the Nixon administration sought private psychiatric information about Daniel Ellsberg (who had released the Pentagon Papers to several newspapers) for public dissemination as a form of reputational attack. It also sought Internal Revenue Service (IRS) audits of those who were critical of the administration. And no matter how honest the government would be in restricting its uses of the data, many citizens would become more cautious in their activities, including being less outspoken in their dissent to governmental policies, if the government were free to check all sorts of records in their names. Recent amendments of the long-standing guidelines reduce the threshold for undertaking a full investigation beyond a "reasonable indication" that a crime has been committed; they now also permit a full investigation where there is a reasonable indication that someone may attempt to or conspire to commit a crime in the future.

We seek to continue the limitations on the power of government to compel access to records of activity of an identified individual by explicitly limiting such access to situations where the data sought would be pursuant to an authorized investigation of an individual already reasonably suspected of terrorism. Thus, we would seek to align the access government seeks, for example, to library records, with traditional criminal law standards.

REQUIRED SECRECY CONCERNING DELIVERY OF RECORDS

•**The court ordering the revelation of records may forbid the nongovernmental custodian of documents to reveal that the government has demanded them,** but only upon a showing of cause and for a limited, renewable period.

•**Any requirement that a nonjudicial demand, such as a National Security Letter, be kept secret shall be valid for only sixty days** but can be renewed by a court on a particularized showing of the need for continued secrecy.

Finally, it is essential that the government be allowed to forbid the nongovernmental custodian from revealing that the government has demanded the records, lest the focus of its suspicions be discovered by terrorists themselves. The burden would be on the government, however, to show cause why such access should remain secret—and only for a limited, renewable period. In the context of nonjudicial demands, the secrecy should only be permitted for sixty days (the requirement now is permanent) and should be renewed only after a showing to a court.

Chapter 7

Identification of Individuals and Collection of Information for Federal Files

The 9/11 Commission Report recommends that the Department of Homeland Security should "lead the effort to design a comprehensive screening system (with)...common standards" for both external borders and for other checkpoints like those at airports or government buildings. The commission recommends federal standards for identification documents like driver's licenses and birth certificates to "be integrated into a larger network of screening points that includes our transportation system and access to vital facilities such as nuclear reactors."[1]

Nothing in these recommendations is objectionable, but the specifics of such a system should not be left vague. As the technology becomes available, we should implement, under strict procedures and oversight, systems of biometric identification (BId), such as a fingerprint or a retinal scan, a facial or a hand pattern or even DNA, to make the use of an alias far more difficult and less helpful to terrorists in the United States.

The desire to remain anonymous animates a growing public concern about the government's ability to collect, use, and make available to others vast amounts of information about specific individuals. Many U.S. citizens object to uncontrolled government access to and use of records of even lawful activity. Still, no individual has a right to protect his privacy by misleading the government about his identity, particularly if he seeks entry or access to sensitive sites or resources. Wherever it is appropriate for authorities to ask a person to identify himself so that records can be checked, it is also appropriate to take steps to prevent false identification. The remedy for fears of invasion of privacy is to limit the occasions of checking records, not to hide identities on occasions when checking records is necessary.

A legal system should take both anonymity and the need for security into account. By demanding identification needlessly and then recording

---

1. The National Commission on Terrorist Attacks, *The 9/11 Commission Report: Final Report of the National Commission on Terrorist Attacks upon the United States* (New York: W.W. Norton, 2004), p. 387.

the transaction or event, the government may develop extensive records of a high proportion of the activities of any individual, creating government files that are neither needed nor guaranteed against improper exploitation. Without the capacity to check identity on appropriate occasions, the government's most elaborate systems for protecting information, facilities, and people could be readily defeated by terrorists.

Explanation and Background

The specific legal rules regarding the appropriate use of BIds are unexplored, with very little consideration of the privacy concerns that such use may raise. Indeed, the greatest obstacle to the extensive use of BIds now is not the law, but administrative convenience and tradition. Presently, the federal government can and does insist on security clearances as a condition of access to certain information or physical resources that are under its control. It can and does sometimes use biometric identification to verify that the person before it is indeed the person who received the security clearance. With the threat of terrorism, this is likely to increase beyond the area of security clearances to a far broader system of file checks—a change requiring consideration of the privacy concerns. There are five important factors to consider in this regard.

First, the U.S. government has or could obtain information that would allow it to put aliens and citizens into categories relevant to terrorism such as: (1) of unknown or unrevealing background; (2) known to be trustworthy ("cleared"); (3) suspected of planning terrorism; or (4) wanted for arrest or some other form of detention. The categories—admittedly too few but illustrative—are set forth in a rough order of frequency; those individuals falling in the last two categories would be far less numerous than those in the first two. The underlying information would not be totally reliable, and so the categorization would not be either.

Second, many people in the last two categories (either suspected of planning terrorism or wanted for arrest or detention) could avoid the consequences that we would like to attach to those categories—additional investigation, denial of access, or detention—by adopting an alias and procuring false identification documents (such as a driver's license or passport).

Third, there are systems which make the use of an alias far more difficult and less helpful to terrorists. If, when an individual presents himself as seeking access to what may be a terrorist target or resource, he is asked for a biometric identification, the BId can be matched with any history or record currently filed under the same BId. A different name would not be useful.

Fourth, business organizations, state and local governments as well as the federal government have frequent need to match individuals with their own records. Sometimes it is just for bookkeeping purposes. Whenever one of these organizations plans to act one way or another depending on how the individual with whom they are dealing has behaved in the past, the organization must make and keep a record of the relevant activities on which it hopes to base decisions in the future. The record is, however, useful only if it can be accurately matched with the individual to whom it pertains. There are a variety of techniques the organization can use for accomplishing this, depending often on whether the individual is present or is seeking access by telephone or other remote contact. The techniques range from signatures to seeking a series of answers that only the right individual would know. These organizations outside the federal government will increasingly rely on BIds as it becomes more common and more easily digitalized.

Fifth, the same systems that allow a rapid check of, for example, a fingerprint against a file of information organized in terms of fingerprints will allow making and keeping a record of when the file was checked, by whom it was checked, where this was, and for what purpose. That information can readily be added to the file itself. In other words, the very system that makes BIds reliable also allows their use to add to an individual's file.

PERMISSIBLE DEMANDS FOR BIOMETRIC INFORMATION

•Biometric or other systems of identification are necessary and appropriate for reliably matching federal "files" of accumulated information on an individual with the current activities of that individual (1) whenever the federal government, a state or local government, or a private facility can appropriately check all or part of a file maintained by the federal government before deciding whether to give an individual access to a sensitive resource or target of a terrorist attack; (2) in order to keep a reliable federal record of requests for access to sensitive resources and targets, whether such a record is developed by obtaining information from another organization or governmental unit or by electronically or otherwise recording requests for access to federal facilities; and (3) whenever an individual is either visiting or returning to the United States.

There is no doubt that a business has very broad discretion to check its records on an individual before deciding whether to engage in a pending transaction with him. State and local governments may do the same thing in this and many other situations (such as granting liquor or other licenses). No one should have the right to produce false identification in a sit-

uation where it is proper for a state or local government to demand identification to check records. Thus, BIds can legitimately be demanded on
many different types of occasions by a variety of nonfederal, governmental organizations, and this power should not be widely restricted by federal legislation.

Yet, in a legal system that permits the use of a BId, it is also appropriate to prohibit its more general use by the federal government. Federal
use of BIds or other systems of identification are neither necessary nor
appropriate when an individual is not seeking access to a sensitive
resource or target. Absent reasonable suspicion of criminal behavior,
demands for BIds at places that are generally open to the public would be
unprecedented and would likely leave an impression of total monitoring
by the federal government. A rule that limited the federal use of BIds to
the context of when a prior record of the applicant's activities is relevant to
the question of whether he should be granted or denied access to a particular resource or target is more compatible with our everyday expectation
that only certain places require greater levels of security and justify
breaching people's anonymity.

Thus, we would limit the use of biometric or other systems of identification to only those situations where a government (federal, state, or
local) or a private facility can appropriately use prior records in deciding
issues of access. In this situation, the records are useless unless the entity
has the capacity to match them to the individual seeking access. The federal capacity to match reliably should be limited to areas where the individual seeks access to a sensitive resource or potential target of a terrorist
attack, such as an airplane or federal facility.

The federal government would also be free either to record access to
or requests for access to sensitive resources and targets or to solicit information available to other levels of government and to private organizations arising from requests to them for access to sensitive resources or
targets. In this way, the U.S. government could sometimes determine
whether a plot to target specific sites is underway.

Clearly, deciding what is a "sensitive" resource or target is difficult,
and the conclusion may require specific designation by an agency such as
the Department of Homeland Security. Designations like these are
presently performed in a variety of other contexts. Admittedly, the designation of a site may inevitably move terrorists to target less secure places,
but a well-structured designation plan would help in minimizing the most
catastrophic of attacks.

The United States is presently requiring many foreign nations to utilize BIds on their passports, a requirement that has met with tremendous
resistance. Requiring current and valid identification (including BIds) for

anyone visiting or returning to the United States is an appropriate application of the technology.

IMPERMISSIBLE DEMANDS FOR BIOMETRIC INFORMATION

•**Biometric or other systems of identification are neither necessary
nor appropriate for matching federal "files" of accumulated information on an individual with the current activities of that individual during random requests for identification when an individual
is neither seeking access to sensitive resources or targets nor seeking to enter the country.** In these circumstances (where demanding
identification is not appropriate) no federal records of individual
activity should be created or maintained.

The privacy concerns associated with identification systems focus far
more on the appropriateness of using files (rather than on the use of BIds)
to deny access or information about activities. While our recommendation
addresses the core issue of reliable identification, the overall appropriateness of the underlying use of such files presents four extremely important
questions.

First, should the United States be allowed to exclude individuals from
certain federal facilities, which are generally open to the public, on the
basis of recorded information indicating that the individuals may be dangerous, although they are not subject to arrest or other detention? Denying
access to facilities generally open to the public even on the basis of federal government files reflecting suspicions of terrorist connections will have
widespread social consequences for the individual rejected by placing him
in the latter of two classes of citizens or residents: the vast majority who
are trusted and believed loyal versus the few who are untrusted and suspected. The determination could be based on unreliable facts and deduc-
tions, yet the underlying information will not generally be subject to a
review for errors by the individual suspected because of national security
concerns about its sources. These unfortunate consequences may be
unavoidable in regulating access to sensitive locations—though rights to
appeal the denial of access and rights to compel the government to correct
any underlying mistakes in its records should be assured. These consequences are, however, unnecessary, ineffective, and doubly harmful when
the issue is access to resources or locations generally open to the public.

Second, in which situations should the United States be allowed to
require businesses or state or local governments to apply federal standards or seek federal approval in deciding whether to permit certain transactions or activities that involve dangerous access to certain locations or
resources (such as guns, airplanes, or explosives)? On which occasions
should the United States be allowed to furnish information from its files to

private, state, or local "gatekeepers" who either want or are required to assess risks of terrorism before engaging in a transaction or authorizing an activity?

Requiring federal standards to be applied by a nonfederal private or public organization in determining whether to allow an individual access to certain potential targets or resources for terrorism is appropriate, but risks serious mistakes if the decision relies on whatever information is otherwise available to a business or nonfederal government. The determination would often be based on even less reliable information than a federal categorization.

The cost of nonfederal bodies using less reliable information can be eliminated by authorizing the United States to furnish information from its files to private, local, or state "gatekeepers" who are seeking to protect facilities against the dangers of terrorism or to deny certain resources (like guns or explosives) to terrorists. Indeed, since the federal government is far more likely to possess such information, protection of nonfederal facilities or resources may depend upon making such information available. Since the sources and methods of acquiring the information are unlikely to be transmitted along with the information, it will frequently be unchallengeable. The political costs of rejecting the federal government's explicit or implicit conclusions as to risk will be great enough to create a federally dominated system with the dangerous (but perhaps necessary) consequences described above.

Third, should federal, state, or local governments be allowed to require individuals to produce verifiable identification whenever requested by local or federal law enforcement officers? Additional concerns are raised by judicial decisions and federal or state statutes that allow law enforcement officers to demand identification of anyone within the jurisdiction of the officer. It would enable local and federal law enforcement authorities to gather—and make available to each other—information on the ordinary daily activities of individuals who, because they are not suspected of any crime or terrorist activity, could not be the subject of an investigation under the Attorney General's Guidelines. Whether or not information is retained in such innocent circumstances, it will needlessly convey the notion that there is risk of governmental reprisal for dissent or for unpopular, but entirely legal, activities.

Last, on which of these occasions should the United States be allowed to add to its records the information that access was sought, thus keeping track of the activities of the individual? The federal government's right to seek information from private, state, or local organizations as to who is seeking access to nonfederal facilities that are considered sensitive enough to require checks for terrorist connections is reasonable. Patterns of unexplained access may reveal hostile intent. This is not true of someone who has been stopped by local police on a hunch alone. Both situations create the danger of encompassing federal files on non-suspects that can be misused. But while the former may be justified by the importance of the occasion and the limited set of records created, the latter cannot. The issue is thus a near relation of that presented by the use of vast systems of business or state records in seeking to discover dangerous patterns of activity.

Chapter 8

Surveillance of Religious and Political Meetings

The historical reluctance to permit federal agents to attend religious and political meetings for surveillance and information-gathering purposes reflects this nation's commitment to the sanctity of speech and free expression, as well as concern about how such authority might be abused. After 9/11, however, the Department of Justice altered long-standing practices and permitted the monitoring of open religious and political meetings without any basis for believing that a crime of political violence was being planned, supported, or executed by members of an organization, and without any basis for believing that violence was being advocated there. While the First Amendment sharply limits any prohibition against advocating violence or political hatred, it does not limit investigations on that basis.

Yet, there are few advantages and many disadvantages to allowing federal agents to attend political and religious meetings without any specific reason to suspect involvement in terrorism or advocacy of violence. The mere possibility that federal agents may be monitoring groups or speech will silence minority viewpoints and discourage exercise of the rights guaranteed in the First Amendment. Any authorization to monitor religious and political groups, as well as the keeping of records based on that monitoring, should be more carefully defined.

Explanation and Background

Under the U.S. Constitution, speech alone cannot be forbidden unless it incites imminent lawless action and is likely to produce that action. There is no constitutional bar, however, to using incitement to violence or hatred of segments of our populations as the occasion and reason for an investigation. There also would be no constitutional bar to monitoring the activities of an individual or an organization on a hunch alone, without any factual basis for suspecting criminal or other terrorist activities. The costs in terms of civil liberties and democratic values would come into play as policy issues, not matters of constitutional law.

Much of the advantage of monitoring the activities of an organization without having any factual basis for believing it is involved in terrorism or other forms of crime depends upon the assumption that the meetings of that organization or the activities of that organization provide an attraction that will bring together people who are likely to engage in political violence or support political violence. To the extent that people who attend the meetings of a particular political or religious organization are themselves far more likely than others to engage in violence, knowledge of their identities would be advantageous. Indeed, even if the individuals were not much more likely to engage in political violence without the encouragement of a charismatic religious or political leader, they may be significantly more likely to engage in political violence if they have attended and been subjected to that form of encouragement.

Information about meetings of, attendance at, and support of an organization urging violence may be of limited value; the great majority of those attending the occasion may have no intention of engaging in violence. This information may, however, be very valuable when combined with other information (for example, about the purchase of explosives) which may be available in private commercial files, in the hands of state and local governments, or in the files of other federal agencies. Furthermore, an investigator's attendance at such meetings may provide the necessary basis for undercover efforts to discover prosecutable recruitment and planning. However, the costs of the surveillance of religious and political meetings may also be quite high. For minority or unpopular groups, the federal government's attendance at meetings may sharply discourage attendance and vocal opposition to government policies. It may antagonize entire communities.

The ability of federal agents to attend public meetings is part of a larger question involving the extent to which we want the federal government, anonymously, to surf the Internet, use commercial data sources, and visit public places. The animating philosophy before 9/11 was "no," based in large measure on historic abuses by the FBI regarding the surveillance of political and religious organizations and meetings, especially during the period of demonstrations against the war in Vietnam and during the Civil Rights movement. In a 1989 report investigating the FBI's broad surveillance of political groups supporting political change in Latin America, the Senate Select Committee on Intelligence noted that "unjustified investigations of political expression and dissent can have a debilitating effect upon our political system. When people see that this can happen, they become wary of associating with groups that disagree with the government and more wary of what they say and write. The impact is to undermine the effectiveness of popular self-government." That sentiment changed dramatically after 9/11, as federal officials argued that FBI guidelines were being interpreted too narrowly and that they appeared to bar reasonable surveillance activities unless expressly authorized. The result was a dramatic change in current FBI guidelines—a pendulum swing that, upon reflection, appears to have gone too far.

MONITORING RELIGIOUS AND POLITICAL ORGANIZATIONS

• **An investigation of a religious or political organization pursuant to the rules regarding domestic intelligence investigations may be authorized where there is a reasonable and articulable basis for suspecting that a group, or leaders of a group, are** (1) planning terrorist activity; (2) recruiting participation in an organization involved in such activity; (3) actively advocating political violence; or (4) actively advocating hatred against another group.

• **The authorization shall be governed by the following conditions:**

1. The request for authorization shall be made, in writing, to be approved by a senior official at FBI Headquarters.

2. It shall last for only sixty days, renewable upon written evidence that the information acquired during the authorization continues to satisfy the conditions in the above section.

3. The number of such authorizations shall be furnished publicly to the members of the House and Senate Judiciary committees.

The Attorney General's Guidelines on general crimes, racketeering enterprise, and terrorism enterprise investigations require, as a predicate for any investigation, "facts or circumstances [that] reasonably indicate that a federal crime has been, is being, or will be committed." That standard has and does "require specific facts or circumstances indicating a past, current, or future violation. There must be an objective, factual basis for initiating an investigation; a mere hunch is insufficient." When the FBI has, however, received information that does not indicate a "reasonable indication" of criminal activities, "responsible handling" may still require "some further scrutiny...." "In these cases...the FBI may initiate a preliminary 'inquiry' in response to the allegation or information 'indicating the possibility of criminal activity.'" In addition, even when further investigative activity is not required by "responsible handling" of limited information inadequate to open a full investigation, something even less than a "preliminary inquiry" is allowed—"the prompt and extremely limited checking out of initial leads."

Obviously a broad range of investigative activity was authorized even with relatively slight predicates. The Attorney General's Guidelines did, however, accomplish two things. First, they made clear that only the suspicion of criminal activity or of foreign-supported terrorism could proper-ly motivate an investigation and that even that suspicion could not be based on prejudice or bias alone. Second, as applied to domestic intelli-gence investigations of possible terrorist activity, these provisions provid-ed some assurance to individuals that they would not be monitored for merely attending meetings of political or religious organizations whose proposed actions are not criminal. Thus, until the Guidelines were modi-fied, FBI agents could attend the meeting of a religious or political organ-ization only if that step was based on a reasonable suspicion that a crime of political violence was being planned, supported, or executed by the members of an organization.

If attendance at a meeting of a religious or political organization led to the use, by an individual working for the FBI, of an assumed name or cover identity to further an investigation into the activities of the organization, the special agent in charge of the field office had to obtain the approval of FBI headquarters under the Attorney General's Guidelines for undercover investigations. That process required the approval of an undercover review committee, which includes attorneys from the Department of Justice who can raise the propriety of the undercover operation with the attorney general. The structure allowed tentative investigative steps to be taken with minimal factual predicates. The structure did, however, exclude general monitoring of the activities of particular political or reli-gious groups based on the closeness of their views to the views of those presently engaged in terrorism.

That critical assurance is unnecessarily undermined by the Attorney General's Guidelines on General Crime, Racketeering Enterprise, and Terrorism Enterprise Investigations. Most important, the Guidelines are made inapplicable to meetings that are opened to the public. For the pur-pose of detecting or preventing terrorist activities, the FBI is authorized to visit any place and attend any event that is open to the public, on the same terms and conditions as the members of the public generally. No informa-tion obtained from such visits shall be retained unless it relates to poten-tial criminal or terrorist activity. Since many if not most meetings of political and religious groups are open to the public, this provision allows monitoring of the meetings, although without retention of information that does not somehow relate to potential criminal or terrorist activity. In effect, the general rules limiting investigative activity no longer apply to public meetings if the government's purpose is to detect terrorist activities. Indeed, the amendments to the Guidelines duplicate the British practice in allowing FBI agents "to visit any place or attend any event that is open to the public, on the same terms and conditions as members of the public generally."

Guidelines also make clear that "statements . . . made in relation to or in furtherance of an enterprise's political or social objectives that threaten or advocate the use of force or violence for political purposes may themselves justify a preliminary inquiry or, perhaps with little more, the opening of an investigation."

At the outset, it is important to note that the issue here is not changing the predicates for criminalization of certain types of speech. Encouragement of generalized violence or group hatred is, indeed, criminalized as incitement in a number of democracies, including the United Kingdom, France, and Israel. The First Amendment to the U.S. Constitution would prevent making such speech a crime in the United States.

What is at stake here are the standards that should govern federal agents in determining whether surveillance of religious and political groups is merited. Without any specific reason to suspect involvement in terrorism or advocacy of violence, federal agents are now permitted to attend any religious or political meetings open to the public.

The recommendation here presents an alternative between a complete bar to attendance (how federal agents appeared to interpret the Attorney General's Guidelines before 9/11) and unrestricted attendance (the standard in the present Attorney General's Guidelines). The proposal would amend the requirement for terrorism investigations that there be the traditional basis for criminal or intelligence investigation—some defensible basis for suspecting the particular organization of planning political violence. It would also allow monitoring of any political or religious groups whose leaders were actively advocating violence or group hatred (although under the U.S. Constitution, such generalized advocacy or incitement cannot itself be a crime).

In reaching this compromise, we reject authorizing agents to attend any meetings open to the public. The advantages of allowing federal agents to attend political and religious meetings without reason to suspect either that the particular organization is involved in terrorism or that its leaders are inciting violence in a way likely either to draw or inspire an unusually dangerous audience are minimal. This form of monitoring, without any predicate, amounts to mere patrol. In the great majority of cases where there is no basis for suspecting the particular organization, the organizational activity will be completely legal and safe, but the prospect of surveillance will still deter attendance and participation.

Even if, unexpectedly, the meeting is a step in incitement or planning of political violence, the possibilities for useful action by federal investigators are extremely limited if the organization is at all careful about how it moves from incitement and encouragement to recruitment, planning, and complicity. If the latter activities are arranged so that they take place in secret conversations and locations and not during public meetings, investigative presence at the public meeting cannot provide much assistance. The primary effect will be in terms of an overbroad form of deterrence, not in terms of a better focused investigation.

On the other hand, permitting FBI attendance at a public meeting where there is incitement or encouragement—albeit in generalized form—of political violence will not greatly deter public attendance at other meetings of organizations whose activities may be unpopular but are legal and democratic. There is little reason to regret deterrence of advocacy of political violence. Moreover, in the present context of terrorist attacks on U.S. citizens, the audience drawn to advocacy of violence would be a group whose likelihood of engaging in terrorism would be substantially greater than that of others in the public. It remains true that there will be little that can be done on the basis of information on attendance alone, but that information, combined with other data, may be valuable.

The recommendation would require, however, approval at the highest level of the FBI and a time limit to ensure that attendance would no longer continue if the basis for the initial monitoring was not satisfied. As is required for any foreign intelligence electronic surveillance, the quantity of such surveillance shall be disclosed publicly.

RECORDS OF RELIGIOUS AND POLITICAL GROUP MONITORING

•In instances where federal agents are permitted to attend religious and political meetings under the above section, the keeping of records is appropriate so long as it is limited to persons engaged in the activities of the above section or who support and encourage these activities.

As described above, changes to the Attorney General's Guidelines address the question of record keeping. Under the Guidelines, Attorney General John Ashcroft specified that, when agents attend an event on grounds that it is open to the public, "no information obtained from these visits will be retained unless it relates to potential criminal or terrorist activity." The new Guidelines provide some valuable assurances. Assuming that the term "relates to" is applied with some measure of strictness, this standard provides substantial reassurance to those considering a meeting of an organization whose views are likely to be antithetical to the government. The standard also incorporates a sensible interpretation of the provisions of the Privacy Act of 1974, which state that a government agency shall "maintain no record of how any individual exercises rights guaranteed by the First Amendment...unless pertinent to and within the scope of an authorized law enforcement activity." A rule that would allow the recording of any information, including the names and descriptions of individuals, obtained while lawfully attending a political or religious meeting is, to U.S. citizens, exceptionally undesirable. A rule that no information will be retained unless it relates to potential criminal activity is presumably the practice applied by many states and localities with regard to the activities of their law enforcement agencies, except where court orders have discouraged the development of intelligence files.

The new Guidelines do not address the difficulty of identifying specific individuals—the leaders—whose conduct or statements may be worthy of some review. Thus, while we would curb the likelihood that federal investigators would attend public meetings, we would interpret the Privacy Act and modify the Attorney General's Guidelines in order to permit the creation and maintenance of records reflecting the advocacy by a group leader, even in some generalized form, of political violence or group hatred, as described in the above section. Such records would have some use in dealing with hate crimes, public disturbances, and terrorist attacks. It is, in any event, likely to be collected by state and local law enforcement and thereafter made available to federal agents, particularly to those working on joint state-federal antiterrorism task forces. Knowing who are community leaders, for good or bad, is part of the job of policing. In addition, denying federal agencies the right to maintain records of those urging such potentially dangerous activity is likely to lead to governmental forms of evasion, defeating the purpose of the prohibition.

Chapter 9

Distinctions Based on Group Membership

The question of "profiling" has animated national security discussions since the 9/11 attacks. The nineteen hijackers were all from the Middle East, and they were all Muslims. But these indisputable facts tell us less than many believe.

Present governmental guidelines regarding profiling in the context of terrorism- or national security–related cases should be revised to give explicit guidance as to the lawful and legitimate use of a "profile" in domestic intelligence investigations. Broad profiles based on the national origin of a U.S. citizen—or on the race or religion of any individual—are neither legitimate nor effective in combating terrorism.

Distinguishing U.S. citizens from others in granting access in dangerous situations is generally appropriate. The hardest cases will arise when distinctions are made among different categories of aliens, such as giving different treatment to people from the United Kingdom than to those from Saudi Arabia.

Nationality is, admittedly, a crude distinction, both over- and underinclusive. Yet, the use of the current nationality of an alien can provide an effective and easily administered distinction that may be utilized in appropriate circumstances by domestic law enforcement agents. There is a certain clarity and objectivity to a designation based on nationality. There is also some fair and rational basis for assuming that, with the possession of a passport from a certain country, the passport holder has a loyalty to that particular country. The circumstances for such distinctions must be carefully tailored and explicitly delineated.

Explanation and Background

In the fall of 1999, 81 percent of those interviewed in a national poll claimed that they disapproved of "racial profiling," defined as the practice of targeting certain groups because police officers believe that these groups are more likely than others to commit certain types of crimes.

After 9/11, 79 percent of respondents to a national poll stated that they approve of some sort of profiling, insofar as it pertains to national security measures and terrorism investigations.

The tremendous change in popular opinion is not surprising. Nineteen Arab men, a vast majority from Saudi Arabia, entered the United States and planned the most catastrophic terrorist attack on U.S. soil. Terrorist groups, at least the ones that seek to harm large numbers of Americans, are for now more likely than not to be Arab and Muslim.

Given what we know about terrorist organizations, who and how they recruit and how they plan their attacks, groups of persons identifiable by some unchosen characteristic may reduce the pool of people on which law enforcement must concentrate. The designation will not be perfect; it will, of course, be both under- and over-inclusive, but in a world of limited resources, it may provide sufficient means to focus law enforcement attention.

Much of the debate surrounding "profiling," however, is often truncated because of a failure to adequately define which characteristic is being "profiled" and whether that characteristic is appropriately linked to the activity law enforcement is trying to prevent.

Our focus is solely on the issue of acceptable profiles based on the foreign nationality of a person. In investigations related to terrorism, profiling based on nationality is different from racial or religious profiling. First, there is a certain clarity and objectivity to a designation based on nationality. Creating a profile based on a formal matter, such as a passport, provides standards for the government officials who will be authorized to act on the profile. Simply put, it limits discretion. Second, such a profile does not divide the U.S. population, as would occur with other forms of profiling based on unchosen characteristics or legitimate expressions of political or religious belief. It does not pit U.S. citizens against each other.

A distinction based on nationality also has some rational justification in terms of combating terrorism. It is not unreasonable to assume, that, with the possession of a passport from a certain country, the passport holder has a loyalty to that particular country. If such a state is a terrorist-supporting state, or at least tolerant of terrorism against the United States, then people holding its passport are more likely to be supporting terrorist groups. Moreover, recent surveys of international attitudes toward the United States suggest that very significant percentages of people within certain countries support suicide bombings and believe the killing of U.S. citizens to be a valid act. We need not ignore that sign of danger. Profiling based on nationality will not always be accurate in regards to a particular passport holder. It is, however, logical to suspect a presumed sympathy with the attitudes of the country of passport.

Even assuming that some sorts of exclusions are permissible based on where an individual's passport is from, the passport will in some instances be different from the place of birth of the immigrant. On the one hand, that place of birth may still command much of the loyalty of someone who has adopted a different citizenship. On the other, emigration—unless used to facilitate terrorism—is strong evidence of abandoned loyalties. In light of the danger of emigration for terrorist purposes, we would allow consideration of the original nationality where the newly adopted nation is less than vigorous in opposing terrorism.

DISTINCTIONS REGARDING U.S. CITIZENS

•**Broad profiles based on national origin of a U.S. citizen, or on the race or religion of any individual, are never permissible.** Affiliation with a religious or political group may be considered if there is reason to suspect that group of either advocating violent or illegal activities (pursuant to our recommendation on "Surveillance of Religious and Political Meetings") or being an agent of a foreign power.

•**Lawful permanent resident aliens should be afforded the protections of U.S. citizens for purposes of this recommendation,** unless they have been in the United States less than the required time (presently five years) for becoming naturalized citizens.

•**Distinctions based on the fact that an individual is not a U.S. citizen, such as in employment at sensitive sites or locations, are legitimate.** It is customary and rational to limit certain privileges to U.S. citizens.

Any existing legal rules that appear to apply to questions of "profiling" are very vague. The U.S. government has announced that it will not tolerate profiling by race or ethnicity in traditional law enforcement activities. In the June 2003 Guidance Regarding the Use of Race by Federal Law Enforcement Agencies issued by the Department of Justice, the government states that "racial profiling at its core concerns the invidious use of race or ethnicity as a criterion in conducting stops, searches and other law enforcement investigative procedures."

The guidance, however, provides exceptions for national security and border protection: "In investigating or preventing threats to national security or other catastrophic events (including the performance of duties related to air transportation security), or in enforcing laws protecting the integrity of the U.S. border, federal law enforcement officers may not consider race or ethnicity except to the extent permitted by the Constitution and the laws of the United States." The criteria for such exceptions is, as stated in the guidance, largely dependent on the circumstances at hand

and appears so vague as to permit almost any consideration of race or ethnicity.

As the attorney general, like most people, discusses "profiling," there is an additional implicit exception to the prohibition on profiling. This exception, unlike the broad exception for national security measures, we choose to adopt. Few people consider "profiling" questionable if there is specific evidence relating a prospective act of terrorism to a member of the group—we accept this form of profiling. For example, if there were evidence that an unidentified Asian person acted suspiciously and was present on the occasion of a particular explosion, focusing the investigation on Asians is not considered questionable profiling. With somewhat less clarity, if a threatened terrorist act is believed to share the characteristics previously associated with members of particular groups—such as suicide bombing—many believe that it is appropriate and not invidious to focus investigative attention on those groups. The distinctions from invidious labeling are that the suspicion is limited to a particular event or a particular type of event and that, unlike group generalizations that may remain in place long after they are no longer accurate, it depends upon a specific, time-bound, factual connection.

We reject profiling based on distinctions among U.S. citizens in terms of their national origin. In large part, wide-spread opposition to this is based on the tragic history of the Japanese-American internment during World War II. It is unfair to people who had no choice of origin and have made a choice to be citizens of the United States. It is divisive and dangerous. With all these disadvantages, it has few benefits as a strategy for dealing with terrorism. All these considerations apply with at least equally strong force to reject the use of race as a basis for suspicion. Here, too, U.S. history provides powerful lessons.

For somewhat different reasons, we reject making a distinction among U.S. citizens based on their affiliation with a religious or political group. We want all individuals within the United States, citizens or aliens, to feel as free as possible to engage in expressions of their religious or political beliefs and to form or join groups based on such beliefs. That is what our First Amendment guarantees. To allow distinctions based on perfectly legitimate religious or political activity as the basis for denying access or encouraging investigation would have a powerful, chilling effect on these protected activities. We recognize only a limited exception: where the religious or political group is reasonably suspected of advocating criminal or terrorist activity as described in the recommendation on "Surveillance of Religious and Political Meetings" or is itself an agent of a foreign power as defined in the Foreign Intelligence Surveillance Act, the government may consider affiliation with a religious or political group.

In addition, not being a U.S. citizen is an appropriate basis to limit certain privileges, such as employment at sensitive sites. It is legitimate to require certain registration for aliens entering this country and to apply conditions to their activities while in the United States.

Throughout this recommendation, we have treated legal permanent residents the same as U.S. citizens, under the terminology of "U.S. persons" as it has generally been used in our national security laws. Permanent resident aliens are, as a legal matter, somewhere between U.S. citizens and mere visitors. This designation includes people who are seeking U.S. citizenship as well as those who come to live in the United States lawfully, for an extended period of time, but are not in the process of seeking U.S. citizenship. There may be a continuing loyalty of a resident alien to the country of origin. On the other hand, such resident aliens are present in the United States, with all sorts of ties to the community, work, and schools and have satisfied some formal inquiry. Thus, as a means to mirror already-existing law, which requires these resident aliens to domicile in the United States before seeking citizenship, we would treat permanent resident aliens as citizens for these purposes if they have resided in the United States for five years or more.

DISTINCTIONS REGARDING GROUPS OF NONCITIZENS WITHIN THE UNITED STATES

• **As a trigger for further review, distinctions among aliens based on their nationalities, such as those from the United Kingdom as compared to those from Iran, are permissible in situations in the U.S. where there already exists a discretionary level of review before access or entry is permitted,** such as at an airport or a sensitive facility.

• **While enough to trigger more careful review, the fact that someone is a national from a particular country associated with a terrorist threat will generally hold little weight in determining whether that specific individual should be denied access.** Thus, the fact that a high proportion of terrorists come from a particular country may make its citizens subject to additional review, even though only a minuscule portion of that population will generally be a threat.

• **Despite the high risk of error, when the facts of a particular terrorist incident suggest the culpability of a state or its citizens, it is appropriate to give disproportionate attention in the initial stages of investigation to the citizens of that state.**

Distinctions made among aliens from different countries—for example, burdens placed on those from Iran as compared to those from the United Kingdom—raise harder issues. The absence of any discussion in the Department of Justice Guidelines about when and in what context nationality profiling among aliens is permissible suggests that, in all contexts, it is a permissible use of law enforcement and gate-keeping techniques to profile on the basis of nationality, regardless of the place, duration, context, or effectiveness.

There are a number of contexts where judgments based at least partially on the particular, foreign nationality may be appropriate—nationality still affects who gets into the country. The more difficult question, in the normal case, is whether in the United States a particular foreign nationality can be used to trigger a special investigation, or more intensive review at specific sensitive sites, or can be used during a criminal investigation as a means to focus law enforcement efforts.

The benefits of using nationality for these purposes depend upon there being a much higher probability that law enforcement and "gate-keepers" will find what they are looking for in the group defined by the profile than elsewhere. That higher probability results from the country of citizenship, or a high proportion of its citizens, being hostile to the United States or at least tolerant of persons who are extremely hostile to the United States. In those circumstances, the citizenship may be relevant, though only of limited value. That value will generally be inadequate to do more than trigger a search for other information about the person. The other information may be available to other federal agencies or other foreign governments or may be based on the passport holder's particular conduct, such as attempts to enter secure sites or purchase certain products.

This picture overstates the benefits in one crucial regard. One real danger of using a nationality profile is that terrorists will recognize the profile and develop devices to circumvent the more intensive review. If certain populations were targeted, we may expect that terrorists will seek to recruit from other parts of the world and from other passport holders. Indeed, there are reports that this has become a central strategy of al-Qaida. The result of nationality profiling would then be for terrorists to enjoy a less-than-normal chance of full investigation.

The logical response of the United States and other states to this possibility is to use citizens outside the profiled class as undercover agents, "offering" to assist terrorist organizations but actually working for the FBI or its counterparts abroad. The cost to terrorists of a system that examines more carefully a class from whom they can recruit more safely is that they have to recruit from less reliable classes. In those categories, the United States should find it far easier to recruit informants who would appear to al-Qaida as promising potential members.

The costs of nationality profiling flow from the domestic and foreign effect of conveying a message of suspicion about an entire population of people. Profiling by national origin will affect large numbers of innocent members of a group in a very public way. It will keep members of families apart.

Denying disproportionate numbers of some group of persons certain protections based on their passport is a very public gesture. Others outside the profiled group —individuals, employers—may mimic what the government is doing, justifying their own profiles based on the lessons of government conduct, even if the government's profiling is limited in scope and context. Prejudice against U.S. persons who had come from suspect countries would be encouraged.

Governmentally focused suspicion of citizens of one particular nation will have consequences for U.S. relationships with that nation and for law enforcement's relationship with U.S. persons whose backgrounds included that nationality. It will engender serious rifts between persons who could provide helpful information and the investigators who would like to know that information. Such profiling may have serious consequences for our relations abroad, both in the context of continuing support for our war on terrorism and for our citizens who are traveling and living abroad but who may be subject to similar profiles and restrictions if other countries follow our policies.

Thus, when access is provided to places or resources without any checks or investigation for U.S. citizens, there should generally be no check for lawfully admitted aliens except in the rare circumstance described in the third point under "Distinctions Regarding Groups of Noncitizens within the United States" of our recommendation. There are, more commonly, a variety of situations in which specific places or specific conduct require some sort of clearance or investigation. Entry to parts of the White House, the CIA, Congress, or a nuclear facility or the purchase of certain quantities of explosives would all be examples. Everyone will be checked in some fashion; one cannot simply walk into the State Department. In this context, a nationality profile to trigger a more thorough category or type of investigation of all persons from that country is appropriate. Since some sort of review is already occurring before entry, access, or a specific purchase is permitted, the attitudes of or within the state of nationality would be relevant to the inquiry, but not determinative, as to how intensive a review is required.

But, assuming that there is some general investigation or criteria for entry or purchase, how much weight should the nationality of the person seeking access be given in that review? Although there are specific targets and resources that may be of high value to terrorist organizations, a complete prohibition of certain nationalities would be both unfair and likely unhelpful. Nationality of particular states would be relevant, however, in that it would provide some background context, as part of a normal investigation, as to the potential risk of the person seeking to enter a facility or purchase certain products. It could provide useful information to law enforcement agencies in conjunction with additional inquiries.

Finally, to investigate a specific terrorist incident before it occurs requires credible and reliable information that illegal and harmful activity is likely to occur. It cannot be based on a general assumption that we are always in danger. To investigate a specific terrorist incident after it occurs requires that evidence directs investigators to specific avenues of inquiry and questioning.

Under these circumstances—terrorism investigations before or after a terrorist incident has occurred—nationality profiling may be somewhat relevant, but only when the circumstances of the incident suggest the involvement of the particular state or its citizens. Given both the nature of terrorism today, and the greater likelihood that the threat comes from nationals from specific countries, it is impractical to say that present nationality cannot be considered at all in determining where investigators may look to prevent or respond to a terrorist attack. On the other hand, it is equally impractical, and certainly harmful, to use even such nationality as a trigger for assuming that everybody who falls into that category is a potential suspect. After 9/11, nationals from specific countries were burdened—from increased interrogations to detentions—based solely on their nationality status. The method was not productive and caused serious harms within communities in the United States as well as with foreign governments, who viewed the response as draconian and unwieldy.

Thus, despite the potentially high risk of error, when the facts of a particular terrorist incident suggest the culpability of a state or its citizens, it is appropriate to give disproportionate attention in the initial stages of investigation to the citizens of that state. Nationality may be one factor, albeit a small factor, in investigating specific terrorist incidents. To give it too much weight would be akin to simply making an entire nationality suspect; to give it no weight would likely hamper investigations. In permitting nationality some role in investigations, however, it would not be enough simply to state that terrorism investigations are always ongoing merely because the threat is always ongoing. A particular incident (past or expected) must be the subject of the investigation.

Chapter 10

Oversight of Extraordinary Measures

In a democratic society that is adopting new and exceptional powers and taking unprecedented actions, there is a need to ensure that systems of oversight are robust. Often such oversight takes the form of judicial review, as the courts decide cases involving individuals who are the subjects of new enforcement powers. Oversight of the effectiveness as well as the fairness of any extraordinary measure, however, must also be carried out by other entities. This nonjudicial role belongs to both Congress and the executive branch itself. As an initial matter, extraordinary measures describe departures from traditional laws, regulations, or actions taken pursuant to the needs of combating the terrorist threat. They are inclusive of the measures in this Report, but also include additional actions that have been or will be taken.

This recommendation addresses appropriate systems of oversight. Much has been said about congressional oversight, and much of it has been critical. The 9/11 Commission concluded that the diffusion within Congress of oversight and budgetary responsibility over issues of terrorism and homeland security was dysfunctional and called on the Congress to coordinate its own functions. Whether that happens or not, it is important to recognize that congressional committees have already begun to exercise their oversight responsibilities in a new way—by creating special commissions when the task is too much or too prolonged for more familiar committee hearings and when it requires unusual assurance of nonpartisanship. The problem that we hope to address is how to use this new mechanism to institutionalize legislative oversight over the executive's use of extraordinary powers—oversight both for effectiveness and for fairness, but oversight that does not expose national security secrets to our enemies or interfere with ongoing investigations.

Our country must find a way to assess, with some transparency, the effectiveness of new measures to combat terrorism, whether they are provisions that soon will be retired under a sunset stipulation or simply ones that are shown by experience to be unwise. Given the frequent needs for secrecy in national security matters, democratic transparency is particularly difficult to assure. The purpose of the following recommendations is to describe how best to find facts in a way that is credible to the public and to reach conclusions that a wide segment of the public will find reasonable when what is at issue is whether particular extraordinary measures are proving to be useful in fighting terrorism and whether they are proving to be dangerous to democratic freedoms—and to do this in a way consistent with protecting secrets when that is truly necessary.

Explanation and Background

The fundamental understanding behind all of our recommendations is that there must be trade-offs among the goals of protecting national security, assuring democratic liberties, and enjoying the cooperation of other nations. We reject the views of those who think that civil liberties are immutable despite the great risks revealed by the 9/11 attacks, and of those who believe that everything that furthers our safety, no matter how little, is justified. Neither position is defensible.

The trade-offs are and will be difficult. Some of them, like the decisions about detention, involve a very complicated balance of a sizeable number of considerations, none of which can be adequately measured. There will, therefore, long be disputes about where the balance should be struck. We do not have to agree on precisely where the balance falls, however, or on precisely what the trade-off should be, to know that there must be simultaneous consideration of our safety at home and abroad, our commitment to democratic liberties, and indeed, our respect for the sovereignty of nations whose cooperation we need and value.

It is equally obvious that the trade-offs cannot be made without periodically assessing the effectiveness of the particular measures adopted to deal with the dangers of catastrophic terrorism. The extraordinary measures that we as a nation decide to take, if they are to be justified as needed to protect our national security despite their costs, can not be defended simply by noting the extraordinary danger of al-Qaida or global terrorism. Justification also depends on the capacity of the measures to reduce that danger. These points can hardly be disputed.

In this, we are insisting that there should be the types of review that the military does after a war, considering how well the tactics, equipment, organization, and strategy have worked. We must do the same thing, not simply in order to fight the next war better, but also in order to know how much our safety has actually been enhanced and, equally important, to reach intelligent judgments about whether a measure's effectiveness is worth its costs. A similar notion lies behind the sunset provisions of the USA PATRIOT Act.

This is why the United States should be periodically reviewing the extraordinary measures that we have decided to take since 9/11. But recognizing the need for review does not answer several remaining questions: Who should decide which measures are so extraordinary as to require review? When and how often should the review be undertaken? Who should evaluate the effectiveness of the measures, and how can they deal with classified information? With what factual basis can the evaluation be sensibly carried out?

Again, the role of Congress is essential in this regard, but also, we believe, the role of internal checks within the executive branch ought to be increased.

CONGRESSIONAL OVERSIGHT OF NEW COUNTERTERRORISM LAWS AND PRACTICES HAVING SIGNIFICANT EFFECTS ON TRADITIONAL RIGHTS OF INDIVIDUALS

•**As ongoing extraordinary measures are retained by legislation or acquiescence, the congressional leadership should establish a five-year nonpartisan commission to make findings and recommendations regarding the continuing need for these measures for consideration by the Congress and the relevant committees of each House.**

•**With regard to any extraordinary measure for addressing the dangers of terrorism that the Congress determines to have or have had significant effects on the liberties of citizens, the commission should establish a system of continuing review.**

1. The list of extraordinary measures to be reviewed should include measures undertaken by the president with or without congressional authority.

2. The frequency of review should be at least annual.

3. The members of the commission should be subject to security clearance procedures and then provided access to classified information on terms similar to those now applicable to the Intelligence Committees.

4. At an absolute minimum, such assessments should examine the case for and against the efficacy of an extraordinary measure in light of:

-The use, or lack thereof, of the measure;

-The likelihood of the assumptions under which the extraordinary measure would be effective;

-The likelihood of the rival assumptions under which it would fail;

-The history and experience that may throw light on these relative probabilities;

-The experience of other democracies in utilizing similar measures; and

-The adequacy of oversight of these extraordinary measures.

5. The published results of the review should not contain classified information that was made available to the commission acting on behalf of the relevant congressional committees. While as much detail as possible should be furnished, even a review that merely reaches unclassified conclusions, if carried out by a credible body, would be valuable.

In 2004, Senators John McCain and Joseph Lieberman proposed the creation of a panel of five people from outside the government, appointed by the president and subject to Senate approval, who would report to Congress on whether to retain or enhance a particular governmental power, like provisions of the USA PATRIOT Act. This proposal, in many ways, mirrors recommendations of the 9/11 Commission that sought the creation of a board within the executive branch to protect civil liberties and privacy rights, with disinterested individuals who would have full access to techniques and collection practices. The president has already appointed a twenty-person advisory panel on these matters, but all are executive branch employees, and the panel has no investigatory role. Thus, the president's response does not provide a suitable check.

We should not shy away from a thorough investigation of the effectiveness of measures that are intended to protect our national security, especially those that implicate personal liberties. There are ample historical precedents. The President's Foreign Intelligence Advisory Board (PFIAB) is an entity that exists in order to provide the president with essential information regarding intelligence and national security matters. Its purpose is to offer guidance—outside the traditional agency-based system—and to investigate matters that have public import in the intelligence area. All members are independent. One important example of their work was PFIAB's review of security at our national laboratories, a review that had tremendous influence on legislative action in this matter.

Though PFIAB has come under some criticism regarding its assessment in the lead up to the war in Iraq, its model provides a good starting point in determining what in fact Congress may need to assess extraordinary measures—their effectiveness and their need. The traditional manner of congressional oversight has proved to be inadequate for a variety of reasons. The 9/11 Commission emphasized the dispersion among committees of counterterrorism measures. The politics of ordinary oversight will also inhibit serious review. Instead, we need a set of long-term assessments and an enduring commitment—both characteristics are somewhat inconsistent with election cycles.

The 9/11 Commission's recommendations to overhaul committee oversight structure are important but exceedingly difficult to implement. Committee structures are difficult to change, even in emergency situations such as ours. Congress still has no adequate system to determine a number of important questions regarding the balance of democratic freedoms and security in the war on terrorism. Government Accountability Office (GAO) reports tend to be limited in their scope. No mechanism for a comprehensive review exists, despite the fact that a number of provisions of the USA PATRIOT Act are set to expire.

Effectively assessing any specific measure calls for a comprehensive review: Did it work? Was it utilized? Was it abused? Our solution would take the review out of the political context of congressional debate and create a congressional equivalent of a PFIAB review for the extraordinary measures that either exist now or that may be proposed. Any conclusion about whether a policy should stay or be rejected would, of course, remain with elected officials. That is necessarily a legislative function. To the extent that relevant facts are not clearly known by the public, or even by Congress, however, this group would have the capacity, the credibility, and the stability to fill that gap.

The Board would not simply meet on one matter (as is the case with most congressional commissions) or exist forever (as is the case with PFIAB), but would be in place during this time of massive legal change (for no less than five years.) During that time, it would be charged with providing information and recommendations to Congress, at least annually, on both the substantive measures that have been taken by the executive branch (either pursuant to congressional mandate or without it) and the frequency and utility of use of such measures.

This assessment would provide Congress with valuable information regarding the need for any particular policy or legislation. It should include provisions of the USA PATRIOT Act that are continuing subjects of debate. This review should take into account the frequency of use of any measure, the assumptions that led to the initiation of such measures, the history and experience of the executive branch agencies in dealing with this extraordinary measure, the experience of other democracies and, most significantly, the adequacy of oversight of these measures (if there are any) as they are applied in individual cases. Indeed, this framework is appropriate as Congress immediately takes up the sunsetted provisions of the USA PATRIOT Act.

The information available to this Board would be the same as the information available to the relevant committees, including the Intelligence Committees. To the extent practicable, the board should provide unclassified information and unclassified recommendations, for public consumption and debate.

Overall, this recommendation seeks to do two things: first, to create an entity that is empowered to find the facts regarding the use of a variety of extraordinary measures and, second, through that entity, to provide the Congress and the public with as much of the information and analysis as national security allows so that we can use democratic institutions for lawful governance.

EXECUTIVE OVERSIGHT OF SUBSTANTIVE LEGAL REFORMS

- **Congress shall enact legislation that provides that each inspector general (IG) shall conduct a systemic review of the use made of each of a list of provisions granting extraordinary powers to the IG's agency.** The review shall include their effectiveness and their costs (intangible as well as tangible) to those affected as well as to the agency, on an annual basis, for no less than five years. This list shall include, but not be limited to, any provisions with sunset clauses in past legislation. While present statutory authority would not preclude reviews of the civil liberties impact of an agency's counterterrorism activities by an inspector general, specific statutory authority and responsibility should be explicitly granted to all relevant IGs as it has already been to the inspector general of the Department of Justice. In both the reviews of effectiveness and of the impact on civil liberties, the IG's authority should extend to reviews of private sector and state and local government conduct, when done pursuant to a mandate from or agreement with the Department.

- **Any new legislation granting extraordinary authorities should include requirements that the relevant inspector general conduct annual reviews, in a classified and unclassified form, of the efficacy of any measure.**

- **To provide a coherent review of (1) extraordinary power vested in more than one agency; and (2) the effect of using different extraordinary powers of different agencies for a shared purpose, the Congress should authorize and fund an interagency committee of IGs that would establish criteria** for any investigation that would involve more than one department or agency and create structures to allow joint-OIG reviews and recommendations.

The proposal for an independent congressional Board should be coupled with the following recommendation regarding executive oversight of its own actions. The Offices of Inspector General (OIGs) have played a very useful role in a relatively noncontroversial way, since the passage of the Inspector General Act of 1978 (IG Act) authorized the creation of offices whose mission it was to detect and prevent fraud, waste, and abuse in their respective departments and agencies across the executive branch. Amendments to the Act in 1988 created IGs in the Treasury and Justice Departments. There are now fifty-six statutory Offices of Inspector General.

The need for aggressive and reliable executive branch oversight is a relatively non-controversial point. OIGs have the responsibility for conducting special investigations of broad public interest and importance. Uniquely situated to understand and describe an agency's conduct, the IG is also in a unique position to help Congress and the public assess the necessity of extraordinary powers to deal with terrorism.

In the difficult areas regarding national security and liberty, the OIG can play a critical role in ensuring that there are internal mechanisms for the executive branch to correct itself. This was evidenced by the Department of Justice's (DOJ) own internal OIG reviews of its treatment of the post–9/11 detainees (and more recently of the Arabic language deficiencies of the FBI). While the report on detention was most notable for its verification of many of the allegations regarding detainee abuse, it is also important that every recommendation proposed by the OIG was adopted by the FBI and the DOJ. That investigation was done pursuant to language in the USA PATRIOT Act, which authorized the OIG to initiate internal investigations based on civil rights and civil liberties complaints. That language may not have been necessary (the OIG could have initiated an investigation pursuant to his normal oversight powers) but was certainly an important mechanism to ensure that there would be an OIG investigation. Having a clear congressional mandate that this type of review was part of the OIG's agenda was of great political importance and likely encouraged the adoption of the recommendations by the DOJ.

Unlike whistleblower protection laws, offices of privacy, and offices of civil rights within a number of departments and agencies, OIGs have broad authority to investigate governmental employee conduct, to recommend institutional changes, and to assess their efficacy. With enduring and reasonable fears of terror attacks, it is important to ensure that each individual OIG is not only impartial, adequately staffed, and active, but also that it is given the explicit statutory authority to investigate important issues related to both efficacy and individual rights.

Experience shows that effectiveness of any extraordinary new executive power is an issue that should not only be reviewed by outside entities (Congress, GAO, etc.) but also by internal ones. It was the IG of Justice who pointed out the prevalence and the uselessness of electronic surveillance that is not translated from Arabic. The IG is in a very good position to determine whether the department is measuring up to its own expectations—here the specific demands of the FBI Director—especially regarding its effectiveness in carrying out the mandate it has been given.

That is only part of the role an IG can play. Many of these new executive powers obviously touch on concerns regarding civil liberties, civil rights, and privacy in ways that are unique and that should also be clearly described and measured. An OIG review, for example, of waste or fraud of a contractor is different in kind than one that seeks to determine whether a new agency power is unduly restricting certain rights or expectations of individuals. Sometimes IG reviews cannot be so easily compartmentalized. For example, a recent Department of Homeland Security (DHS) IG review of the controversial visa security program was exceptionally critical, finding the DHS had not committed enough resources or personnel to ensure that visa clearances of visitors were adequately reviewed.

It is for these reasons that we seek to buttress IG review by a variety of means. First, Congress should require that each individual IG office conduct a systematic review of its agency's use of extraordinary measures, including any sunset provisions. These reviews would be annual, continuing for no less than five years, and would provide the executive branch its own mechanism of internal review so that it can assess its own conduct and effectiveness.

These reviews would require that there be an effectiveness assessment, along with an assessment of the impact any procedure has had on the liberties of citizens or others within the United States. As compared to reviews of intelligence agencies abroad, which are complicated and highly classified, such data is easily accessible, questions of covert or secretive operations are less likely to limit an IG review, and final documents and assessments can more readily be released to the Congress and the public. These reviews would also extend to the conduct of private sector contractors and state and local governments, where such entities perform federal government functions pursuant to a mandate from or agreement with an executive agency.

Finally, one of the unintended consequences of the massive overhaul of government agencies since 9/11—the proliferation of new agencies and duties all related to combating terrorism—suggests that a variety of counterterrorism measures have no clear home base. The question "who's in charge" is still too often unanswerable. This poses problems for counterterrorism enforcement in general, and specifically for issues concerning individual liberties and rights; it makes the work of individual IG's less comprehensive than what we need. OIGs, by statute, have the ability to obtain any and all records only from any component of their agencies without a subpoena. In a variety of contexts, however, many agencies have jurisdiction over a specific substantive power that may affect individual rights and privacy.

This dispersion of counterterrorism functions has led to a lack of a single oversight structure, not simply in Congress, but also within the executive branch. There have been historic attempts to unify IG mandates, given the rules regarding an IG's jurisdiction. At the very least, there should be a formalized interagency IG group that would establish criteria for any investigation pursuant to this recommendation that involves more than one agency or that would require compliance by more than one department or agency. Such mechanisms tend to exist on a case-by-case basis. A more formalized process is required given the magnitude of the issues involved.

Appendix A

Counterterrorism Policies in the United Kingdom

Tom Parker

Coercive Interrogations

"...secret, illegal, not morally justifiable and alien to the traditions of what I believe still to be the greatest democracy in the world."[1]

Coercive interrogation techniques had historically been a feature of the British response to colonial insurgencies in places such as Kenya, Cyprus, Malaya, and Aden, but their use had long been outlawed at home.[2] As the United Kingdom confronted escalating nationalist terrorism in Northern Ireland in the early 1970s, however, these methods were briefly adopted by the British security forces in the interrogation of interned IRA suspects to great public opprobrium. The British government subsequently admitted that the use of these methods had been authorized at a "high level"[3] and unsuccessfully sought to justify this decision before the European Court of Human Rights (ECHR).

COERCIVE INTERROGATION AND INTERNMENT

In the immediate aftermath of the introduction of internment in August 1971, twelve detainees were selected for "interrogation in depth."[4] The location, or locations, where these interrogations took place has never offi-

---

1. Minority report of Lord Gardiner, *Report of the Committee of Privy Counselors appointed to consider authorized procedures for the interrogation of persons suspected of terrorism* (London: Her Majesty's Stationery Office (HMSO), March 1972).
2. Peter Taylor, *Provos: The IRA and Sinn Fein* (London: Bloomsbury, 1997).
3. *Case of Ireland v. United Kingdom*, European Court of Human Rights Series A, No. 25 (1978) and Taylor, *Provos*. Stormont Prime Minister Brian Faulkner was apparently briefed by Royal Ulster Constabulary (RUC) and military personnel who were directly involved in the interrogations and was assured that the "appropriate authorities" in London had signed off on the use of these methods.
4. *Case of Ireland v. United Kingdom*.

cially been identified.[5] At least two additional suspects who were detained in October 1971 went through the same process, and a few other less well-documented cases were likely. Royal Ulster Constabulary (RUC) interrogators working "under the supervision" of the British Army[6] applied five well-established techniques which had previously been practiced in the course of colonial emergencies: (1) hooding, (2) wall-standing, (3) subjection to noise, (4) relative deprivation of food and water, and (5) sleep deprivation.[7] Although never put down on paper, these techniques had apparently been orally taught to members of the RUC at a seminar run by the British Intelligence Centre in April 1971.[8]

The terms used are fairly self-explanatory. Hooding meant that a prisoner's head was covered with an "opaque cloth bag with no ventilation"[9] except during interrogation or when in isolation. The prisoner would often also be stripped naked to enhance his feeling of vulnerability. Wall-standing consisted of forcing prisoners to stand balanced against a cell wall in the "search position" for hours at a time, inducing painful muscle cramps. One prisoner was forced to remain in this position for forty-three and a half hours, and there were at least six other recorded instances of prisoners being kept like this for more than twenty hours.[10] Subjection to noise meant placing the prisoner in close proximity to the monotonous whine of machinery such as a generator or compressor for as long as six or seven days. At least one prisoner subjected to this treatment, Jim Auld, told Amnesty International that having been driven to the brink of insanity by the noise, he had tried to commit suicide by banging his head against metal piping in his cell.[11] Food and water deprivation meant a strict regimen of bread and water. Sleep deprivation was practiced prior to interrogation and often in tandem with wall-standing. Detainees were usually subjected to this conditioning over the course of about a week. Although only relatively few detainees received the full "in depth" treatment, some of these techniques were also

---

5. Amnesty International tentatively identified Palace Barracks in Holywood near Belfast as one of these centers.

6. Owen Bowcott, "General Fought Plan to Intern Suspects," *The Guardian*, January 1, 2002.

7. Donald Jackson, "Prevention of Terrorism: The United Kingdom Confronts the European Convention on Human Rights," *Journal of Terrorism and Political Violence*, Vol. 6, No. 4 (Winter 1994), p. 509.

8. *Case of Ireland v. United Kingdom.*

9. Amnesty International, *Report on Allegations of Ill-Treatment Made by Persons Arrested Under The Special Powers Act After August 8, 1971*, October 30, 1971.

10. See Jackson, *Prevention of Terrorism.*

11. Amnesty International, *Report on Allegations of Ill-Treatment*; and Alex Richardson, "Iraq Abuse Images Stir Memories in N. Ireland," Reuters, May 14, 2004.

applied more widely for several months in the Regional Holding Centres.[12]

Many of 342 individuals arrested with the introduction of internment were released within forty-eight hours, and with their release came the first stories about the ill-treatment of those detained.[13] On August 31, 1971, British Home Secretary Reginald Maudling responded to growing public concern by appointing Sir Edmund Compton to investigate complaints made by forty suspects detained on August 9, 1971. These included complaints of ill treatment made by detainees not selected for "in depth" interrogation. Additional complaints involved the practice of forcing detainees to run an obstacle course over broken glass and rough ground while being beaten and, perhaps most seriously of all, deceiving detainees into believing that they were to be thrown from high flying helicopters. In reality, the blindfolded detainees were thrown from a helicopter that hovered approximately four feet above the ground.[14] Despite accepting that these events did indeed take place Sir Edmund reported: "Our investigations have not led us to conclude that any of the grouped or individual complainants suffered physical brutality as we understand the term."[15]

The Compton Report came in for considerable criticism both in the United Kingdom and overseas. The former *Derry News* columnist John McGuffin described it as "one of the shabbiest and incompetent attempts at whitewash since the Warren Report in the USA."[16] Amnesty International rejected the report's findings out of hand commenting: "The allegations are of such a nature as to provide a *prima facie* case of brutality and torture in contravention of Article 5 of the Universal Declaration of Human Rights and Article 5 [sic] of the European Convention on Human Rights."[17]

On November 16, 1971, Maudling bowed to the inevitable and announced that a further Committee had been set up under the chairmanship of Lord Parker of Waddington to consider "whether, and if so in what respects, the procedures currently authorized for interrogation of persons suspected of terrorism and for their custody while subject to interrogation require amendment."

---

12. Taylor, *Provos*.

13. *Case of Ireland v. United Kingdom.*

14. Sir Edmund Compton, *Report of the Enquiry into Allegations against the Security Forces of Physical Brutality in Northern Ireland arising out of events on the 9th August 1971* (London: HMSO, November 1971).

15. Compton, *Report of the Enquiry into Allegations against the Security Forces of Physical Brutality in Northern Ireland arising out of events on the 9th August 1971.*

16. John McGuffin, *Internment* (Tralee, Ireland: Anvil, 1973).

17. Amnesty International, *Report on Allegations of Ill-Treatment*. Presumably the author of the report meant to refer to Article 3 of the European Convention on Human Rights.

The Parker Report contained both majority and minority reports. The majority report concluded that the application of the techniques, subject to some recommended safeguards against excessive use, need not be ruled out on moral grounds. The minority report by Lord Gardiner, however, disagreed that such interrogation procedures were morally justifiable, even in emergency terrorist conditions. Both the majority and the minority reports consider the methods to be illegal under domestic law, although the majority report confined its view to British law and to "some if not all the techniques."

Prime Minister Edward Heath addressed Parliament on March 2, 1972, following the publication of the Parker Report: "[The] Government, having reviewed the whole matter with great care and with reference to any future operations, have decided that the techniques ... will not be used in future as an aid to interrogation. The statement that I have made covers all future circumstances. If a Government did decide ... that additional techniques were required for interrogation, then I think that ... they would probably have to come to the House and ask for the powers to do it."[18]

In April 1972, new British Army instructions and RUC Force Order 64/72, concerning, respectively, arrests under the Special Powers Regulations and the treatment of prisoners, directed that excessive force should never be used. In June 1972, the Attorney General gave a ministerial directive on the proper treatment of persons in custody, making it clear that any form of ill treatment would be prosecuted by the authorities. Further Army and RUC instructions of August 1972 relating to arrests and interrogations expressly prohibited the use of the "five techniques" and of threats and insults.[19]

The matter did not end there, however. On December 16, 1971, the Republic of Ireland had filed an application with the European Commission on Human Rights alleging that the emergency procedures applied against suspected terrorists in Northern Ireland violated several articles of the European Convention on Human Rights.[20] It is depressing to note that little more than a decade earlier Dublin had been the United Kingdom's ally in combating cross-border IRA activity.[21]

In its February 1976 report to the Committee of Ministers of the Council of Europe, the commission unanimously found that the "five techniques" amounted to "a modern system of torture" and a violation of

---

18. *Case of Ireland v. United Kingdom.*
19. Ibid.
20. Jackson, "Prevention of Terrorism."
21. Peter Smith, *The Difficult Subjects: The Northern Ireland Experience*, Harvard Long-Term Legal Strategy Project; and Taylor, *Provos.*

Article 3 of the convention.[22] The case was referred to the ECHR for adjudication.

Ireland v. United Kingdom was the first interstate case ever brought before the European Court.[23] Reviewing the evidence in December 1977, the court found the "five techniques" to be "cruel, inhuman and degrading" and thus breaches of Article 3 of the convention but stopped short of describing them as torture, noting that "they did not occasion suffering of the particular intensity and cruelty implied by the word torture."[24]

The actual utility of coercive interrogation was addressed at some length in the course of *Ireland v. United Kingdom*. The British government sought to argue that it had been necessary to introduce such techniques to combat a rise in terrorist violence. The government claimed that the two "operations of interrogation in depth" addressed by the court had obtained a considerable quantity of actionable intelligence, including the identification of seven hundred members of both IRA factions and the discovery of individual responsibility for about eighty-five previously unexplained criminal incidents.[25] Other well-informed sources were, however, more skeptical. Former British Intelligence officer Frank Steele, who served in Northern Ireland during this period, told the journalist Peter Taylor: "As for the special interrogation techniques, they were damned stupid as well as morally wrong... in practical terms, the additional usable intelligence they produced was, I understand, minimal."[26] Certainly the last quarter of 1971, the period during which these techniques were most employed, was marked by mounting, not decreasing, violence—a fairly obvious yardstick by which to measure their efficacy.[27]

Finally, it should be noted that in the mid-1970s, at least fourteen former detainees subjected to the "five techniques" were subsequently able to institute civil proceedings in the British courts seeking damages from the government for wrongful imprisonment and assault for which they ultimately received compensation awards ranging from £10,000 to £25,000.[28]

COERCIVE INTERROGATION AND THE WAR ON TERROR

At a hearing before the European Court on February 8, 1977, the British Attorney General made the following declaration: "The Government of the United Kingdom have [sic] considered the question of the use of the

---

22. Jackson, "Prevention of Terrorism."
23. Ibid.
24. *Case of Ireland v. United Kingdom.*
25. Ibid.
26. Taylor, *Provos.*
27. Philip Thomas, "Emergency and Anti-Terrorism Power: 9/11: USA and UK," *Fordham International Law Journal*, Vol. 26 (April 2003), pp. 1223–1224.
28. *Case of Ireland v. United Kingdom.*

'five techniques' with very great care and with particular regard to Article 3 of the Convention. They now give this unqualified undertaking, that the 'five techniques' will not in any circumstances be reintroduced as an aid to interrogation."[29]

The Attorney General's undertaking notwithstanding, there have been continued complaints from members of the nationalist community that physical and mental abuse have remained a feature of interviews conducted by the officers of the RUC. [30] Between 1993 and 1996, the Independent Commission for Police Complaints (ICPC) investigated 384 allegations of assaults by RUC officers during police interviews, as well as sixty-five additional complaints of assault alleged to have occurred after arrest.[31] The ICPC did not uphold a single one of these complaints, although some commentators have observed that the impartiality of these investigations was substantially undermined by the fact that they were conducted by serving members of the RUC.[32] No evidence suggests, however, that these alleged police abuses, either in Northern Ireland and on the mainland, occurred with official sanction; thus, any such abuses, even if proven, would fall outside the scope of this paper.

Prime Minster Edward Heath's 1972 statement to the House of Commons remains the official position of the British government to this day. In the wake of the revelations regarding the abuse of Iraqi detainees by U.S. military and civilian personnel in Baghdad's Abu Ghraib prison, the Parliamentary Under-Secretary of State for the Ministry of Defence, Lord Bach, told the House of Lords: "The training in methods of questioning is of a high standard and is well within the terms of the Geneva Convention. The joint services intelligence organization's training documentation states that the following techniques are expressly and explicitly forbidden: physical punishment of any sort; the use of stress privation; intentional sleep deprivation; withdrawal of food, water or medical help; degrading treatment, including sexual embarrassment or religious taunting; the use of what is called 'white noise'… and torture methods such as thumbscrews. I repeat: all those are expressly and explicitly forbidden."[33]

The secretary of state for defense, Geoff Hoon, recently admitted that the hooding of prisoners, a practice notably omitted from Lord Bach's

---

29.   Jackson, "Prevention of Terrorism."

30.   Indeed, a government report found evidence of what it termed "a coordinated and extensive campaign" to discredit the RUC. Judge H.G. Bennett, *Report of the Committee of Inquiry into Police Interrogation Procedures in Northern Ireland* (London: HMSO, 1979).

31.   Michael O'Connor and Celia Rumann, "Into the Fire: How to Avoid Getting Burned by the Same Mistakes Made Fighting Terrorism in Northern Ireland," *Cardozo Law Review*, Vol. 24, (April 2003), p. 1686.

32.   Ibid.

33.   House of Lords Debates, *Hansard*, May 10, 2004.

statement, had been used in the course of British military operations in Iraq, but went on to report that the ban on its use had been reinstated in late 2003.[34]

Indefinite Detention

"Internment… brought together men from all parts of the country and bonded them, even those innocent of any involvement in political conspiracy, into an organic unit."[35]

The internment of suspected terrorists without trial is an emergency power that has been made available to British security forces both in the context of Northern Ireland and now more recently in the "war on terrorism." It has been applied with mixed results and there has been a long-standing and vigorous debate in the United Kingdom about its utility as a counterterrorist tool. As a result, the legislative framework governing internment has been subject to frequent review.

INTERNMENT IN THE CONTEXT OF IRISH TERRORISM

Internment was first used in Ireland in the twentieth century under the Defence of the Realm Act of 1914.[36] This wartime act was invoked to intern 2,519 suspected rebels following the Dublin Easter Uprising of 1916.[37] Internees were screened by the Advisory Committee on the Internment of Rebels established in London in a vain attempt to identify the remaining leaders of the Republican movement. One of those interned was the charismatic Michael Collins, who used his time in the Frongoch internment camp in North Wales to recruit likely volunteers into the hardcore of the Irish Republican Brotherhood (IRB) underground. The treatment of the internees provoked a public outcry in both the United Kingdom and the United States, pressuring the British government to declare an amnesty in December 1916. Collins went on after his release to create the Republican terrorist cell known as "The Squad," which intimidated and murdered members of the local security forces with spectacular success in

34. Duncan Walker, "Name, Rank and Number," *BBC News*, May 13, 2004, http://news.bbc.co.uk/2/hi/uk_news/magazine/3707763.stm.

35. Brian Feeney, *Sinn Fein: A Hundred Turbulent Years* (Madison: University of Wisconsin Press, 2002), p. 60.

36. This was not a new tactic, prior to the Easter Uprising, detention without trial had been used to suppress the United Irishmen in the 1790s, and the habeas corpus was suspended to combat nationalist activity in Ireland on four occasions in the nineteenth century.

37. Tim Pat Coogan, *Michael Collins* (London: Arrow, 1990) p. 49.

1919–1920. The Squad's first leader was another Frogoch alumnus, Mick McDonnell.[38]

After the partition of Ireland, the new Stormont Government included a provision on internment in the Civil Authorities (Special Powers) Act (Northern Ireland) of 1922. This Act was renewed annually until 1928, then extended for a five-year period and finally made permanent in 1933.[39] The Special Powers Act remained in force until the end of 1972, when it was superseded by the Emergency Powers Act. The Special Powers Act was invoked on numerous occasions to intern suspected terrorists, and the practice of internment was considered to have been particularly effective in disrupting the IRA's 1956–1962 border campaign.[40]

The widescale use of internment in the early 1970s, however, proved to be much more controversial. Faced with escalating violence in the province, Unionist Prime Minister of Northern Ireland Brian Faulkner persuaded the British government of the day that internment might bring the situation under control.[41] On August 9, 1971, British troops mounted Operation Demetrius—a series of raids across Northern Ireland which resulted in the detention of 342 IRA suspects in Regional Holding Centres in Ballykinler, Girdwood Park, and Magilligan.[42] Army intelligence was so poor that those detained even included veterans of the Easter Uprising now in their eighties—most of the serious Republican players had been tipped off prior to the raids and had already gone to ground.[43]

On August 16, 1971, Joe Cahill, then Chief of Staff of the Provisional IRA and a prominent target of Operation Demetrius, taunted the authorities by surfacing to hold a press conference in Belfast, during which he claimed

---

38. Ibid., p. 116.
39. Michael O'Connor, "Into the Fire: How to Avoid Getting Burned by the Same Mistakes Made Fighting Terrorism in Northern Ireland," *Cardozo Law Review,* Vol. 24 (2003), p. 1657.
40. Smith, *The Difficult Subjects;* and Taylor, *Provos.* The successful use of internment during 1956–1962 campaign can largely be ascribed to the fact that it was applied simultaneously by governments on both sides of the Irish border. Effective cooperation between London and Dublin meant that the IRA was deprived of a safe haven south of the border. Such cooperation was significantly absent when internment was resurrected in the 1970s—indeed the Irish government was ultimately to take the British government first to the European Commission on Human Rights and then subsequently to the European Court of Human Rights over the treatment of IRA detainees (*Ireland v. United Kingdom*).
41. In fairness to Prime Minister Edward Heath, the British government only followed Faulkner's advice reluctantly. British military commanders also initially opposed internment on the grounds that it could not be "justified by any military necessity" before acquiescing to political direction. Peter Taylor, "Heath's Fateful Decision," *The Guardian,* January 1, 2002, http://politics.guardian.co.uk/.
42. Compton, *Report of the Enquiry into Allegations.*
43. Taylor, *Provos,* p. 93; and Paul Wilkinson, *Terrorism and the Liberal State* (London: Macmillan, 1986).

that only thirty of the men who had by now been detained were actually members of the IRA.[44] The government was increasingly embarrassed by revelations about the paucity of the intelligence directing internment, which had already led to 105 of the initial 342 detainees being released after questioning.[45] This intelligence did not appear to improve over time; by November 1971, 508 of the 980 suspects detained had been released.[46]

Within Northern Ireland, internment further galvanized the nationalist community in its opposition to British rule, and violence immediately surged against the security forces. Twenty-seven people had been killed in the first eight months of 1971, prompting the introduction of internment; in the four remaining months of the year, 147 people were killed. In 1972, 467 people were killed as a result of terrorist action.[47] In the words of the former British Intelligence officer Frank Steele, who served in Northern Ireland during this period: "[Internment] barely damaged the IRA's command structure and led to a flood of recruits, money and weapons. It was a farce."[48]

In response to mounting public criticism, further fueled by reports of the mistreatment of detainees, a wide-ranging commission of inquiry was established in 1972 under Lord Diplock to review the legal procedures used to counter Irish terrorism. In its report, the commission recommended, *inter alia*, a number of changes to the practice of internment, which it witheringly described as "imprisonment at the arbitrary Diktat of the Executive Government."[49] Although it stopped short of recommending some degree of judicial oversight, the Diplock Commission called for the process to involve the civilian authorities operating within the context of a prescribed procedure. The commission considered it vital that steps be taken to reverse the appearance of arbitrariness which had hitherto characterized the process.

The Emergency Powers Act of 1973 adopted Lord Diplock's recommendation by requiring that a *prima facie* case establishing the suspect's "involvement in terrorism" and the existence of an "ongoing danger to the community" be made to the Secretary of State for Northern Ireland before an interim custody order could be issued. The secretary of state was empowered to issue an order detaining a terrorist suspect for up to twenty-eight days, after which the case would have to be referred to an independ-

---

44. *Internment–A Chronology of the Main Events*, CAIN Web service at http://cain.ulst.ac.uk/events/intern/chron.htm.
45. Compton, *Report on Allegations of Ill-Treatment*.
46. Ibid.
47. Philip Thomas, "Emergency and Anti-Terrorism Power: 9/11: USA and UK."
48. Taylor, *Provos*, pp. 129–130.
49. Lord Diplock, *Report of the Commission to consider legal procedures to deal with terrorist activities in Northern Ireland* (December 1972).

ent commissioner should a longer period of detention be sought. The government was not required to inform the internee of the reason for his detention until at least one week prior to any determination hearing. Evidence could be presented by the government in secret to the commissioner without any requirement to disclose this material to the detainee or his counsel. Internment was to continue in Northern Ireland until December 5, 1975, by which time a total of 1,981 people had been detained—1,874 Republicans and 107 Loyalists.[50] The British Army estimated that up to 70 percent of the long-term internees became re-involved in terrorist acts after their release.[51]

The option of internment remained dormant on the statute books, but it was increasingly seen as a relic of a discredited past. This attitude was perfectly encapsulated in the Review of the Northern Ireland (Emergency Provisions) Acts 1978 and 1987 led by Viscount Colville of Culross in 1990, which reported to Parliament: "The provisions relating to detention without trial have not been in use since 1975, and the practice is widely condemned in other countries. The provisions should not be re-enacted."[52] The decision was finally taken to discard the power of internment in the Northern Ireland (Emergency Provisions) Act of 1998. Junior Northern Ireland Minister Lord Dubs told the House of Lords: "The Government have [sic] long held the view that internment does not represent an effective counter-terrorism measure…. The power of internment has been shown to be counter-productive in terms of the tensions and divisions which it creates."[53]

PREVENTIVE DETENTION IN THE WAR ON TERROR

"We reluctantly accept that there may be a small category of persons who are suspected international terrorists who cannot be prosecuted, extradited or deported and therefore will have to be detained."[54]

The Anti-Terrorism, Crime, and Security Act (ATCSA) of 2001 was introduced to Parliament in the wake of the 9/11 attacks with the aim of further strengthening the Terrorism Act of 2000. While there was widespread recognition that the Terrorism Act brought long overdue and coherent reform to

---

50. *Internment–A Chronology of the Main Events*, CAIN Web service at http://cain.ulst.ac.uk/events/intern/chron.htm.
51. Wilkinson, *Terrorism and the Liberal State*.
52. Viscount Colville of Culross, *Review of the Northern Ireland (Emergency Provisions) Acts 1978 and 1987*, HMSO (July 1990).
53. Lord Dubs, House of Lords Hansard Debates, January 12, 1998. In further House of Lords debate in March 1998, he added: "I remember when internment was last used…how the whole issue became a recruiting sergeant for the IRA."
54. Home Affairs Committee, First Report Session 2000-01: Terrorism, Crime and Security Bill 2001, Report with Minutes of Proceedings, together with Minutes of Evidence and Appendices, HC 351 19 (November 2001).

the United Kingdom's antiquated and *ad hoc* anti-terrorism legislation, ATCSA was less well received—as was amply illustrated by the fact that the House of Lords made seventy amendments to the original bill, although most were subsequently reversed in the House of Commons.[55]

Much of the criticism leveled at ATCSA has been directed at Part IV, Sections 21–23 of the act, which allows for the indefinite detention of foreign nationals suspected of involvement in terrorism where it is not possible to deport them because they would be at risk of torture or death if returned to their country of origin.[56] Unlike the practice of internment in Northern Ireland, such detentions occur within the framework of immigration law.[57] Detainees need not be charged with an offense. Sixteen individuals have been detained under ATCSA since December 2001.[58]

The provisions contained in Part IV were denounced by Amnesty International as "a perversion of justice."[59] On the same day that ATCSA was brought before Parliament, the British Home Secretary David Blunkett laid a Human Rights Derogation Order in respect of Article 5 of the European Convention on Human Rights, which prohibits detention without trial.[60] The United Kingdom was the only European country to enter a derogation from the convention as a result of the 9/11 attacks.[61] In December 2004, Law Lords ruled in an 8-1 decision that Section 23 of the ATCSA was incompatible with the European Convention on Human Rights because the provision "unjustifiably discriminate[s] against foreign nationals on the grounds of their nationality or immigration status."[62] A month later, in response to the House of Lords ruling, Home Secretary Charles Clarke announced a series of proposed measures that would authorize the Secretary to impose house arrest, curfews, and other restrictions on anyone—including British citizens—suspected of involvement in terrorism.[63]

---

55. Philip Thomas, "Emergency and Anti-Terrorism Power," p. 1218.

56. Deportation in such circumstances would be in violation of Article 3 of the European Convention on Human Rights.

57. Both Immigration Officers and the Home Secretary have wide powers to detain persons subject to immigration control under the Immigration Act of 1971. These powers were previously used during the first Gulf War to intern a number of aliens believed to pose a potential security threat—notably student members of the Iraqi Ba'ath Party—for the duration of the conflict.

58. Campaign Against Criminalising Communities website at http://www.cacc.org.uk/PRSIAC291003.htm and "Hundreds Arrested, Handful Convicted," *BBC News*, April 23, 2004 at http://news.bbc.co.uk/1/hi/magazine/3290383.stm.

59. *Justice perverted under the Anti-terrorism, Crime and Security Act 2001*, AI Index EUR 45/029/2003, December 11, 2003.

60. Thomas, "Emergency and Anti-Terrorism Power," p. 1217.

61. Ibid.

62. Beth Gardiner, "U.K.'s Highest Court Rules Against Holding Terror Suspects Without Trial," Associated Press, December 16, 2004.

63. "Terror Suspects Face House Arrest," *BBC News*, January 26, 2005.

The power to detain indefinitely a terrorism suspect who falls within the criteria defined by the act rests with the Home Secretary, who must certify that he reasonably suspects that the individual in question poses a threat to national security. This category is broad enough to include individuals who have "links with" an "international terrorist group." Section 21(4), however, further defines "links" as supporting or assisting that group, which would apparently rule out mere association. The Home Secretary has since given an undertaking that these powers would only be exercised for the purposes of the emergency which was the subject of the derogation, which presumably restricts their use to individuals with links to al-Qaida or its international affiliates.[64] Sections 21–23 are temporary provisions subject to renewal. Section 29(7) also contains a sunset clause which provides that Sections 21–23 will cease to have effect on November 10, 2006, unless renewed by primary legislation.

Certification can be challenged on points of fact and law at the Special Immigration Appeals Commission (SIAC), which was originally created in 1997 to hear appeals relating to deportation cases made on national security grounds.[65] ATCSA also provides that the commission must automatically review the lawfulness of each detention after six months initial detention, and thereafter every three months. Special procedures apply to the handling of cases before the SIAC to enable a proper review of executive power but also to prevent the disclosure of sensitive intelligence material. A security-cleared "special advocate" appointed by the commission represents the detainee in addition to a legal representative of the detainee's own choosing. Unclassified or "open" material is heard before the commission in public with the full participation of the detainee's nominated advocate. Sensitive or "closed" material is heard in a private hearing in which the "special advocate" represents the detainee's interests. The "special advocate" is barred from discussing "closed" material with his client without the authorization of the commission. To date only one detainee, a thirty-seven-year old Libyan, known only as "M," has mounted a successful appeal and been released.[66] "M" was held in Belmarsh High Security prison for sixteen months.[67]

---

64. Kavita Modi and John Wadham, "Anti-Terrorism Legislation in the United Kingdom and the Human Rights Concerns Arising from it," *Liberty*, March 31, 2003.

65. Madeleine Shaw and Vaughne Miller, *Detention of Suspected International Terrorists –Part 4 of the Anti-Terrorism, Crime and Security Act 2001*, House of Commons Library, Research paper 02/52, September 16, 2002.

66. A second detainee, 'G,' has been released on mental health grounds, and two detainees have voluntarily left the country.

67. Audrey Gillan, "Defeat for Blunkett as Judges Free Detainee," *Guardian*, March 19, 2004.

A number of aspects of the operation of the SIAC have drawn criticism from civil liberties advocates. Particularly controversial is that SIAC decisions are not subject to judicial review and that habeas corpus is not available.[68] Furthermore, is crucially not at liberty to question the validity of the Home Secretary's assessment of what constitutes a threat to national security. In *Secretary of State for the Home Department v. Rehman*, the House of Lords held that the assessment of the threat to national security was essentially a matter for the executive rather than the courts.[69]

Bodies such as the Immigration Law Practitioners Association have raised concern over the "discriminatory treatment" of non-British nationals.[70] In *A and Others v. the Home Secretary*, nine detainees appealed against their detention citing Article 14 of the Human Rights Act (1998) which specifically prohibits discrimination between nationals and non-nationals. Their argument was initially accepted by SIAC, which ruled their detention was indeed unlawful, but this decision was successfully overturned by the government in the Court of Appeal.[71]

Perhaps most damaging of all was the public resignation of a lay member of the SIAC, Sir Brian Barder, in January 2004. Sir Brian told *The Guardian* newspaper that SIAC's decisions were being undercut by the Home Secretary,[72] adding in his resignation statement: "SIAC can't really be regarded as a reliable safeguard against abuse of the detention power, and the whole procedure is so flawed and objectionable that I finally decided that... I couldn't conscientiously have any further involvement in it."[73]

Although such concerns persist and politicians from across the political spectrum have spoken out against ATCSA, it appears to be popular with the British public. An independent poll conducted for the British Broadcasting Corporation (BBC) published on April 26, 2004, found that 62 percent of the 510 people questioned backed the existing indefinite detention of foreign terrorist suspects without charge, 63 percent would support extending such action to the detention of British suspects, and 58 percent would support the detention of those associating with suspects.[74]

---

68. Shaw and Miller, *Detention of Suspected International Terrorists.*
69. Modi and Wadham, "Anti-Terrorism Legislation."
70. http://www.ilpa.org.uk.
71. Modi and Wadham, "Anti-Terrorism Legislation."
72. Audrey Gillan, "Terror Tribunal Member Quit over Blunkett," *Guardian*, March 16, 2004.
73. http://www.barder.com/brian/1pointofview/SIACresignation.htm.
74. "Terror Measures Backed in Survey," *BBC News*, April 26, 2004, http://news.bbc.co.uk/1/hi/uk/3658767.stm.

Targeted Killing

By all accounts, it has been many years since the United Kingdom has considered assassination as a possible tool of government policy; however, that is not to say that there have not been occasions in the past thirty years in which the British government has been accused of espousing the use of lethal force by its intelligence agencies and security forces.

In late 1981, the Headquarters Mobile Support Unit (HMSU) of the Royal Ulster Constabulary was involved in three shootings that resulted in six fatalities—three Provisional Irish Republican Army (PIRA) operatives, two Irish National Liberation Army (INLA) operatives, and one individual with no previous known terrorist affiliation.[75] The incidents gave rise in May 1984 to the first of several inquiries into persistent allegations that British security forces were operating what became known as a "shoot-to-kill" policy in Northern Ireland. Eleven RUC officers were investigated by John Stalker, the Deputy Chief Constable of Greater Manchester, and his successor Sir Colin Sampson; four officers were subsequently charged with murder, but all four were acquitted at trial.

In addition to the spotlight brought to bear on the RUC, the British Army's activities in Northern Ireland have been called into question. Between 1976 and 1987, a standing force of approximately 150 British special forces soldiers—members of the Special Air Service (SAS) and 14 Intelligence Company—killed 30 PIRA and 2 INLA operatives in intelligence-led operations.[76] In the same period, regular British Army units in Northern Ireland—a force which never dropped below 9,000 men—killed a total of 9 PIRA and 2 INLA members.[77] Journalist Mark Urban points out that no Loyalist terrorists were killed in the same period by the security forces, noting that in 1990, there were 260 Nationalist and 130 Loyalist prisoners in the government's maximum security Maze Prison, which he considers to be a proportionate guide to the level of active engagement of both sides in the Northern Ireland crisis.[78] Urban believes that these figures are suggestive of a different official approach to the threat posed by each side, although he was unable to prove the formal existence of such a policy. At the end of an exhaustive study of the SAS's involvement in Northern Ireland, Urban concluded that the key role in advocating

---

75. Peter Taylor, *Brits: The War Against the IRA* (London: Bloomsbury, 2001), pp. 241–253.

76. Mark Urban, *Big Boy's Rules: The SAS and the Secret Struggle Against the IRA* (London: Faber, 1992), pp. 243, 253. SAS troops also accidentally killed six innocent bystanders in the course of these operations.

77. Urban, *Big Boy's Rules*, p. 238.

78. Ibid., p. 239.

"ambushes" was played by middle-ranking police and Army officers rather than by politicians.[79]

The involvement of Special Forces troops in counterterrorist operations was not confined to the province of Northern Ireland. On March 6, 1988, an SAS team shot dead three members of a PIRA Active Service Unit in Gibraltar, claiming that they had adopted an aggressive stance when challenged. The three PIRA members proved to be unarmed at the time of the shooting, although a car linked to the trio discovered in nearby Marbella was subsequently found to be packed with explosives. There was widespread criticism of the SAS's failure to apprehend three unarmed suspects without loss of life. Allegations of "a shoot-to-kill policy" resurfaced—primarily in a controversial television documentary entitled *Death on the Rock,* in which two alleged eyewitnesses claimed that the British soldiers had opened fire on the PIRA trio without warning. An inquest held on Gibraltar found that the soldiers had acted lawfully, however.

The families of the PIRA members killed in Gibraltar took the case to the European Court of Human Rights in Strasbourg, France.[80] In September 1995, the court narrowly ruled in a 10–9 majority decision that the PIRA team had been "unlawfully killed" in breach of Article 2 of the European Convention on Human Rights—the right to life.[81] The British deputy prime minister, Sir Michael Heseltine, angrily rejected the court's ruling and stated that the government would not be taking any further action regarding the case.[82] The ECHR was again called to rule on four separate cases in which fourteen people had been killed in Northern Ireland between 1982 and 1992, allegedly by or with the collusion of the security forces.[83] On this occasion, however, the court stopped short of finding that the fourteen had been unlawfully killed, commenting instead in May 2001 that the post fact proceedings for investigating the use of lethal force by the security forces had sufficient shortcomings for the United Kingdom to be in breach of the procedural obligations imposed by Article 2, but nothing more.[84]

The most extensive, long-term examination of the security forces' activities in Northern Ireland has been conducted in the course of three linked inquiries undertaken by the current head of the Metropolitan Police

---

79. Ibid, p. 241.
80. *McCann and Others v. the United Kingdom* (no. 18984/91).
81. Amnesty International, *European Court of Human Rights Condemns Killings in Gibraltar in 1988,* AI index EUR 45/10/95, September 28, 1995.
82. Ibid.
83. *McKerr v. the United Kingdom* (no. 28883/95), *Hugh Jordan v. the United Kingdom* (no. 24746/94), *Kelly and Others v. the United Kingdom* (no. 30054/96) and *Shanaghan v. the United Kingdom* (no. 37715/97).
84. http://news.bbc.co.uk/1/hi/northern_ireland/1311724.stm, May 4, 2001.

Service, Sir John Stevens, into alleged collusion between members of the security forces and loyalist paramilitaries. Taken together, these three inquiries comprise the largest investigation ever undertaken in the United Kingdom, the team took 9,256 statements, recorded 10,391 documents, and seized 16,194 exhibits. As Stevens himself observed, all three inquiries "operated from the premise that those involved in policing and security duties in Northern Ireland work to and are subject to the rule of law."[85]

The first Stevens Inquiry was initiated in October 1988 to investigate allegations that security documents held by the Ulster Defence Regiment had been passed to Loyalist paramilitaries to enable them to identify Nationalist targets for assassination. It led to the conviction of a British Army source, Brian Nelson, for thirty-five serious terrorist offenses. The second inquiry was prompted by a BBC documentary entitled *Dirty War,* screened in 1992 and revisited Nelson's activities. The third inquiry, initiated in April 1999 following the compilation of a confidential report by British Irish Rights Watch,[86] investigated the Loyalist murders of Belfast solicitor Pat Finucane, who had helped defend a number of PIRA suspects, and Brian Adam Lambert, a young Protestant student who had apparently been killed in error. In all, the three Stevens inquiries have so far resulted in 144 arrests and 94 successful convictions for a wide variety of offenses. The Stevens inquiries were characterized by "widespread" obstruction of the investigation by parts of the British Army and RUC.[87] Beyond criticizing the probity of potentially inflammatory remarks made by one former government minister, Douglas Hogg, Stevens was not able, however, to link any members of the executive to the events under investigation. Again, it would appear that for the most part the officials involved took matters into their own hands without direction from the political sphere.

In addition to British activities relating to the troubles in Northern Ireland, there have been allegations that the United Kingdom has at least been indirectly involved in two attempts to assassinate foreign leaders known to be sponsors of international terrorist groups. The renegade former British Security Service officer David Shayler claimed in 1995 that the British Secret Intelligence Service (SIS) provided £100,000 to a Libyan agent codenamed 'Tunworth' in full knowledge that he was planning to use the these funds to recruit members of the Militant Islamic Group (MIG), led by Abdallah al-Sadeq, to assassinate the Libyan leader Colonel

---

85. *Stevens Inquiry: Overview and Recommendations,* April 17, 2003.
86. "Deadly Intelligence: State Involvement in Loyalist Murder in Northern Ireland," *British Irish Rights Watch,* February 1999.
87. *Stevens Inquiry,* p. 13.

Muammar Qaddafi.[88] In February 1996, the MIG planted a bomb near Sirte on a route used by Qaddafi's motorcade. Several of Qaddafi's body-guards were killed when the device was detonated, although the Libyan leader himself escaped unscathed. Reporting on the episode for the BBC's flagship current affairs program *Panorama*, Mark Urban claimed that he had been told "categorically" that the British Foreign Secretary at the time had not been informed in advance about the operation which had been authorized internally within SIS.[89]

SIS is also reported to have played a major role in an attempt by the Iraqi National Accord (INA) to overthrow Saddam Hussein in 1996.[90] In January 1996, SIS allegedly persuaded a coalition consisting of the United States, Saudi Arabia, Kuwait, and Jordan to support a military coup mas-terminded by a retired Iraqi Special Forces General Mohammed Abdullah al-Shahwani. The plot has been described by Con Coughlin as "undoubt-edly the most extensive ever attempted," but the plotters were ultimately exposed by the Iraqi Special Security Organization in June 1996 before the plan could be put into effect. Given the violent history of regime change in Iraq, there can be little doubt that, had it been within their power, the plot-ters would have sought to kill Saddam and his sons. Indeed, among eight hundred suspects detained in the aftermath of the plot's exposure were two presidential chefs who reportedly confessed to having been tasked by al-Shahwani with poisoning Saddam.[91]

On balance, it would appear that in the last thirty years or so, succes-sive British governments have not seen a need to employ targeted assassi-nation as a tactic to combat terrorism either at home or abroad. Such a policy would in any event run contrary to British law and the United Kingdom's obligations under the European Convention on Human Rights. On occasion, however, state officials have been complicit in such acts but seemingly on their own authority and without direction from the execu-tive. Where this has occurred, public inquiries have, in most instances, been established to investigate such wrongdoing. On its official website, the British Security Service states baldly: "We do not kill people or arrange their assassination. We are subject to the rule of law in just the same way as other public bodies."[92] There is no reason not to believe that this prin-ciple also holds true for the United Kingdom's other intelligence and secu-rity agencies.

---

88. Mark Hollingsworth and Nicolas Fielding, *Defending the Realm: MI5 and the Shayler Affair* (London: Deutsch, 1999), pp. 149–150.
89. Ibid., p. 150.
90. Con Coughlin, *Saddam: The Secret Life* (London: Macmillan, 2002), pp. 303–305.
91. Ibid., p. 305.
92. See http://www.mi5.gov.uk/output/Page119.html#3.

Information Collection

The British debate on the pros and cons of opening government-held files to data-mining is still in its infancy, but a number of both technical and institutional obstacles to the development of such a practice currently exist. Some evidence suggests, however, that the current Labor government intends to come to grips with the issue.[93]

Interplay between the layers of legal regulation is complex.[94] Historically, the interaction between legislative and administrative powers has largely been left to individual public bodies to interpret on an *ad hoc* basis according to the statutes by which those bodies have been established. Some statutory bodies are expressly prevented from sharing data—even with the consent of the data subject[95]; others have more freedom of action. As a result, in the past, a great deal of institutional confusion has surrounded a given organization's ability to share data and, for the most part, government departments and other statutory bodies have tended to err on the side of caution, leading to poor interdepartmental communication.

The situation is further complicated by the Data Protection Act of 1998. The Act identifies eight universal Data Protection Principles by which all government (and commercial) record managers are bound. Principles 2 and 5 are particularly inimical to the concept of data-mining. Principle 2 ensures that personal data can only be obtained for clearly specified purposes and must not be further processed in any manner incompatible with those stated purposes. Principle 5 ensures that personal data should not be kept for any longer than is necessary to meet the purpose for which it was collected. Article 12 of the Act confers certain protective rights on data subjects in relation to "automatic decision-taking" which seems a clear reference to data-mining. The Data Protection principles are policed by an information commissioner who is ultimately empowered to take enforcement action against any serious transgressions by data controllers.

---

93. *Privacy and Data-sharing: The Way Forward for Public Services*, A Performance and Innovation Unit Report, April 2002.

94. For example, eight different Acts of Parliament with sections bearing on the data-sharing powers of the Department for Work and Pensions (DWP) have been passed since 1999 alone.

95. The Local Government Finance Act of 1992 prevents local authorities from using any data gathered in the course of administering the Council Tax for any other purpose. Taken as a whole this material could provide other government departments with the most up-to-date nationwide information on residential occupancy.

It is also worth noting that the United Kingdom lags behind many developed countries in the adoption of information technology systems, and a number of key areas, most notably the paper-based civil registration system, simply lack any capacity for electronic data-mining.[96] As a result, certain requests for information can be both extremely time consuming and needlessly labor intensive. Furthermore, many departmental information technology projects have, in the past, been developed on a piecemeal basis and often interface poorly with other systems. The Police Service, Crown Prosecution Service, magistrates courts, Courts Service, Prison Service, and National Probation Service still lack the integrated technology to allow individual criminal cases to be effectively tracked electronically through the Criminal Justice System.[97] In 2001, the government announced the allocation of £1 billion (UK) over the next ten years to address this shortcoming.

A possible glimpse of the future can be found in a wide-ranging and detailed Performance and Innovation Unit (PIU) report entitled "Privacy and Data-Sharing," which was published in April 2002. Produced under the auspices of the Cabinet Office and endorsed in a foreword by Prime Minister Tony Blair, the report outlines a coherent data-sharing strategy to support the online provision of government services, a project known within Whitehall as "e-government."[98] It sets government the complimentary objectives of enhancing privacy and making better use of personal information (including health records, tax returns, welfare benefits, law enforcement records, and driving license information) to deliver a wide range of smarter public services.[99] As with the "Entitlement Card" proposal, the government has sought to head off criticism that it plans to create "a Big Brother state" by highlighting the anticipated improvement in public services that the e-government initiative would deliver.

The PIU report only deals obliquely with antiterrorism measures and does not consider the potential national security benefits that would

---

96. It is still notoriously easy to obtain a British passport fraudulently because the UK has yet to cross refer its birth and death records and make this information available to the UK Passports Agency in a form that it can easily use. According to the Cabinet Office report "Identity Fraud: A Study" published in July 2002 between April 2000 and March 2001, the Passport Agency detected 1,484 fraudulent applications. Of these, 301 used the identities of dead people—the so-called "Day of the Jackal" method. Other key identity documents are just as easy to obtain. In January 2003, The *BBC* journalist Paul Kenyon was able to acquire a copy of David Blunkett's birth certificate from the family records office and use it to obtain a provisional driving license using the home secretary's details, even though he is registered as being blind.

97. See also *Criminal Justice: The Way Ahead* (London: HMSO, February 2001), pp. 107–111.

98. *Privacy and Data-sharing.*

99. Ibid., pp. 4–17.

inevitably arise from the initiatives that it describes. The report does, however, consider possible non-consensual law enforcement applications—such as ensuring that pedophiles are prevented from working with children and tackling benefit fraud.[100] One intriguing possibility suggested by the report is that more effective electronic exchange of information between National Health Service General Practioners (GPs), coroners, and local registrars (recording births, deaths, and marriages) may have led to earlier detection and apprehension of the serial killer Dr Harold Shipman.[101] The fact that the government is thinking along these lines suggests that investigators working on cases with national security implications could reasonably expect access to most forms of data held by government departments.[102] The report argues strongly for the adoption of secondary legislation to create "data-sharing gateways" to allow enforcement agencies to obtain relevant personal information held elsewhere in government without informing either the individual concerned or gaining his or her consent.[103]

The PIU report is sensitive to the potential for abuse in an integrated system of data-sharing gateways and calls for any attempt to produce such secondary legislation to be both proportionate to the public policy objective and to include effective oversight mechanisms. The report also notes that any new legislation would have to negotiate the Human Rights Act of 1998, which enshrines the right to a private life assured by Article 8 of the European Convention on Human Rights in British law for the first time.[104] As yet, this provision has only been tested in courts in the context of celebrity challenges to media reporting. It is still too early to say what consequences, if any, this constitutional development may have for the governmental collection, retention, and review of personal data.[105]

---

100.   Ibid., pp. 99–107.

101.   Dr. Shipman, a GP in the Greater Manchester area, was convicted in January 2000 for the murder of fifteen elderly patients; a subsequent Public Inquiry into his activities completed in 2002 suggested that he was responsible for at least 215 deaths between 1975 and 1998, making him by a wide margin the United Kingdom's worst serial killer.

102.   The government took a significant step in this direction with the introduction of the Anti-Terrorism, Crime and Security Act of 2001. Government agencies such as Her Majesty's Customs and Excise and the Inland Revenue are now formally able to pass information to police forces and the Security Service where national security is an issue. Also, under the act communication service providers are no longer obliged to erase call information when no longer needed for billing purposes, creating under a voluntary code of practice a significant archival resource for investigators.

103.   *Privacy and Data-sharing,* pp. 106–107.

104.   Ibid., at p. 107.

105.   The use of intrusive surveillance techniques by the intelligence and security services are exempted from the same provision under the Regulation of Investigatory Powers Act of 2000.

Governmental records that are becoming increasingly computerized and proposals to join up government-data retention systems have long provoked the concern of British civil liberties organizations. Most see a danger of functional creep and an increasing desire on government's behalf to control every facet of national life. A report produced by Charter 88 in the mid-1990s estimated that private information on the average adult living in the United Kingdom existed in over two hundred separate publicly or commercially held data files.[106]

Concerns have also been expressed about the potential security risks of so much personal information being held in common. Liberty has noted a National Audit Office (NAO) report published in March 1995 which found that instances of hacking involving the government's developing information technology network had increased 140 percent in 1994 alone. Most of the 655 cases in 1994 involved government staff abusing their positions to obtain information on members of the public to disclose to outsiders.[107] Many members of the public continue to remain skeptical about the government's ability to guarantee information security.[108] In May 2002, the Inland Revenue was forced to suspend its online self-assessment service after some users found that they could view details of other people's tax returns.

OPEN SOURCE DATA-MINING
The suggestion that law enforcement or national security agencies should be barred from exploiting openly available sources of information such as the Internet would be met by most British observers with near disbelief. So long as the data mined fits one of the recording categories under which a government agency operates—for example, in the Security Service (MI5), this may simply be that the material is somehow germane to an investigation of suspected terrorist or espionage activities—there are no restrictions on British agencies in this regard.

Identification of Individuals and Collection of Information for Federal Files

Speaking on September 14, 2001, British Home Secretary David Blunkett announced that in the wake of the terrorist attacks on Washington and New York, the British government was considering the reintroduction of a nation-

---

106. Caroline Ellis, "Identity Cards and the Slow Death of Parliamentary Government," *Violations of Rights in Britain*, Series 3, No. 29.
107. *Mistaken Identity!* Liberty ID Cards Briefing (1996) at http://www.charter88.org.uk/publications/briefings/idcards.html.
108. "The Problem with e-government," Bill Thompson, *BBC News*, June 7, 2002.

al identity card. Supporters of the move pointed out that citizens from eleven out of the fifteen nations of the European Union already carried identity cards as part of their everyday life. A Marketing & Opinion Research International (MORI) poll conducted on September 21, 2001, found that 85 percent of the British population supported the reintroduction of identity cards.[109]

Although Blunkett's announcement was broadly greeted with enthusiasm by the law enforcement community, it also provoked an outcry from British civil liberties groups such as Liberty, Charter 88, and Privacy International. As the impact of the 9/11 attacks faded, public enthusiasm for the introduction of an identity card also cooled, and the government quietly let the suggestion drop in the face of mounting opposition while it sought a more acceptable alternative.

The United Kingdom has twice operated a national identity card scheme in the past. During World War I, a statutory registration scheme was introduced and operated until 1919. The relevant Acts were eventually repealed by the Statute Law Revision Act of 1927. An identity card system (consisting of nine distinct civilian cards) was again introduced as security measure in September 1939 after the outbreak of World War II, but it was abolished in 1952 by the Conservative government of Sir Winston Churchill.

The two main identity documents currently issued by the British government are the passport and the photo–driving license introduced by John Major's Conservative government in 1996. It should be noted that not all UK residents qualify for these documents, and only an estimated ten million photo–driving licenses are currently in circulation.[110] The United Kingdom is a nation of approximately sixty million people. The various mainland United Kingdom police forces generally have no powers to require a person to provide them with information about their identity. A constable may, however, arrest a person on suspicion of committing an offense which would not normally be subject to powers of arrest if the identity of the person cannot be readily be ascertained or there are reasonable grounds for doubting whether the name and address supplied are genuine.[111] In Northern Ireland, the police and army have the power to demand proof of identity at any time—a privilege which was renewed by the Anti-Terrorism, Crime and Security Act of 2001.

---

109. http://www.mori.com/polls/2001/notw-id.shtml.
110. The paper driving license, which remains in much wider circulation, is little use as an identity document as it does not contain a photograph or date of birth—only the holder's name and address.
111. Section 25, Police and Criminal Evidence Act (1984).

The introduction of some form of national identity card has been a regular feature of public debate in the UK for the past two decades. Legislators have floated proposals to use identity cards to combat football hooliganism, human trafficking, Irish terrorism, illegal immigration, and benefit fraud. Between 1988 and 1994 alone, the House of Commons considered four separate identity card–related bills brought forward by backbench Members of Parliament (MPs), and numerous related departmental studies have been conducted under the aegis of successive Conservative and Labor administrations.[112]

When the current Labor government returned to the issue in 2002, very little mention was made of the potential benefits that an identity card scheme may have for national security; indeed, the term "identity card" itself was scrupulously avoided. The debate has focused primarily on benefit fraud and illegal immigration. In January 2002, the British government introduced Application Registration Cards (ARC) for asylum seekers arriving in the United Kingdom. The ARC is a smart card containing an asylum seeker's finger prints, a photograph, and details about their age and nationality, as well as some data that can only be accessed by immigration officials. The system has been criticized since its introduction because the application forms for the card, consisting of a single piece of paper, have proved to be easily falsified.

In July 2002, the government launched a six-month consultancy period concerning a detailed proposal to introduce a non-compulsory national "Entitlement Card" as "a more efficient and convenient way of providing services, tackling illegal immigration and illegal working and combating identity fraud."[113] The government admitted in its consultation paper that it was "debatable whether an entitlement scheme on its own would have an effect on other types of crime."[114] The consultation paper contained no specific reference to terrorism and only one mention of "very serious crimes."[115] The formal deadline for the submission of comments on the Consultation Paper was January 31, 2003, and the government has yet to publish the results.

Civil Liberties groups have interpreted the Entitlement Card as an attempt to introduce an identity card by stealth and have reacted strongly to the Consultation Paper. Liberty and Charter 88 have organized a "no2id" campaign, essentially marshalling their arguments around the four key areas identified by Adrian Beck, lecturer in Security Management

---

112. *Mistaken Identity!*
113. http://www.homeoffice.gov.uk/comrace/entitlements/fraud.html.
114. *Entitlement Cards and Identity Fraud—A Consultation* at www.homeoffice.gov.uk/comrace/entitlements/fraud.html.
115. Ibid.

at the University of Leicester, in the course of his work on the use of national identity cards in the European Union: (1) the possible impact of the introduction of ID cards on crime; (2) the way that it may affect the relationship between the police and ethnic minority groups; (3) the dangers of functional creep; and (4) logistical hurdles such as the frequency with which many members of the population change their address.[116]

In addition to opposing the introduction of any national registration scheme on principle, "no2id" campaigners have noted that there is no evidence to suggest that the use of identity cards by many of the United Kingdom's European partners has led to any appreciable reduction in crime. The Home Office's own figures reveal that only 5 percent of benefit fraud is identity fraud.[117] The Liberal Democrat Home Affairs spokesman Simon Hughes questioned whether there would be any tangential reduction of the terrorist threat, noting that "those responsible for the September 11th attacks had legitimate identification."[118] Campaigners have also latched onto a statement made by the Conservative peer Earl Ferrers in the House of Lords on behalf of the Major Government in May 1994, in which he commented that he "could not recall any terrorist offence which would not have taken place if the terrorists had been required to carry ID cards."[119] Finally, a significant number of advocacy groups have expressed concern that ethnic minorities, recent immigrants, and socially excluded groups such as the homeless or mentally ill may be unfairly singled out and possibly disadvantaged by the entitlement scheme.

Surveillance of Religious and Political Meetings

In principle, there are no legal restraints on either UK police forces or the British Security Service (MI5) attending or otherwise monitoring any political or religious gathering. In practice, where necessary, such activities are mostly carried out either remotely through human or technical sources or in person by local Special Branch (SB) officers[120] under the direction of the Security Service.

Section 1(2) of the Security Service Act of 1989 defines the role of the Security Service as "the protection of national security and, in particular,

---

116. *No Id Cards,* Campaign Pamphlet produced by Liberty and Charter 88 (2002) at http://www.no2id.com.
117. Ibid.
118. Ibid.
119. *House of Lords Debates*, Vol. 545cc 1650-1, quoted in *Mistaken Identity!*
120. The Special Branch is effectively a small unit of local Detective Officers, sometimes consisting of fewer than ten men, found within each Police Authority Area which deals, *inter alia*, with classified material relating to intelligence and related investigations.

its protection against threats from espionage, terrorism, and sabotage, from the activities of agents of foreign powers and from actions intended to overthrow or undermine parliamentary democracy by political, industrial, or violent means." The only significant restraint placed on the Service in this regard by the 1989 Act can be found in Section 2(2)(b) which requires that "the Service does not take any action to further the interests of any political party." The 1989 Act also empowers the Security Service to protect the "economic well-being" of the United Kingdom from external threats, and the Security Service Act of 1996 extended its role still further to support law enforcement agencies in the prevention and detection of serious crime. The Service is predominantly self-tasking and makes its own judgments about the magnitude and nature of the various threats to national security and how best to deploy its resources in response. As the Security Service website notes, however, its judgments in this regard are subject to validation by the Home Secretary and the external scrutiny of Parliament.[121]

Within the Security Service, a system of "internal mechanisms" has been designed to ensure that it only investigates genuine threats to national security. There are detailed criteria governing the opening of files on individuals and organizations. These criteria specify the circumstances in which opening a file and initiating inquiries are justified within the terms of the Service's statutory responsibilities. They are kept under review and are formally checked every year to ensure that they remain up to date and relevant. Inactive files fall dormant and are then closed after a relatively short period. External review exists in the form of the Intelligence and Security Committee (ISC) of the House of Commons and the Security Service commissioner established by the 1989 Act. The commissioner submitted a detailed report on the Service's filing system in 1991 which has since been made public,[122] and the ISC apparently continues to take "a close interest" in the Service's file keeping policies.[123]

Since 2000, the manner in which the Security Service carries out its duties has also been subject to the Regulation of Investigatory Powers Act (RIPA). RIPA presents no obstacle to investigators either openly attending a public meeting or to their recording relevant information gathered in such a manner. RIPA does, however, regulate the use of covert methods to gather intelligence. Section 28(3) identifies a number of circumstances that may authorize the use of surveillance or human intelligence sources against a target which include, *inter alia*, the interests of national security,

---

121. Official Security Service (MI5) website, http://www.mi5.gov.uk.
122. HMSO (Cm 1946).
123. Official Security Service (MI5) website, http://www.mi5.gov.uk.

preventing and detecting crime, preventing disorder, and protecting public safety. Clearly the intent of RIPA is to convey broad powers of investigation on both law enforcement and the intelligence agencies. Section 5(3) identifies a more limited, but still relatively broad set of circumstances in which the interception of communications may be authorized by a warrant issued by the home secretary: national security, the prevention or detection of serious crime, safeguarding the economic well-being of the United Kingdom, and meeting a mutual international assistance agreement.[124]

In summary, if sufficient reason exists to believe that a political or religious group poses a threat to the national security of the United Kingdom, the state can deploy the full battery of resources in its armory to monitor and further investigate that group's activities. Although the monitoring by the Security Service of such organizations as the Campaign for Nuclear Disarmament (CND) during the 1980s was extremely contentious, Parliament has not seen fit to introduce legislation to limit the Service's freedom of action in this regard. Furthermore, as Part 5 of the Anti-terrorism, Crime and Security Act of 2001 specifically extended "racially aggravated offences" to include "religiously aggravated offences" as well, it is also extremely doubtful that British legislators wish religious groups to enjoy any special protection under the law.

Distinctions Based on Group Membership

The debate concerning racial profiling in the United Kingdom essentially revolves around crime and public order issues, rather than terrorism *per se*, and it is dominated by the charge of "institutional racism" leveled against the [London] Metropolitan Police in Sir William MacPherson's landmark 1999 report on the findings of the Stephen Lawrence Inquiry.[125] MacPherson also singled out countrywide racial disparities in the use of stop-and-search powers as perhaps the most visible manifestation of "racist stereotyping" in the police service.[126] Thus, any consideration of racial profiling in the United Kingdom must inevitably take the operation of stop-and-search powers as its point of departure.

The Police and Criminal Evidence Act (PACE) of 1984 was the first act of legislation to properly consolidate the search powers available to police

---

124. The act further stipulates that the circumstances surrounding the mutual international assistance agreement must involve the prevention or detection of serious crime.
125. Sir William MacPherson chaired the Home Office–sponsored Stephen Lawrence Inquiry into events surrounding the botched police investigation into the South London murder of a young black student, allegedly by a gang of local white youths.
126. *The Stephen Lawrence Inquiry, Report of an Inquiry by Sir William MacPherson of Cluny* (February 1999) at 6.45(b).

officers in England and Wales. Under Section 1 of PACE, police have the power to stop and search an individual if they have "reasonable grounds" to suspect that individual may have stolen or prohibited articles in his or her possession. This power was further extended by Section 15(3) of the Prevention of Terrorism (Temporary Provisions) Act of 1989 to include circumstances where there were "reasonable grounds" for suspecting a person to be guilty of a terrorist offense or concerned in the commission, preparation, or instigation of an act of terrorism. In addition, under common law, police have the right to search any individual that they have under arrest and the discretion to carry out searches where consent is freely given.

The current code of practice for police officers issued by the Home Office in 1999 (PACE Code A) sets out guidance as to what constitutes reasonable grounds for suspicion:

> Whether a reasonable ground for suspicion exists will depend on the circumstances in each case, but there must be some objective basis for it... the decision to stop and search must be based on all the facts which bear on the likelihood that an article of a certain kind will be found... Reasonable suspicion can never be supported on the basis of personal factors alone without supporting intelligence... nor may it be founded on the basis of stereotyped images of certain persons or groups as more likely to be committing offences.[127]

The protection afforded to members of the public by the 'reasonable grounds' formula in PACE was, however, substantially eroded by the passage of the Criminal Justice and Public Order Act of 1994. Originally introduced with soccer hooliganism in mind, Section 60 allows senior police officers[128] reasonably anticipating "serious violence" within their area of responsibility to authorize exceptional stop-and-search powers for a twenty-four-hour period. A police officer operating in a Section 60 zone is thereby empowered to stop any person or vehicle and make any search he thinks fit "whether or not he has any grounds for suspecting that the person or vehicle is carrying weapons or articles of that kind." Section 81 gave senior police officers[129] the power to authorize the exercise of extensive stop-and-search powers, for a period not exceeding twenty-eight days, if "expedient to do so in order to prevent acts of terrorism."[130] Again, this power could

---

127. PACE Code A (Home Office, 1999c).
128. Of Superintendent rank and above.
129. Of Commander or Assistant Chief Constable rank and above.
130. Terrorism is defined in Section 20(1) of the Prevention of Terrorism (Temporary

be exercised by uniformed officers in the complete absence of any reasonable grounds for suspicion.

The possibility for the abuse of these new powers has been somewhat mitigated by the Race Relations (Amendment) Act of 2000, which effectively extended the original 1976 Act to cover regulatory and enforcement action by public bodies. This made chief police officers vicariously liable for acts of discrimination carried out by officers under their direction and control and provides for compensation, costs, or expenses awarded as a result of a claim to be paid out of police funds. Equally significant, the Act also removed from ministers the power to issue conclusive certificates in race claims to the effect that an act of race discrimination was done for the purposes of national security and was therefore not unlawful.

Further protection is offered to members of minority groups by Article 14 of the European Convention on Human Rights (The Prohibition of Discrimination) which was ratified by the United Kingdom in 1951 and incorporated into British law under Paragraph 1(1)(a), the Human Rights Act of 1998. The provisions in Article 14 are intended to be of an accessory nature and can only be invoked in conjunction with one of the other rights protected by the Convention.

The *Guardian* and *Observer* newspapers have maintained a high level of interest in the question of "institutional racism" in the police service, which has led them to question the utility of stop-and-search as a crime prevention tool and to highlight its ongoing discriminatory quality. The reporting by these two newspapers has produced a battery of interesting statistics. Only 100,000 of the one million people stopped in 1998 under police stop-and-search powers were found to be breaking the law in some regard.[131] A black person is still six times more likely to be stopped by police in England and Wales than a white person. Although the overall number of people stopped by police has fallen dramatically since 1998, between October 2001 and October 2002, the proportion of black people stopped by the police rose by 4 percent while the number of whites stopped in the same period fell by 18 percent.[132]

Immigration policy is another important factor in this debate. Inevitably, some nationalities (and even faiths) are sometimes singled out in the United Kingdom for tighter immigration controls than others. For example, in January 2003, the government introduced a visa regime for Jamaican nationals in an attempt to counter an increase in illegal immigration from this source. Senior immigration officers at the port of entry have

---

Provisions) Act of 1989 as "the use of violence for political ends… [including] any use of violence for the purpose of putting the public or any section of the public in fear."

131. "When Being Black and Driving a Jaguar Makes You a Criminal," *Observer*, February 23, 2003.

132. Kamal Ahmed, "Met launches new 'sus' patrols," *The Observer*, October 6, 2002.

the discretionary right to refuse visitors admission to the United Kingdom,[133] and the exercise of this power is frequently controversial. In February 2002, six Islamic students from Newark, New Jersey, were denied entry into the United Kingdom under the Immigration Act of 1971 because immigration officers were not satisfied that their intention to study in the United Kingdom was genuine.[134] Similarly, visa applications and applications for 'leave to remain' in the United Kingdom from the nationals of a number of Middle Eastern countries are routinely vetted by the Security Service—as were applications from East Europeans during the Cold War — and the Service has the right to recommend a refusal on national security grounds. The home secretary has the power, most recently under the Immigration and Asylum Act of 1999, to issue an order to refuse an individual "leave to enter" the United Kingdom directly, although mechanisms exist to challenge such an order in the British courts. The Nation of Islam leader, Minister Louis Farrakhan, has been banned since 1986 by successive Labor and Conservative home secretaries from entering the United Kingdom because of his "notorious opinions."[135] Finally, the Asylum, Immigration and Nationality Act of 2002 conferred new powers on the home secretary to withdraw British nationality from dual nationals deemed to pose a threat to national security. This power was used for the first time in early April 2003 to withdraw British citizenship from the controversial London-based Muslim cleric Sheikh Abu Hamza.[136]

To date, there have been no serious proposals to single out any group in government or military service for special attention as security risks, as suggested by the academic Daniel Pipes in the United States.[137] Overall policy on vetting is set by the Cabinet Office, which is also responsible for other aspects of government protective security policy. The "developed vetting" procedure for those regularly handling secret material in the United Kingdom is already stringent. Each individual applying for a high-level security clearance is treated individually and a whole range of personal circumstances are taken into account in the course of a year-long investigation. The most recent high profile cases of members of the intelligence services breaking their commitments under the Official Secrets Act —those of Richard Tomlinson (SIS) and David Shayler (MI5)—both involved white, middle-class career officers who betrayed details of classi-

---

133. "Immigration Rules" (April 2003), http://www.ind.homeoffice.gov.uk/default.asp?PageId=3185.
134. "Islamic students refused entry to Britain," *BBC News*, February 26, 2002.
135. "Farrakhan banned from Britain," *CNN.com*, April 30, 2002.
136. "Cleric stripped of citizenship," *BBC News*, April 5, 2003.
137. See, for example, Daniel Pipes, "To Profile or Not to Profile," *New York Sun*, September 21, 2004.

fied operations to the media, apparently motivated by nothing more than poor performance evaluations and bruised egos.

Appendix B

Torture and Coercive Interrogations

Thomas Lue

Despite the longstanding commitment of the United States against the use of torture, the 9/11 terror attacks have kindled a serious discussion among legal academics and the general public about whether U.S. troops should engage in torture to obtain information that could help thwart terrorist attacks and save lives.[1] This debate was thrust into the forefront of the nation's consciousness by media reports and photographs documenting the use of coercive interrogation techniques by U.S. troops in Iraq, Afghanistan, and elsewhere.[2] These interrogation practices, though some

---

This appendix was completed in May 2004. Since then, a number of documents—including legal memoranda from the Department of Justice and the Pentagon—have clarified (and in some instances, revised) the position of the U.S. government on coercive interrogation. This article is descriptive in nature, and takes no position on the validity of the U.S. government's arguments, or on the relative merits of the various legal arguments discussed herein.

---

1.   Much of this debate has focused on the moral, philosophical, and legal arguments for and against the use of torture. See, for example, Martin E. Andersen, "Is Torture an Option in War on Terror?" *Insight on the News*, May 27, 2002, available at http://www.insightmag.com/main.cfm/include/detail/storyid/253614.html (last visited May 13, 2004); Alan M. Dershowitz, *Why Terrorism Works: Understanding the Threat, Responding to the Problem* (New Haven, Conn.: Yale University Press, 2002), pp. 131–164; Seth F. Kreimer, "Too Close to the Rack and the Screw: Constitutional Constraints on Torture in the War on Terror," *University of Pennsylvania Journal of Constitutional Law*, Vol. 6 (November 2003), p. 278; Sanford Levinson, "'Precommitment and Postcommitment': The Ban On Torture In The Wake of September 11," *Texas Law Review*, Vol. 82 (June 2003), p. 2013; John T. Parry, "What Is Torture, Are We Doing It, and What If We Are?" *University of Pittsburgh Law Review*, Vol. 64 (Winter 2003), p. 237; and "Torture: Ends, Means, and Barbarity," *Economist*, January 9, 2003.
2.   The publication of photographs revealing sexual humiliation, threatened electrocution and other prisoner abuses at the Abu Ghraib prison outside Baghdad focused an intense spotlight on coercive interrogation techniques used by U.S. military and intelligence personnel. See, for example, Seymour M. Hersh, "Torture at Abu Ghraib," *New Yorker*, May 10, 2004, p. 42; Dana Priest and Barton Gellman, "U.S. Decries Abuse But Defends Interrogations," *Washington Post*, December 26, 2002, p. A1; and Eric Schmitt, "There Are Ways to Make Them Talk," *New York Times*, June 16, 2002, §4, p. 1.

are technically not torture,[3] nonetheless involve a level of physical and psychological coercion that, at the very least, would implicate serious constitutional concerns if applied to criminal suspects on U.S. soil. For example, the use of hooding, prolonged standing or kneeling in uncomfortable positions, sleep and light deprivation, and the temporary withholding of food, water, and medical attention have all reportedly been used against detainees overseas and are considered "acceptable" techniques by the U.S. government.[4] Moreover, strong evidence exists that the United States "renders" uncooperative prisoners to Egypt, Jordan, and other countries that are willing to use more aggressive questioning, including torture, to get information from suspects.[5]

In light of current U.S. interrogation practices, a serious discussion of the issues surrounding torture must also consider the use of other coercive techniques that fall short of the formal statutory and treaty definition of torture. Before analyzing the legality of current U.S. interrogation practices, it is necessary to provide a brief sketch of what is currently known about these practices. What is particularly salient is that the use of coercive interrogation by U.S. forces has largely been cloaked in secrecy. As of mid-2004, only one official document had been released to the public discussing the interrogation techniques being used by U.S. forces,[6] and they are currently unregulated by public guidelines or statute. Various press reports have uncovered the existence of an official documented policy at both the Department of Defense and the CIA authorizing the use of coercive techniques.[7]

---

3. Some of the more extreme methods used at Abu Ghraib (unleashing dogs, beating prisoners, etc.) likely do qualify as torture, but many of the methods (sleep deprivation, hooding, etc.) that have reportedly been approved by the Department of Defense and used by U.S. troops in Afghanistan, Guantanamo Bay, and elsewhere, likely do not rise to the level of torture. See text accompanying notes 62–65.
4. Don Van Natta Jr., "Questioning Terror Suspects In a Dark and Surreal World," *New York Times*, March 9, 2003, § 1, p. 1. See also Jess Bravin, "Interrogation School Tells Army Recruits How Grilling Works," *Wall Street Journal*, April 26, 2002, p. A1.
5. See Eric Lichtblau and Adam Liptak, "Questioning to Be Legal, Humane, and Aggressive, The White House Says," *New York Times*, March 4, 2003, p. A13.
6. The Senate Armed Services Committee in 2004 made public a list of interrogation techniques approved for use by U.S. forces in Iraq. The list was released in connection with hearings concerning prisoner abuses at the Abu Ghraib prison outside Baghdad. See Dana Priest and Dan Morgan, "Rumsfeld Defends Rules for Prison," *Washington Post*, May 13, 2004, p. A1.
7. In contrast to the recent public disclosure of the Department of Defense's interrogation techniques, much remains unknown about the methods used by the CIA. Recent media reports describe the use of "graduated levels of force" against Khalid Shaikh Mohammed, including "a technique known as 'water boarding,' in which a prisoner is strapped down, forcibly pushed under water and made to believe he might drown." Dana Priest and Joe Stephens, "Pentagon Approved Tougher Interrogations,"

According to media reports, a classified list of about twenty "physically and psychologically stressful methods" was approved in April 2003 "at the highest levels of the Pentagon and the Justice Department" for use at the Guantanamo Bay prison.[8] These techniques included making detainees disrobe entirely for questioning, "reversing the normal sleep patterns ... and exposing them to heat, cold and 'sensory assault,' including loud music and bright lights."[9] According to Department of Defense officials, "The use of any of these techniques requires the approval of senior Pentagon officials—and in some cases, of the defense secretary. Interrogators must justify that the harshest treatment is 'militarily necessary'.... Once approved, the harsher treatment must be accompanied by 'appropriate medical monitoring.'"[10]

Similar guidelines on the use of coercive techniques have also been approved for use by U.S. military forces against detainees in Iraq.[11] The Senate Armed Services Committee has released a once-secret list of interrogation techniques, which contains two categories of measures—those approved for all detainees and those requiring special authorization by the commander of U.S. forces in Iraq. Among the items included in the latter

---

Washington Post, May 9, 2004, p. A1. According to the *New York Times*, "These techniques were authorized by a set of secret rules for the interrogation of high-level Qaeda prisoners ... that were endorsed by the Justice Department and the CIA. The rules were among the first adopted by the Bush administration after the September 11 attacks for handling detainees and may have helped establish a new understanding throughout the government that officials would have greater freedom to deal harshly with detainees." James Risen, David Johnston, and Neil A. Lewis, "Harsh C.I.A. Methods Cited in Top Qaeda Interrogations," *New York Times*, May 13, 2004, p. A1.

8. Priest and Stephens, "Pentagon Approved Tougher Interrogations," p. A1.

9. Ibid.

10. Ibid.

11. The similarity of the techniques approved for use in Iraq and Guantanamo may at least be partially explained by the fact that the chief of interrogations and detentions in Iraq (beginning in August 2003) was General Geoffrey D. Miller, the same general who had previously been in charge of detainees at Guantanamo Bay. Tim Golden and Eric Schmitt, "General Took Guantanamo Rules To Iraq for Handling of Prisoners," *New York Times*, May 13, 2004, p. A1. A critical distinction between the detainees held in Guantanamo and Iraq, however, is that the latter enjoy the full protections of the Geneva Conventions. In contrast, the Bush administration has classified detainees at Guantanamo as "illegal combatants" who enjoy only very limited protection under the Geneva Conventions. See note 30. This distinction may help explain why the Department of Defense recently revised their interrogation policy in Iraq to prohibit the use of any "extraordinary" interrogation methods (sleep deprivation, diet manipulation, stress positions, use of dogs to threaten detainees, etc.). The only exceptions are "putting prisoners alone in cells or in small groups segregated from the general prison population for more than thirty days." Bradley Graham, "New Limits on Tactics at Prisons," *Washington Post*, May 15, 2004, pp. A1, A16.

category are "sensory deprivation," "stress positions," "dietary manipulation," forced changes in sleep patterns, isolated confinement, and use of dogs.[12]

Despite the existence of these internal guidelines, however, some of the interrogation techniques used by U.S. troops at Abu Ghraib prison appear to have gone far beyond those authorized by the Pentagon. In an internal U.S. Army report not meant for public distribution, Major General Antonio M. Taguba found "sadistic, blatant, and wanton criminal abuses" of prisoners at Abu Ghraib between October and December of 2003, including:

> Breaking chemical lights and pouring the phosphoric liquid on detainees; pouring cold water on naked detainees; beating detainees with a broom handle and a chair; threatening male detainees with rape ... sodomizing a detainee with a chemical light and perhaps a broom stick, and using military working dogs to frighten and intimidate detainees with threats of attack, and in one instance actually biting a detainee.[13]

The media has also reported that uncooperative detainees at Bagram air base in Afghanistan are "sometimes kept standing or kneeling for hours, in black hoods or spray-painted goggles.... At times they are held in awkward, painful positions and deprived of sleep with a 24-hour bombardment of lights."[14] Similarly, suspected al-Qaida members are sometimes beaten, bound in painful positions, and deprived of sleep.[15] Medical treatment has been "selectively" withheld from at least one suspect, and "blunt force trauma" has been reported as a contributing factor to the deaths of two Afghan men in U.S. custody.[16] The Department of Defense has admitted that twenty-five Iraqi and Afghan war detainees had died in U.S. custody between January 2003 and May 2004.[17]

---

12. Priest and Morgan, "Rumsfeld Defends Rules for Prison," pp. A1, A19.
13. Hersh, "Terror at Abu Ghraib," p. 43 (citing Taguba report). Although the Taguba report states that military personnel used these methods to help military intelligence officers gain information during interrogations, at least one Iraqi claims that the abuse he suffered was not for interrogation purposes, but rather was "punishment for bad behavior, in this case a jail-yard fight." Ian Fisher, "Iraqi Recounts Hours of Abuse by U.S. Troops," *New York Times*, May 5, 2004, pp. A1, A18.
14. Priest and Gellman, "U.S. Decries Abuse But Defends Interrogations," p. A1. For a description of the use of hooding, prolonged standing in "stress positions," and protracted interrogations, see Jess Bravin and Gary Fields, "How Do U.S. Interrogators Make a Captured Terrorist Talk?" *Wall Street Journal*, March 4, 2003, p. B1.
15. See Priest and Gellman, "U.S. Decries Abuse But Defends Interrogations," p. A15.
16. Ibid, p. A14; and April Witt, "U.S. Probes Death of Prisoner in Afghanistan," *Washington Post*, June 24, 2003, p. A18.
17. Editorial, "The Military Archipelago," *New York Times*, May 7, 2004, p. A30.

The use of psychological coercion techniques by U.S. interrogators has also been documented. U.S. officials often feign friendship, respect, or sensitivity[18] or use female interrogators to question devout Muslims.[19] Some interrogators seek to convince a prisoner that he is being held by a country that employs torture or have even made threats to use specific methods of torture.[20] The *Wall Street Journal* has reported on an "interrogation school" set up by the U.S. Army where "interrogators ... are authorized not just to lie, but to prey on a prisoner's ethnic stereotypes, sexual urges and religious prejudices, his fear for his family's safety, or his resentment of his fellows."[21] According to one of the instructors at the school, the techniques are "just a hair's-breadth away from being an illegal specialty under the Geneva Convention."[22]

Finally, an unknown number of detainees who refuse to cooperate are "rendered ... to foreign intelligence services whose practice of torture has been documented by the U.S. government and human rights organizations."[23] Egypt, Morocco, Jordan, and Saudi Arabia are particularly well-known destinations for suspected terrorists.[24] The *Washington Post* quotes "one official who has been directly involved in rendering captives into foreign hands" as explaining that "we send [people] to other countries so they can kick the [expletive] out of them."[25]

In summary, in addition to the methods described in the Taguba report, all of the following techniques have been reportedly used or taught by U.S. military personnel:

---

18. Ibid.
19. Van Natta Jr., "Questioning Terror Suspects In a Dark and Surreal World," p. 1.
20. See Priest and Gellman, "U.S. Decries Abuse But Defends Interrogations," p. A1; and Bravin and Fields, "How Do U.S. Interrogators Make a Captured Terrorist Talk?" p. B1 (noting that U.S. interrogators have threatened to send detainees to countries where they will be tortured).
21. Bravin, "Interrogation School Tells Army Recruits How Grilling Works," p. A1.
22. Ibid.
23. Priest and Gellman, "U.S. Decries Abuse But Defends Interrogations," p. A1.
24. "[In 2003], U.S. immigration authorities, with the approval of then–acting Attorney General Larry Thompson, authorized the expedited removal of Maher Arar (suspected of having ties to al-Qaida) to Syria, a country the U.S. government has long condemned as a chronic human rights abuser." Dana Priest and Joe Stephens, "Secret World of U.S. Interrogation," *Washington Post*, May 11, 2004, pp. A1, A12.
25. Priest and Gellman, "U.S. Decries Abuse but Defends Interrogations," p. A14. Although Stephen Cambone, the undersecretary of defense for intelligence, recently testified that the Pentagon has not rendered any suspects to Saudi Arabia, Jordan, Morocco, or Syria, the rendering of detainees is often carried out by the CIA rather than the Department of Defense. Indeed, in testimony before the 9/11 Commission, CIA Director George J. Tenet acknowledged that the agency had participated in more than seventy renditions in the years before the 9/11 attacks. In 1999 and 2000 alone, the CIA and Federal Bureau of Investigation (FBI) participated in two dozen renditions. Priest and Stephens, "Secret World of U.S. Interrogation," p. A12.

- putting on smelly hoods or goggles
- subjection to noise
- deprivation of sleep
- deprivation of food and drink
- deprivation of medical treatment
- exploiting sexual urges or religious prejudices
- preying on fears of the safety of relatives or family
- putting rats or cockroaches in cells
- keeping the prisoner naked and isolated
- threat of indefinite detention

The processes of public debate, public legislation, and public oversight are crucially important to the proper functioning of an official practice of coercive interrogation. The United States is only now, however, beginning to engage in an open discussion on the use of coercive techniques. As one scholar noted:

> Congress has not voted to give the Executive branch specific authority to engage in torture or other cruel, inhuman, or degrading treatment. The President has not signed legislation creating a section in the United States Code for torture as a method of interrogation. Nor, for that matter, has the administration made a public accounting of the interrogation practices it has authorized in the absence of legislation. As a result, we are a country that appears to have adopted a policy of coercive interrogation but is not willing to admit that fact to the world or even to ourselves.[26]

If media reports are correct, U.S. forces are currently employing coercive interrogation techniques against many if not most detainees overseas, and yet none of these practices is subject to public guidelines or regulations. As a result, the full scope and content of U.S. interrogation practices is unknown. Perhaps this ignorance is a conscious choice: "We let the executive branch do what it has to do, and we will not ask questions because, frankly, we do not want to know."[27]

The Status of the Law

In 2004 testimony before the Senate Armed Services Committee, Defense Secretary Donald Rumsfeld indicated that U.S. forces in Iraq and

---

26. Parry, "What Is Torture, Are We Doing It, and What If We Are?" p. 261.
27. Ibid.

Afghanistan "are under orders to observe the [Geneva] Conventions."[28] In contrast, President George W. Bush has used the term "illegal combatants" to describe detainees (such as members of the Taliban or al-Qaida) captured in the war on terrorism.[29] This categorization effectively removes those protections of the Geneva Convention that apply only to prisoners of war (POWs).[30] U.S. citizens who are deemed illegal combatants may have additional constitutional protections, but to date, only a handful of detainees—out of thousands—have a claim of citizenship. The remaining detainees, who are neither POWs nor U.S. citizens, are likely protected only by U.S. international commitments.

INTERNATIONAL LAW

The UN Convention Against Torture and Other Cruel, Inhuman or Degrading Treatment or Punishment (CAT) entered into force in 1987 and

---

28. Priest and Stephens, "Secret World of U.S. Interrogation," p. A1. The Taguba report cited the lack of proper training of military police on the Geneva Conventions as a major factor contributing to prisoner abuses at Abu Ghraib. See Ariel Sabar, "Army Faults Leadership for Abuse of Prisoners," *Baltimore Sun*, May 4, 2004, pp. 1A, 11A; and Jackie Spinner, "Soldier: Unit's Role Was to Break Down Prisoners," *Washington Post*, May 8, 2004, pp. A1, A16 (Quoting an Army military police officer charged with abusing detainees at Abu Ghraib: "The Geneva Convention was never posted, and none of us remember taking a class to review it.... The first time reading it was two months after being charged. I read the entire thing highlighting everything the prison is in violation of. There's a lot.").

29. Press conference of President George W. Bush and British Prime Minister Tony Blair, "President Bush, Prime Minister Blair Discuss War on Terrorism," July 17, 2003, press release available at http://www.whitehouse.gov/news/releases/2003/07/20030717-9.html. Previously, the Bush administration had used the term "enemy combatant" to describe captured detainees. See letter from William J. Haynes II, general counsel, Department of Defense, to Kenneth Roth, executive director, Human Rights Watch, April 2, 2003, available at http://www.hrw.org/press/2003/04/dodltr040203.pdf.

30. Article 17 of the Geneva Convention prohibits the "physical or mental torture" of POWs, and "any other form of coercion.... Prisoners of war who refuse to answer may not be threatened, insulted, or exposed to any unpleasant or disadvantageous treatment of any kind." *Geneva Convention Relative to the Treatment of Prisoners of War*, Aug. 12, 1949, art. 17, 6 U.S.T. 3316, 3332, 75 U.N.T.S. 135, 148 [hereinafter Geneva Convention]. It is important to note, however, that some provisions of the Geneva Convention apply to all captured persons, not just prisoners of war. For example, Article 5 of the Geneva Convention requires that "[s]hould any doubt arise" as to whether any individual meets the requirements for POW status, the person "shall enjoy the protection" of the convention until his or her status has been determined by a "competent tribunal." Moreover, Article 75 of Protocol I (1977) supplementing the Geneva Convention requires that even for non-POWs, any means of interrogation involving "violence to the life, health, or physical or mental well being of persons," including torture, corporal punishment, and humiliating or degrading treatment is forbidden. The United States has signed this protocol but has not ratified it and thus is not formally a party to the treaty. Although signature of a treaty under the 1969 Vienna Convention on the Law of

has been ratified by 134 countries, including the United States.[31] Article 2 forbids "torture," or acts that inflict "severe pain or suffering, whether physical or mental" for the purpose of obtaining information or confession, inflicting punishment or other prohibited purposes.[32] Article 16 also imposes an obligation to "undertake to prevent ... other acts of cruel, inhuman or degrading treatment or punishment ... which do not amount to torture." This distinction between "torture" and "cruel, inhuman or degrading treatment" is significant. The Torture Convention bans torture absolutely: "No exceptional circumstances whatsoever, whether a state of war or threat of war, internal political instability or any other public emergency, may be invoked as a justification of torture."[33] A similar prohibition of any derogation applies to both torture and cruel, inhuman or degrading treatment in the International Covenant on Civil and Political Rights (ICCPR) (Articles 4 and 7). In contrast, although states must "undertake to prevent" cruel, inhuman, or degrading treatment, the "no exceptional circumstances" language of the UN Convention Against Torture does not explicitly apply to such practices. As a result, some commentators have suggested that states may engage in cruel, inhuman, or degrading conduct and still arguably fulfill their obligations under the Convention Against

---

Treaties (Article 18) requires a state to refrain from acts that would "defeat the object and purpose of the treaty," this is a much lesser commitment than would be required with ratification. In short, it is unclear how much latitude the U.S. government is gaining by placing their captives in the non-POW category of "illegal (unlawful) combatants." See General Sir Hugh Beach, *Geneva and Guantanamo: The Laws of War and the Handling of Prisoners*, ISIS Special Policy Paper (April 2002), available at http://www.isisuk.demon.co.uk/0811/isis/uk/regpapers/nospecial.pdf (last visited May 13, 2004).

31. *Convention Against Torture and Other Cruel, Inhuman or Degrading Treatment or Punishment*, Dec. 10, 1984, 1465 U.N.T.S. 85, available at http://www.un.org/documents/ga/res/39/a39r046.htm [hereinafter *Convention Against Torture*]. Ratification of the treaty by the United States included a significant reservation which will be considered below. See text accompanying note 44. The United States is also a party to the International Covenant on Civil and Political Rights (ICCPR), which explicitly states that "no one shall be subjected to torture or to cruel, inhuman or degrading treatment or punishment." *International Covenant on Civil and Political Rights*, December 19, 1966, art. 7, 999 U.N.T.S. 171, 172 [hereinafter *ICCPR*]. Although the ICCPR binds the United States on the international plane, the covenant is "non-self-executing," and thus cannot be directly enforced by U.S. courts without further action by Congress to implement the treaty. See 138 Cong. Rec. 8071 (1992).

32. *Convention Against Torture*, articles 1–2. Article 14 of the Convention Against Torture requires that each state party provide a civil remedy for victims of torture. In 1992, the U.S. Congress passed the Torture Victim Protection Act (TVPA), Pub. L. No. 102-256, 106 Stat. 73, 28 U.S.C. § 1350 (2004), which provides a civil remedy against torturers acting under the color of law of a foreign nation.

33. *Convention Against Torture*, article 2, para. 2. Thus, a necessity defense cannot be used to justify torture.

Torture so long as exceptional circumstances justify such conduct.[34] Thus, the definition of what constitutes torture and what constitutes cruel, inhuman, or degrading treatment is of vital importance in determining whether a particular practice is permitted under the convention.

Although the convention itself does not provide a definition of "cruel, inhuman or degrading" treatment, various international courts and committees have given some content to the distinctions between torture and cruel and inhuman treatment.[35] The most obvious cases of torture involve the infliction of intense physical pain. Severe beatings with wooden or metal sticks or bars,[36] the combination of beatings, withholding food, and being made to stand all day for days at a time, as well as rape or physical mutilation,[37] have all been recognized by international bodies as torture.

The line separating "torture" from "cruel, inhuman or degrading" practices, however, has been harder to draw. The most famous case parsing this distinction, *Ireland v. United Kingdom*, considered the use of coercive techniques—hooding, sleep deprivation, wall-standing for hours at a time, restrictions on food and water, and excessive noise—by British forces against suspected members of the Irish Republican Army (IRA).[38] The European Court of Human Rights (ECHR) held that such practices, although inhuman and degrading, were not acts of torture. The court specifically noted that the "special stigma" of torture should be reserved for those practices that exhibit a "particular intensity and cruelty," and

---

34. Some disagreement exists among commentators over whether exceptional circumstances can justify cruel, inhuman, or degrading treatment under the Convention Against Torture. See Parry, "What Is Torture, Are We Doing It, and What If We Are?" p. 243, n. 37; and Kreimer, "Too Close to the Rack and the Screw," pp. 279–81 and nn. 9–11. Article 16, paragraph 2 of the Convention Against Torture states that "the provisions of this Convention are without prejudice to the provisions of any other international instrument or national law which prohibit cruel, inhuman or degrading treatment or punishment." As noted in the text, the ICCPR prohibits cruel, inhuman, or degrading treatment absolutely, regardless of whether a "public emergency" exists. *ICCPR*, articles 4, 7.
35. The UN Committee on Human Rights, the European Commission of Human Rights, and the European Court of Human Rights have each given meaning to the phrase "cruel, inhuman or degrading." The UN Committee on Human Rights enforces the UN Convention Against Torture, while the European Commission and the European Court of Human Rights both enforce the European Convention on Human Rights (1950), which also prohibits torture and inhuman treatment. Parry, "What is Torture, Are We Doing It, and What If We Are," p. 240.
36. Ibid. (discussing decision of European Commission of Human Rights in "the Greek case" where the Commission found that Athens police had tortured political prisoners).
37. Ibid. (discussing cases reported by the UN Committee on Human Rights).
38. *Ireland v. United Kingdom*, 25 Eur. Ct. H.R. (ser.A) (1978).

that British practices used against suspected members of the IRA did not rise to such a level.[39]

Significantly, the case of *Ireland v. United Kingdom* was cited by the Landau Commission in 1987 to support Israel's claim that the interrogation methods of the General Security Service (GSS) did not constitute torture. GSS interrogators utilized many of the same techniques used by their British counterparts—including prolonged standing in uncomfortable positions, sleep deprivation, hooding, and constant noise—against suspected Palestinian terrorists in the late 1980s and 1990s.[40] In contrast to the ECHR's ruling in *Ireland*, however, the UN Committee Against Torture and the Special Rapporteur on Torture found that GSS practices did in fact constitute torture.[41] Israel disagreed with these conclusions, however, and although the Israeli Supreme Court banned such practices in 1999,[42] the court continued to insist that GSS practices were not prohibited acts of torture under either Israeli or international law. Indeed, the court explicitly provided for a defense of necessity for interrogators who chose to use such methods.[43]

U.S. STATUTE AND TREATY OBLIGATIONS

In 1994, the U.S. Senate ratified the UN Convention Against Torture and Other Cruel, Inhuman or Degrading Treatment or Punishment. The Senate ratification included, however, a significant reservation that narrowed the definition of torture. Specifically, the U.S. reservation limited the types of mental pain or suffering covered by the convention to:

> ... *prolonged* mental harm caused by or resulting from (1) the intentional infliction or threatened infliction of severe physical pain or suffering; (2) the administration or application, or threatened

---

39. Ibid., paras. 167–168, at 66–67. See also Parry, "What Is Torture, Are We Doing It, and What If We Are?" p. 241.

40. The sole exception was the Israeli practice of shaking, which was not a technique used by British forces. Some critics argue that the methods used by the GSS were much more severe than those used by the British. See Israeli Information Center for Human Rights in the Occupied Territories, *Legislation Allowing the Use of Physical Force and Mental Coercion in Interrogations by the General Security Service* (January 2000), pp. 61–62.

41. Ibid., pp. 37–38. See also Parry, "What Is Torture, Are We Doing It, and What If We Are?" p. 242.

42. *Judgment Concerning the Legality of the General Security Services Interrogation Methods*, 38 I.L.M. 1471, 1489 (1999) (Isr.).

43. "Our decision does not negate the possibility that the 'necessity' defence be available to GSS investigators, be within the discretion of the Attorney General, if he decides to prosecute, or if criminal charges are brought against them, as per the Court's discretion." Ibid. Such a defense of justification could only be (arguably) permissible under the Convention Against Torture if GSS practices did not constitute torture, but were merely "cruel, inhuman or degrading."

administration or application, of mind altering substances or other procedures calculated to disrupt *profoundly* the senses or the personality; (3) the threat of *imminent* death; or (4) the threat that another person will *imminently* be subjected to death, severe physical pain or suffering, or the administration or application of mind altering substances or other procedures calculated to disrupt *profoundly* the senses or personality.[44]

As a result of this reservation, some forms of mental pain or suffering that would be considered "torture" by other countries would be considered only "cruel, inhuman or degrading" treatment by the United States, e.g., the administration of drugs that disrupted (but not "profoundly") one's senses or personality. These practices, under one interpretation of the convention,[45] would be permissible if justified by exceptional circumstances.

With respect to extradition, Article 3 of the convention states that, "No State Party shall expel, return ... or extradite a person to another State where there are *substantial grounds for believing* that he would be in danger of being subjected to torture" (emphasis added). The Senate reservation interpreted the italicized language to prohibit extradition "if it is more likely than not that he would be tortured." Here again, however, the distinction between torture and cruel, inhuman, or degrading treatment is significant. The State Department has stated in the context of international extradition that "torture is an extreme form of cruel and inhuman treatment and does not include lesser forms of cruel, inhuman or degrading treatment or punishment."[46] According to some commentators, this statement implies that although Congress has directed U.S. officials not to deport any person to a country where it is more likely than not that he will be tortured,[47] officials may nonetheless deport persons to countries where

---

44.   U.S. Reservations, Declarations, and Understandings, Convention Against Torture and Other Cruel, Inhuman or Degrading Treatment or Punishment, 136 Cong. Rec. S17491-92 (daily ed., Oct. 27, 1990) (ratified Nov. 20, 1994) [hereinafter U.S. Reservations] (emphases added). This definition is included in federal legislation providing for remedies for torture. See 18 U.S.C. § 2340 (2004) (criminalizing acts of torture committed outside the United States by U.S. nationals or persons later found in the United States); Torture Victim Protection Act of 1991 (TVPA), Pub. L. No. 102–256, 106 Stat. 73, 28 U.S.C. § 1350 (2004) (providing civil remedy against torturers acting under color of law of a foreign nation). Congress enacted both statutes to implement the Torture Convention. See Parry, "What Is Torture, Are We Doing It, and What If We Are?" p. 244, n. 39.

45.   See note 34.

46.   22 C.F.R. § 95.1(b)(7) (2002).

47.   "It shall be the policy of the United States not to expel, extradite, or otherwise effect the involuntary return of any person to a country in which there are substantial grounds for believing the person would be in danger of being subjected to torture, regardless of whether the person is physically present in the United States." Pub. L. No. 105-277, 112 Stat. 2681-822 (1998).

they will face cruel, inhuman, or degrading treatment that would be unconstitutional if applied in the United States.[48]

The Senate also narrowly interpreted the terms "cruel, inhuman or degrading treatment or punishment." According to the Senate resolution ratifying the convention, "the United States considers itself bound by the obligation ... to prevent 'cruel, inhuman or degrading treatment or punishment,' only insofar as the term ... means the cruel, unusual and inhuman treatment or punishment prohibited by the Fifth, Eighth, and/or Fourteenth Amendments to the Constitution of the United States."[49] U.S. treaty obligations concerning "cruel, inhuman or degrading" practices are thus defined not by reference to rulings of international bodies such as the ECHR, but rather through U.S. constitutional jurisprudence.[50]

Because the Senate reservation makes explicit reference to the Fifth, Eighth, and Fourteenth Amendments, any legitimate interpretation of the convention (i.e., one that respects the Senate's legislative intent) must consider seriously the constraints on government action imposed by the U.S. Constitution. As such, there are at least three ways of interpreting "cruel, unusual and inhuman treatment or punishment prohibited by the Fifth, Eighth and/or Fourteenth Amendments." First, this language may be referring to the traditional coerced confession/involuntariness standard under the due process clauses.[51] This standard is not entirely apposite to interrogation in the intelligence context, however, because the primary goal of such interrogation is not criminal prosecution, but rather intelligence gathering. A second possibility is that the Senate language refers to "cruel and unusual" punishment that has been held unconstitutional under the Eighth Amendment.[52] The Eighth Amendment ban on "cruel

---

48. Parry, "What Is Torture, Are We Doing It, and What If We Are?" p. 245, n. 42. Other international law provisions, however, including the ICCPR, support a contrary interpretation of U.S. extradition obligations. Ibid.

49. *U.S. Reservations*, 136 Cong. Rec. S17491.

50. "In other words, taken as a whole, the Senate declared that the Convention banned conduct that was already unconstitutional." Parry, "What Is Torture, Are We Doing It, and What If We Are?" p. 245. For a discussion of the constitutional issues surrounding torture, see Kreimer, "Too Close to the Rack and the Screw," pp. 283–317.

51. Under traditional due process, in order for a confession to be admissible, it must not have been coerced or involuntary. See Joshua Dressler, *Understanding Criminal Procedure* (New York: LexisNexis, 2002), pp. 437–443. See also note 103.

52. Under the Eighth Amendment, an inmate may make a claim for "deliberate indifference" to his serious medical needs (*Estelle v. Gamble*, 429 U.S. 97, 104 (1976)), overly harsh "conditions of confinement" (*Rhodes v. Chapman*, 452 U.S. 337, 347 (1981)), or excessive force constituting "unnecessary and wanton infliction of pain" (*Whitley v. Albers*, 475 U.S. 312, 320-321). A core judicial inquiry is whether force was applied in a good-faith effort to maintain or restore discipline or to cause harm maliciously and sadistically. *Whitley*, 475 U.S. at 217–320.

and unusual punishment" may not be implicated in the interrogation context, however, because that language applies only to "punishment," and the effort to extract information where no judicially imposed punishment is contemplated may lie outside of the prohibition.[53]

The question that arises, then, is whether the due process clauses of the U.S. Constitution, in contexts that do not involve criminal prosecution or punishment, nonetheless prohibit coercive interrogation practices (e.g., sleep deprivation, hooding, etc.) that fall short of torture. In May 2003, the U.S. Supreme Court in *Chavez v. Martinez* had an opportunity to address this question in the context of a 42 U.S.C. §1983 claim against the police.[54] The case involved Oliverio Martinez, who was shot five times (including in the face) following an altercation with police. On the way to the hospital and in the emergency room, a police officer repeatedly interrogated him over a span of forty-five minutes about his interactions with the police. According to Justice Anthony Kennedy, "The officer made no effort to dispel the perception that medical treatment was being withheld until Martinez answered the questions put to him.... Martinez begged the officer to desist and provide treatment for his wounds, but the questioning persisted despite these pleas and despite Martinez's unequivocal refusal to answer questions."[55] Martinez, who was neither read his Miranda rights nor charged with a crime, sued for violation of his Fourteenth Amendment due process rights.[56]

The Court fractured badly in its decision, producing six separate opinions. Five justices could not agree on Martinez's Fourteenth Amendment due process claim and remanded that issue back to the lower court.[57] In Justice John Paul Stevens's view, "the interrogation of [Martinez] was the

---

53. Kreimer, "Too Close to the Rack and Screw," p. 285. "The State does not acquire the power to punish with which the Eighth Amendment is concerned until after it has secured a formal adjudication of guilt in accordance with due process of law." *Ingraham v. Wright*, 430 U.S. 651, 671–672, n. 40 (1977).
54. 538 U.S. 760 (2003). See Marjorie Cohn, "Dropping the Ball on Torture: The U.S. Supreme Court Ruling in *Chavez v. Martinez*," *Jurist*, June 10, 2003, available at http://jurist.law.pitt.edu/forum/forumnew113.php. The following analysis of *Chavez v. Martinez* draws heavily from this article.
55. *Chavez*, 538 U.S. at 798 (Justice Kennedy, concurring in part and dissenting in part).
56. Martinez also sued for violation of his Fifth Amendment privilege against self-incrimination. Six justices held that Martinez could not recover on his Fifth Amendment self-incrimination claim because he had not been criminally prosecuted. Ibid. at 766 (plurality opinion); ibid. at 777 (Justice Souter, joined by Justice Breyer, concurring in the judgment).
57. Because a majority of the court remanded Martinez's substantive due process claim without explanation, see *Chavez*, 538 U.S. at 779–780, the reasons behind the remand remain unclear. It may have been because the majority could not agree on whether a substantive due process violation had occurred, or because the five justices could not agree on whether Martinez had waived that claim by failing to pursue it in the Ninth Circuit below.

functional equivalent of an attempt to obtain an involuntary confession from a prisoner by torturous methods."[58] Justice Anthony Kennedy, writing separately, stated, "A constitutional right is traduced the moment torture or its close equivalents are brought to bear. Constitutional protection for a tortured suspect is not held in abeyance until some later criminal proceeding takes place."[59] Justices Ruth Bader Ginsburg and John Stevens agreed with Justice Kennedy, who wrote that the "use of torture or its equivalent in an attempt to induce a statement violates an individual's fundamental right to liberty of the person," a violation of Fourteenth Amendment due process.[60] Justice Clarence Thomas (writing for Chief Justice William Rehnquist and Justice Antonin Scalia), although acknowledging that "police torture ... is [not] constitutionally permissible [even if] the statements are not used at trial," nonetheless rejected Martinez's due process claim.[61] For these justices, the methods used by the police were not so brutal and offensive to human dignity so as to "shock the conscience" and violate the due process clause.

As a result, although the due process clauses clearly place some limits on the amount of coercion that can be applied, the constitutionality of coercive interrogation practices such as hooding and sleep deprivation remains unknown. *Chavez v. Martinez* involved the perceived withholding of medical treatment from a plaintiff who had been interrogated for forty-five minutes while in pain and awaiting medical treatment after being shot in the face by the police. Whether that, without more, would constitute a violation of the U.S. Constitution was left unclear by the procedural aspects of the case as well as by the possibility, for some justices, that the police activity did not have infliction of pain as its purpose. It is thus unknown which current U.S. coercive interrogation practices would "shock the conscience" of the Court and would therefore be unconstitutional.

LEGAL ANALYSIS OF CURRENT U.S. INTERROGATION PRACTICES

In comparison to cases where international courts or committees have found torture, most of the techniques used by U.S. forces, whether isolated or in combination, likely do not rise to the level of torture.[62] One glaring exception may be the treatment of prisoners at the Abu Ghraib prison in Baghdad, where the beating and sodomizing of detainees, the unleash-

---

58. Ibid. at 783 (Justice Stevens, concurring in part and dissenting in part).
59. Ibid at 789–790 (Justice Kennedy, concurring in part and dissenting in part).
60. Ibid. at 796 (Justice Kennedy, joined by Justices Stevens and Ginsburg, concurring in part and dissenting in part).
61. Ibid. at 773 (opinion of Justice Thomas, joined by Justices Rehnquist and Scalia); and ibid. at 774–75.
62. See Parry, "What Is Torture, Are We Doing It, and What If We Are?" p. 251.

ing of dogs, and the pouring of phosphoric liquid almost certainly qualify as acts of torture. Another exception may be the alleged beatings of suspected al-Qaida members, which would qualify as torture if, as is likely, they would inflict severe pain for the purpose of interrogation or intimidation. Also, the withholding of medical treatment, if prolonged, may also be torture, depending on the severity of the injury.[63]

With the exceptions noted above, however, the methods employed by U.S. forces bear a striking resemblance to those used by British and Israeli interrogators.[64] As such, they likely qualify as "cruel, inhuman or degrading" conduct under at least the international interpretation of the UN Convention (as elucidated by the ECHR, UN Committee Against Torture, etc.), and perhaps under the U.S. interpretation as well (defined by U.S. Constitutional law).[65] Although Article 16 requires states to "undertake to prevent" cruel, inhuman, or degrading conduct, some commentators have suggested that it also arguably permits such conduct if it is justified by exceptional circumstances.[66] Thus, even if one assumes that current U.S. practices are unconstitutional (which is unclear in light of *Chavez v. Martinez*) and constitute "cruel, inhuman or degrading" treatment, it may be that U.S. interrogators can theoretically draw on a necessity or exceptional circumstances defense to rebut charges that they are violating the convention.[67] In addition, although U.S. treaty obligations forbid officials from sending detainees to other countries where it is more likely than not that they will be tortured, it may be permissible under the convention for the United States to "render" detainees to countries where they will only be subject to cruel, inhuman, or degrading treatment.[68] Thus, even if current U.S. interrogation techniques do inflict "cruel, inhuman or degrad-

---

63. Ibid.
64. In contrast to Israeli and British practices, U.S. interrogations of detainees are conducted outside the country. As a result, U.S. interrogators in Afghanistan, Iraq, and elsewhere may not be under the same constitutional constraints that would make their interrogation methods impermissible in the United States.
65. As noted above, however, there is a tenable argument in light of the Supreme Court's ruling in *Chavez v. Martinez* that current U.S. interrogation practices are not unconstitutional and thus do not constitute "cruel, inhuman or degrading" treatment under the U.S. interpretation of the convention. See text accompanying notes 54–61.
66. See note 34.
67. Classification of current practices as "cruel, inhuman or degrading" means that U.S. interrogators are not subject to federal prosecution for "torture" under 18 U.S.C. § 2340A. In addition to the Convention Against Torture, however, the U.S. is also a party to the ICCPR which prohibits any derogation from its ban on both torture and cruel, inhuman, or degrading treatment. *ICCPR*, articles 4, 7.
68. See text accompanying notes 47–48. The ICCPR, however, supports a contrary interpretation of U.S. extradition obligations that would not allow the rendering of detainees to countries where they will be subject to cruel, inhuman, or degrading treatment. See note 48.

ing" treatment,[69] the United States may be able to argue that its interrogation practices do not violate the Torture Convention if it can prove that the exigencies of its war on terrorism justify such treatment.[70]

The Policy Considerations

Whether torture or other methods of coercive interrogation actually work is a question distinct from the legality of such techniques, but it is one that must be considered when contemplating an official program of coercive interrogation. As indicated below, the existing data on the efficacy of coercive interrogation is largely anecdotal and inconclusive; thus, any calculation of the costs and benefits of coercive interrogation is necessarily speculative.

Whether a particular technique is effective—i.e., whether it "works"—can be defined in a variety of ways.[71] For purposes of this analysis, a coercive technique "works" if it succeeds in eliciting truthful information that can be effectively utilized by law enforcement and/or intelligence personnel. The following discussion provides an overview of the existing empirical, theoretical and anecdotal literature on coercive interrogation (i.e., torture and other less coercive techniques such as sleep deprivation, hooding, etc.). As is apparent, very little scientific data exists on the effectiveness of such techniques. Instead, much of the available evidence is anecdotal and points in conflicting directions.

EMPIRICAL EVIDENCE

As may be expected, very little scientific research has been done on torture or other forms of coercive interrogation. Most of the available literature focuses on the effects of torture on both victims and torturers.[72] Some lim-

---

69. See note 65.
70. This is a particularly big "if," however, in light of media reports documenting what appears to be the systematic use of coercive interrogation techniques against detainees. See text accompanying notes 8–25, 67.
71. For example, during the Vietnam War, the North Vietnamese tortured U.S. POWs in an effort to elicit anti-U.S. propaganda statements. Torture "worked" in this context when the soldiers succumbed and agreed to give treasonous statements. See Jean M. Arrigo, "A Consequentialist Argument Against Torture Interrogation of Terrorists," presented at the Joint Services Conference on Professional Ethics, January 30–31, 2003, p. 9. Similarly, in the late 1930s, the Soviet government arrested and tortured 5–10 percent of the population in an attempt to suppress political opposition. Under these circumstances, torture "worked" if it resulted in a confession, regardless of whether the confession was true or false. Ibid., p. 13.
72. See, for example, Stuart W. Turner and Caroline Gorst-Unsworth, "Psychological Sequelae of Torture," in John P. Wilson and Beverley Raphael, eds., *International Handbook of*

ited data suggests the success of torture at eliciting confessions or state-ments (regardless of their truth),[73] but virtually no scientific data exists on whether torture or other forms of coercive interrogation are successful in eliciting truthful information.

In *Ireland v. United Kingdom*, the European Court of Human Rights stated that British interrogators obtained "a considerable quantity of intel-ligence information" through coercive interrogations.[74] Similarly, the Israeli Supreme Court, despite invalidating a number of coercive practices of the General Security Service (GSS), nonetheless recognized that use of such techniques "in the past has [led] to the thwarting of murderous attacks."[75] A report given by Israel to the United Nations claimed that GSS investigations from 1994–1996 foiled ninety planned terrorist attacks (presumably many by the result of coercive interrogations), including "10 suicide bombings; 7 car bombings; 15 kidnappings of soldiers and civil-ians; and some 60 attacks of different types."[76] None of these findings are scientifically rigorous, however, and they do not indicate what the results would have been had other methods been used instead.[77]

THEORETICAL LITERATURE

Like the empirical evidence, the theoretical literature on coercive interro-gation techniques is sparse and largely unsupported by scientific data. Much of the literature focuses on how torture leads to confession or sub-

---

Traumatic Stress Syndromes (New York: Plenum, 1993); Martha K. Huggin, Mika Haritos-Fatouros, and Philip Zimbardo, *Violence Workers: Police Torturers and Murderers Reconstruct Brazilian Atrocities* (Berkeley: University of California Press, 2002); and Francoise Sironi and Raphaelle Branche, "Torture and the Borders of Humanity," *International Social Science Journal*, Vol. 54, No. 174 (December 2002), pp. 539–548.

73. For example, estimates indicate that only 5 percent of the repatriated U.S. POWs held by the Chinese in the Korean War decisively resisted the cognitive disorientation tactics of the Chinese; 15 percent "participated" to the extent they were court-martialed or dishonor-ably discharged. See Arrigo, "A Consequentialist Argument Against Torture Interrogation of Terrorists," p. 9. In contrast, however, Commander James Stockdale estimates that less than 5 percent of his 400 fellow U.S. airmen succumbed to North Vietnamese demands for anti-U.S. propaganda statements during the Vietnam War. Ibid.

74. 25 Eur. Ct. H.R. (ser.A) (1978), para. 98, at 60.

75. See *Judgment Concerning the Legality of the General Security Services Interrogation Methods*, 38 I.L.M. 1471, 1475 (1999) (Isr.); and Levinson, "'Precommitment and Postcommitment,'" p. 2029.

76. UN Committee Against Torture, *Consideration of Reports Submitted by States Parties Under Article 19 of the Convention, Second Periodic Reports of States Parties Due in 1996,* Addendum, "Israel," p. 8, UN doc. Cat/C/33/Add.2/Rev.1 (1997), cited in Levinson, "'Precommitment and Postcommitment,'" p. 2029.

77. See Israeli Information Center for Human Rights in the Occupied Territories, *Legislation Allowing the Use of Physical Force and Mental Coercion in Interrogations by the General Security Service*, p. 67.

mission,[78] rather than the elicitation of truth. One study presents three possible models of how torture interrogation leads to truth-telling,[79] but it relies heavily on anecdotal evidence and provides little empirical data to support its claims. Thus, the actual causal mechanisms of how coercive interrogation leads to truth remain largely unknown.

ANECDOTAL EVIDENCE

A number of dramatic anecdotes are used to illustrate the successful use of torture and other coercive techniques to prevent terrorist acts. For example, a 2003 *Washington Post* article reported that Philippine authorities in 1995 beat a terrorist suspect "with a chair and a long piece of wood, forced water into his mouth, and crushed lighted cigarettes into his private parts."[80] This episode of torture allegedly resulted in the disclosure of information that led to the unraveling of an elaborate plot to assassinate the pope and crash jets into the Pacific Ocean and the Pentagon.[81] Similarly, the *Atlantic Monthly* in January 2002 reported that a Sri Lankan intelligence officer tortured three terrorists suspected of planting a bomb somewhere in the city that was set to explode during the evening's rush hour. After executing one of the terrorists, the officer successfully obtained information that led to the discovery and defusing of the bomb.[82]

Despite the prevalence of these and other "success" stories, many experts, including former U.S. military officers, have argued that torture and other coercive techniques "do not work" and are "counterproductive."[83] In a media interview, New York Police Department (NYPD) interrogator Jerry Giorgio stated, "Everybody knows the Good Cop/Bad Cop

---

78. See, for example, Richard P. Conti, "The Psychology of False Confessions," *The Journal of Credibility Assessment and Witness Psychology*, Vol. 2 (1999), pp. 14–36.

79. See Arrigo, "A Consequentialist Argument Against Torture Interrogation of Terrorists," pp. 3–17. Arrigo describes three models by which torture interrogation can lead to truth: the animal instinct model, the cognitive failure model, and the data processing model. The animal instinct model describes the mechanism by which terrorists give up their secrets in a timely manner to escape immediate pain or death. Ibid., p. 6. In the cognitive failure model of truth telling, torture renders the subject unable to maintain a position of self-interest. As a result, he becomes suggestible or compliant under interrogation. Ibid., p. 9. Finally, the data processing model holds that torture provokes ordinary subjects to yield data (both true and false) on an opportunistic basis, resulting in the identification of truth when data is analyzed comprehensively across subjects. Ibid., p. 5.

80. Doug Struck et al., "Borderless Network of Terror," *Washington Post*, September 23, 2003, pp. A1, A26, quoting Marites Vitug and Glenda Gloria, *Under the Crescent Moon: Rebellion in Mindanao* (Quezon City, Philippines: Ateneo Center for Social Policy and Public Affairs, Institute for Popular Democracy, 2000).

81. Ibid.

82. Bruce Hoffman, "A Nasty Business," *Atlantic Monthly*, January 2002, pp. 49, 51–52.

83. Andersen, "Is Torture an Option in War on Terror?"

routine, right? Well, I'm always the Good Cop. I don't work with a Bad Cop, either. Don't need it."[84] Some interrogators stress the need to create dependency through relationship-based interrogation.[85] Saudi officials reportedly bring radical imams to interrogation sessions to build a rapport with detainees, who are later passed on to more moderate imams. Working in tandem with relatives of the detainees, the clerics try to convince the subjects over days or weeks that terrorism violates tenets of the Koran and could bar them from heaven.[86]

A particularly clear illustration of the disagreement over coercive techniques juxtaposes the experiences of French general Jacques Massu and his deputy Paul Aussaresses, both of whom tortured dozens of suspected terrorists during the 1955–1957 French "Battle for Algiers." In a 2001 interview, Massu confessed that "torture ... isn't indispensable in times of war, and one can very well do without it. When I look back on Algeria, it saddens me.... One could have done things differently."[87] In response to Massu's comments, however, Aussaresses vigorously defended both the necessity and efficacy of torture in Algeria.[88] Such contrasting views on torture from two similarly situated individuals suggest that the question of whether coercive interrogation actually works (and whether it is necessary) may ultimately be a highly subjective inquiry.

METHODOLOGICAL PROBLEMS

As the above overview suggests, the available empirical, theoretical, and anecdotal evidence does not yield a clear answer to the question of whether torture or other coercive techniques work at eliciting the truth. The primary reason for this, undoubtedly, is that many interrogations occur in secrecy, away from the view of inquiring social scientists. Because scientists cannot ethically replicate coercive interrogations through clinical experiments, their empirical data set is necessarily restricted.

---

84. Mark Bowden, "The Dark Art of Interrogation," *Atlantic Monthly*, October 2003, pp. 51, 69.
85. Dana Priest and Thomas E. Ricks, "CIA Poised to Quiz Hussein," *Washington Post*, December 17, 2003, p. A1.
86. Priest and Stevens, "Secret World of U.S. Interrogation," p. A1.
87. Adam Shatz, "The Torture of Algiers," *New York Review of Books*, November 21, 2002, p. 53.
88. Ibid. More recently, Aussaresses has suggested that the United States do the same to suspected al-Qaida terrorists. "In a January [2003] *60 Minutes* program, reporter Mike Wallace asked the aging Aussaresses if, in the case of a suspected would-be Al Qaeda hijacker, 'it would be a good idea to torture information out of him.' Oh yes, responded Aussaresses, 'it would be certainly the only way to have him talk.' Wallace followed up: 'And he could conceivably tell about the group that arranged the attacks on September 11?' Replied Aussaresess: 'It seems to me, it is obvious.'" Andersen, "Is Torture an Option in War on Terror?"

Part of the problem, however, is also methodological. In particular, the existing literature fails to distinguish between torture and less coercive methods of interrogation. Some techniques that fall short of torture (e.g., mild psychological coercion, sleep deprivation, hooding) may be more or less efficacious than the infliction of severe physical or mental pain, but current data does not make any such distinctions. Moreover, the available evidence does not evaluate the efficacy of coercive interrogation in light of the different situations in which it is used. The value of information varies enormously depending on whether governmental authorities have the time to check and rule out false leads.[89] None of the existing evidence evaluates the efficacy of coercive methods used in short-term, ticking-bomb scenarios vs. long-term, strategic intelligence.

Yet despite these limitations, one significant conclusion that can be drawn from the available evidence is that the use of torture is extremely likely to have highly detrimental societal impacts in the long run that may not be immediately apparent. Thus, although torture may yield immediate successes, the "initial gains from torture interrogation are later lost through mobilization of moral opposition, both domestically and internationally, and through demoralization or corruption of the torturers and their constituencies."[90] The most vivid illustration of this is the French experience in Algeria, where "torture not only failed to repress the yearnings for independence among Algerians; it increased popular support for the [National Liberation Front (FLN)] ... contributing to the transformation of a small vanguard into a revolutionary party with mass support." [91] Thus, the use of torture by the French in Algeria quite literally may have won the battle, but lost the war.[92] Indeed, the abuse of Iraqi prisoners by U.S. troops at Abu Ghraib demonstrates that in the modern world, where news and photographs can be transmitted instantly across the globe, the backlash and mobilization of moral opposition can occur literally overnight. Even if the use of torture and highly coercive methods yielded

---

89. For example, assume that torturing a suspect will yield one hundred false positives for every truthful statement. In the context of a short-term, ticking-bomb scenario, use of torture is likely useless as authorities cannot check out all the possibilities in time. This same torture of a suspect (yielding a 1 percent response rate) may, however, be enormously useful in the context of long-term, strategic intelligence gathering.

90. Arrigo, "A Consequentialist Argument Against Torture Interrogation of Terrorists," p. 23. In the words of F. Andy Messing, a retired major in the U.S. Special Forces, "[Torture] is a downhill slope if you engage in it ... every place it has been used ... it comes back and bites you." Andersen, "Is Torture an Option in War on Terror?"

91. Shatz, "The Torture of Algiers," p. 57.

92. For more on the use of torture by the French in Algeria during the "Battle for Algiers," see Pierre Vidal-Naquet, *Torture: Cancer of Democracy* (Baltimore, Md.: Penguin, 1963).

"good information," as some military intelligence officials in the Taguba report claimed it did,[93] it is difficult to fathom what information could be so valuable as to outweigh the tremendous backlash, particularly in Arab countries, that has been generated by the use of coercive (and likely torturous) methods by U.S. troops against Iraqi prisoners.[94]

A SUMMARY OF THE BENEFITS AND COSTS OF COERCIVE INTERROGATION

In light of the paucity of scientific evidence on the efficacy of coercive techniques, making intelligent guesses about the likely benefits of coercive interrogation is an extremely challenging proposition. As the anecdotal evidence indicates, it is implausible to suggest that torture or other coercive techniques *never* work. Yet, whether these techniques will actually lead to useful and timely information is unknown. Moreover, the evidence fails to distinguish between torture and less coercive methods of interrogation, and it also fails to distinguish between two possible goals of interrogation: to stop a "ticking bomb," or to develop—for patient confirmation or eventual discard—strategic intelligence leads about the broad plans, membership, funding, and organization of a terrorist group. This latter distinction is particularly important.

Take, as an example, a bomb feared placed at a crowded athletic event. Coercive interrogation (whether torture or less coercive techniques) can prevent the damage the bomb would do only if all the following circumstances are realized: First, of course, the person interrogated must in fact be someone who knows where the bomb was placed and where it will go off. Second, the interrogation must produce a truthful answer, not just an answer carefully chosen to satisfy the interrogator without revealing the truth. Third, the truth must be obtained in time to prevent the explosion. Fourth, the associates of the persons interrogated must be unable or unwilling to implement a substitute attack, replacing the one aborted as a result of coercive interrogation. All of these are requirements for the tac-

---

93. Hersh, "Torture at Abu Ghraib," p. 45. Despite these claims by military intelligence officials, the fact that several hundred of the detainees were released after the pictures at Abu Ghraib were made public suggests that many detainees possess little or no valuable intelligence information. See Robert Moran, "A Winding Road to Freedom," *Houston Chronicle*, May 5, 2004, p. A18; and "Some Prisoners Freed from Abu Ghraib," CNN.com, May 14, 2004, at http://www.cnn.com/2004/WORLD/meast/05/14/iraq.abuse/index.html (reporting the release of 250 prisoners from Abu Ghraib) (last visited May 16, 2004). A report conducted by the International Committee of the Red Cross quotes intelligence officials who estimate that between 70–90 percent of prisoners in Iraq "had been arrested by mistake." Bob Drogin, "Most 'Arrested by Mistake'" *Los Angeles Times*, May 11, 2004, p. A11 (quoting Red Cross report).
94. See Neil MacFarquhar, "Revulsion at Prison Abuse Provokes Scorn for the U.S.," *New York Times*, May 5, 2004, p. A18.

tical use of coercive interrogation to prevent a particular terrorist attack. Yet rarely would the authorities be sufficiently sure of each of these matters, all of which must be present for coercive interrogation to work. As a result, if the government were to establish a practice of coercive interrogation for ticking-bomb scenarios, most instances of coercive interrogation would be to no avail.

The situation is somewhat different when what is sought is broad, strategic knowledge about the terrorist organization—its membership, strategies, and finances. In such a scenario, two of the aforementioned constraints would not apply. The requirements of prompt results and the absence of a substitution effort by the terrorists drop out of the equation, leaving only the requirements (1) that you have the right person and (2) that you can avoid, by painstaking checking, acting on purposeful lies. As a result, it may be that coercive interrogation applied in this context may yield more beneficial results than in the ticking bomb scenario. In either case—tactical or strategic intelligence—the benefits would have to be adjusted downward to reflect how much of the valuable information could have been obtained another way (i.e., without coercive interrogation).

With regard to the costs of coercive interrogation, the most obvious cost is the suffering borne by the percentage of persons who are innocent but mistakenly believed to know the location of a bomb or valuable strategic information. Although the costs would be correspondingly lower for less coercive methods of interrogation, such persons would still have been subjected to moderate coercion with no societal benefit. The personal experience will be the same for those who do not satisfy the conditions of innocence, but the costs to the guilty may be diminished in such cases by the sense that punishment is deserved in any event.

Two less obvious costs deserve attention as well. There will be detrimental effects (costs) imposed on the interrogator himself in the form of psychological damage (which would vary depending on the severity of coercion that he applied to the suspect).[95] Also, in the significant portion of cases where, to escape the coercion, the person interrogated creates a false but plausible story, innocent people will be victimized, and their interrogators will bear the costs in terms of deep resentment as well as other foregone investigative opportunities.

As Israel's experience with coercive interrogation indicates, the use of coercive methods frequently leads to anger, inciting new recruits to help further terrorist acts. Moreover, coercive interrogation outside the United States will also have the cost of encouraging retaliatory and probably less moderated use of coercive techniques against U.S. military personnel.

---

95. See sources cited, note 72.

More broadly, the limits of U.S. willingness to coerce are likely not to be understood or adopted by other states that will find precedent and justification in U.S. action for abandoning their own treaty obligations.[96]

The long-term institutional costs of coercive interrogation are also substantial. The loss of a sense of moral rightness that comes with extreme forms of coercion can greatly undermine political support for a sustained effort in the country doing the interrogation, as well as among allies whose help may be needed in intelligence gathering. Indeed, France decided to abandon Algeria, in part because of such a loss of domestic support. In states with divided loyalties, where potential terrorists are likely to be found, use of coercive interrogation will likely reduce support for efforts to prevent terrorism. Cooperation in the form of arrest and extradition is also more likely to be avoided and denied by even friendly Western democracies if they believe they are sending individuals to be tortured or subjected to cruel, inhuman, or degrading treatment.

Long-Term Legal Strategy

Given the existing state of knowledge, it is the view of the authors of this book that the harms associated with some "highly coercive interrogation" (HCI) techniques, although potentially large, can nevertheless be sufficiently limited if adequate procedural safeguards ensure that the techniques are applied strictly in the manner and circumstances in which they are authorized. (In contrast, the harms associated with torture would likely be substantially greater than those of HCI, while the added benefits are unclear and speculative at best). A system that utilizes HCI has two important aspects, each of which is addressed in the recommendations on coercive interrogations in Chapter 1.[97] First are the substantive questions regarding which interrogation techniques should be utilized. Second are the procedural protections that ought to be required, assuming that a system of interrogation should be utilized. Presently, there has been scant attention given to either.

---

96. For a description of the "contagion effect" that would result if the United States believed that torture was acceptable as a proper means of fighting the war against terrorism, see Levinson, "'Precommitment and Postcommitment," pp. 2052–2053.
97. See "Recommendations: Coercive Interrogations," in Chapter 1 of this book. It is important to note at the outset that these recommendations assume that the central aim of interrogations conducted overseas is not to gather evidence for criminal prosecution, but rather, to obtain intelligence that can be used to prevent future terrorist attacks. Thus, evidentiary concerns about admissibility are not implicated.

SUBSTANTIVE GUIDELINES

The universe of interrogation techniques can be divided into three categories. On one extreme are those practices that constitute "torture" under U.S. statute and treaty obligations. On the other extreme are techniques that are permissible under the U.S. Constitution or the Geneva Conventions. Finally, there is the range of practices (e.g., sleep deprivation, hooding, etc.) that fall between those two extremes and are currently unregulated by either public guideline or statute.

Article 1 of the UN Convention Against Torture defines "torture" as acts that inflict "severe pain or suffering, whether physical or mental" for prohibited purposes.[98] Torture is prohibited *absolutely* by the Convention— "no exceptional circumstances whatsoever, whether a state of war or threat of war, internal political instability or any other public emergency, may be invoked as a justification of torture."[99] In addition, U.S. treaty obligations forbid officials from deporting persons to countries where they are "more likely than not" to be tortured.[100]

The first recommendation in Chapter 1 states, "Without exception, the United States shall abide by its statutory and treaty obligations that prohibit torture." This position is simple and clear: the U.S. government should not be breaking domestic or international law. If the United States wants to engage in torture, it must publicly withdraw from its international commitments and revise its domestic laws.

As noted above, the harms associated with torture would likely be substantially greater than those associated with other forms of interrogation (e.g., HCI), while the added benefits are unclear and speculative. There is no reliable evidence bearing on how much more effective (if at all) torture would be compared to other forms of interrogation or fact gathering, including highly coercive forms of questioning which are not prohibited by either treaty or statute. In contrast, the costs to be weighed against these uncertain benefits are clear and grave. French horror at torture by its military guaranteed the collapse of support at home for its war in Algeria—the same thing can happen in the United States. Moreover, the consequence of U.S. authorization of torture would be not only to sacrifice the moral high ground among our allies in our conflict with terrorists, but also to undermine drastically our efforts to display respect and friendship toward the other nations and groups within which the terrorists are a small minority. The United States would, in short, be creating large num-

---

98. Recall that the U.S. reservation to the Convention Against Torture (as well as federal statutes) limits the kinds of mental pain or suffering that qualify as torture to four specific types. See text accompanying note 44.

99. *Convention Against Torture*, article 2, para. 2.

100. See text accompanying notes 46–47.

bers of terrorist supporters. The departure of the world's economic, cultural, and military power from a flat prohibition on torture would constitute an invitation to every other country to itself abandon either the pretense or the reality of the worldwide prohibition. This recommendation, therefore, reiterates that the United States should abide by its statutory and treaty obligations and absolutely prohibit practices that fall within the definition of torture.

With regard to extradition, the authors' recommendation in Chapter 1 regarding "Transfer of Individuals" states that if past conduct suggests that a country has engaged in aggressive questioning of suspects, the United States should not render individuals to that country unless it has received adequate assurances that the individual will not be tortured. Under the regulations implementing the UN Convention Against Torture, "The Secretary of State may forward to the attorney general assurances that the Secretary has obtained from the government of a specific country that an alien would not be tortured there if the alien were removed to that country."[101] The attorney general must then decide whether the assurances are "sufficiently reliable" to allow deportation consistent with the convention. This procedure should be used whenever there is evidence that a destination country has previously engaged in torture. Upon deportation, the U.S. government should carefully monitor deportees and strictly hold the other government to its promises.[102]

In addition, there are situations where the United States is likely to benefit from interrogations by foreign governments that are not subject to these same restrictions. The United States should not be in a situation of simply delegating what it would not otherwise do itself. In those situations, where the United States has substantial grounds for believing (based on past conduct or, indeed, what it has been told) that torture will be utilized to obtain the information, Chapter 1 also recommends that the United States should in no way direct or support the interrogation, nor should it encourage other nations to make such transfers in violation of the prohibitions of the Convention Against Torture. The purpose of this recommendation is to ensure that the United States does not subvert the clear statutory and international standards that would apply to its own interrogators.

At the other end of the spectrum, although torture should be absolutely prohibited, any and all techniques that are legal under the Geneva Conventions and the standards for a voluntary confession under the due

---

101.   8 C.F.R. § 208.18 (2004).

102.   See *Immigration Relief Under the Convention Against Torture for Serious Criminals and Human Rights Violators: Hearing Before the House Judiciary Subcomm. On Immigration, Border Security, and Claims*, 108th Cong. 7-8 (2003) (statement of Susan Benesch, Refugee Advocate, Amnesty International).

process clauses of the U.S. Constitution should be permitted under the discretion of executive officials. Article 17 of the Third Geneva Convention requires prisoners of war (POW) to give only their name, rank, date of birth, and serial number when questioned. The article explicitly prohibits "physical or mental torture" of POWs or "any other form of coercion"; POW's "may not be threatened, insulted, or exposed to any unpleasant or disadvantageous treatment of any kind." The standards applied to criminal suspects under the U.S. Constitution are generally more permissive as a certain level of psychological coercion or deception of criminal suspects is permitted under the Fifth and Fourteenth amendments.[103]

An article in the *Washington Post* describing the interrogation methods likely to be used against Saddam Hussein provides a good illustration of the kinds of techniques that fall under this category. For example, the use of "good cop–bad cop" double teaming and false newspaper stories reporting betrayal of top lieutenants would all be constitutional under the Fifth and Fourteenth Amendments.[104] In contrast to hooding or sleep deprivation, these techniques do not constitute "cruel, inhuman or degrading" treatment, and thus are fully permissible under U.S. treaty obligations.[105]

The category of interrogation methods that falls between torture and permissible techniques under the Constitution or Geneva Conventions is difficult to define with precision. Complicating this definitional question is the issue of what label to affix to such practices. At first glance, it seems that this middle category of practices corresponds neatly with the definition of "cruel, inhuman and degrading" treatment under the UN Convention. Indeed, the U.S. reservation defines such treatment as conduct that is prohibited by the Fifth, Eighth, and Fourteenth Amendments

---

103. Among other strategies, a police officer may display false sympathy for the accused, falsely claim to have incriminating evidence proving the accused's guilt, or falsely assert that a co-defendant has implicated the accused in the crime. Dressler, *Understanding Criminal Procedure*, at 453–454). See also, for example, *Illinois v. Perkins*, 496 U.S. 292 (1990) (holding that undercover officer masquerading as burglar in jail cell to purposely elicit incriminating statements from suspect was permissible); *Frazier v. Cupp*, 394 U.S. 731 (1969) (holding that misrepresenting strength of case against suspect was constitutionally permissible).

104. Priest and Ricks, "CIA Poised to Quiz Hussein," p. A35. This may be a particularly salient issue given the classification of Saddam Hussein as a "prisoner of war" subject to the protections of the Geneva Conventions.

105. A more complicated scenario involves "false flag" operations where fake décor and disguises are used to make the individual believe that he is in the custody of a state that uses torture. Ibid., p. A35. Such a practice may very well violate the Convention Against Torture as it seems functionally equivalent to the "threatened infliction of severe physical pain or suffering," which is a category of mental harm prohibited by the Senate reservation to the convention. See text accompanying note 44.

of the Constitution.[106] What is permissible under the due process clauses of the Fifth and Fourteenth Amendments of the U.S. Constitution depends, however, on whether the information obtained from the interrogation is to be used in a criminal prosecution.[107] The authors' recommendation in Chapter 1 regarding "Oversight of the Use of Any Highly Coercive Interrogation (HCI) Techniques" defines all techniques that fall in the category between torture and those traditionally allowed for a voluntary confession under the due process clauses of the Constitution as HCI techniques.[108]

Simply affixing the label of "highly coercive interrogation" to this middle category of practices, however, does not solve the definitional question of which practices fall into this category. As mentioned above, the borders between torture and HCI and those between HCI and permissible practices under the U.S. Constitution and Geneva Conventions, are not marked with bright lines. Perhaps the best that we can do is to provide a list of techniques that are illustrative, but not exhaustive (note: all of the following techniques have been reportedly used or taught by U.S. military personnel):[109]

- putting on smelly hoods or goggles
- wall-standing for long periods of time
- subjection to noise

---

106.   Recall that the Eighth Amendment ban on "cruel and unusual punishment" is not implicated in the interrogation context. See note 53.

107.   Due process requires that in order for a confession to be admissible, it must not have been coerced or involuntary. See Dressler, *Understanding Criminal Procedure*, pp. 437–439. If the individual is not criminally prosecuted, however, the "coerced confession" standard is inapposite; thus, the only due process constraint on governmental action is the prohibition against conduct that "shock[s] the conscience," *Chavez v. Martinez*, 538 U.S. 760, 774 (2003) (quoting *County of Sacramento v. Lewis*, 523 U.S. 833, 846 (1998), which left open the possibility that deprivations of liberty caused by "the most egregious official conduct" may violate the due process clause).

108.   It is important to note that this category of HCI overlaps with the definition of "cruel, inhuman or degrading" treatment under Article 16 of the Convention Against Torture, but is not a perfect fit. The recommendations in Chapter 1 interpret "cruel, inhuman or degrading" treatment under Article 16 as those methods that would violate the due process prohibition against governmental actions that "shock the conscience," a standard which remains unclear after *Chavez v. Martinez*. The definition of HCI, however, includes all techniques that fall between torture and those traditionally allowed for a voluntary confession under the due process clauses. Thus, because some techniques that would result in an involuntary/coerced confession would nonetheless not consist of conduct that "shock[s] the conscience," the category of HCI practices covers a broader range of conduct than the category of "cruel, inhuman or degrading" treatment under Article 16 of the convention.

109.   See sources cited, notes 2–7. Although the combined or prolonged use of some HCI techniques may eventually cause severe pain or suffering amounting to torture, the

- deprivation of sleep
- deprivation of food and drink
- deprivation of medical treatment (borderline)
- exploiting sexual urges or religious prejudices
- preying on fears of the safety of relatives or family
- putting rats or cockroaches in cells
- keeping the prisoner naked and isolated
- threat of indefinite detention

The constitutional status of these and other coercive techniques is unclear in light of the Supreme Court's ruling in *Chavez v. Martinez*[110] and inevitably depends on the duration of their application, whether various techniques are used independently or in combination, and whether the detainee has access to family members or legal counsel. For purposes of this analysis, it is enough to note that HCI practices that shock the conscience are unconstitutional and thus qualify as cruel, inhuman, or degrading treatment under the U.S. interpretation of the UN Convention.

The authors' recommendation in Chapter 1 requires that HCI practices authorized by the president must be consistent with U.S. law and U.S. obligations under international treaties, including prohibitions on "cruel, inhuman, or degrading" treatment.[111] Accordingly, only those HCI techniques that do not "shock the conscience" may be authorized as a general practice. In extraordinary and highly unusual circumstances—amounting to the defense of necessity in criminal law—Chapter 1 also recommends an emergency exception whereby the president, upon a written finding of an urgent and extraordinary need, may authorize the use of HCI techniques that qualify as "cruel, inhuman, or degrading."[112] In no circumstances, however, may the president authorize the use of "torture" as defined by statute and treaty.

In addition to the substantive question of what techniques should be permitted, we must also consider the procedural protections that ought to be required. The experiences of other countries highlight two potentially dangerous slippery slopes that must be addressed when contemplating an

---

recommendations assume that use of these techniques by U.S. interrogators will not reach the level of intensity rising to torture.

110. See text accompanying notes 54–61.

111. See the recommendations in Chapter 1 of this book. Although some disagreement exists as to whether Article 16 of the Convention Against Torture allows countries to engage in cruel, inhuman, or degrading conduct under exceptional circumstances, see note 34, the ICCPR contains language that prohibits any derogation from its ban on both torture and cruel, inhuman, or degrading treatment. *ICCPR*, articles 4, 7.

112. See recommendations in Chapter 1 of this book.

official practice of HCI. First is the slippery slope with regard to the situations in which HCI would be used. For example, should HCI be used only in ticking bomb scenarios or also for long-term strategic intelligence purposes? Should HCI be used against all members of a terrorist cell or only those in charge of militant activities? Even though the Landau Commission recommendations sought to limit the use of coercive techniques, in practice, Israeli GSS personnel used such methods systematically against tens of thousands of Palestinians (with some estimates indicating that 94 percent of those interrogated by the GSS were subjected to ill treatment).[113] A second slippery slope concerns the kinds of techniques that are used by interrogators. As one Israeli human rights group notes, "From the moment that the psychological barrier and the moral-statutory prohibition on force are removed, the transition from psychological pressure to 'moderate physical pressure' and from this to torture is easier."[114]

In full consideration of these potential dangers, as well as the costs and benefits of a generalized practice of HCI, Chapter 1 recommendations permit the use of highly coercive interrogation techniques only under exceptional circumstances, and only under careful procedural safeguards to ensure that HCI techniques are applied strictly in the manner and circumstances in which they are authorized.[115] These procedural safeguards are spelled out in, and form the core of, the authors' set of recommendations in Chapter 1.

---

113. Israeli Information Center for Human Rights in the Occupied Territories, *Legislation Allowing the Use of Physical Force and Mental Coercion in Interrogations by the General Security Service*, p. 44.
114. Ibid., p. 43.
115. See the recommendations in Chapter 1 of this book.

Appendix C

Board of Advisors

The Long-Term Legal Strategy Project for Preserving Security and Democratic Freedoms in the War on Terrorism

All members of the Board of Advisors agreed with the necessity to evaluate the legal terrain governing the "war on terrorism." This final Report is presented as a distillation of views and opinions based on a series of closed-door meetings of the Board. The advisors have from time to time been offered the opportunity to express views or make suggestions relating to the matters included in this Report, but have been under no obligation to do so, and the contents of the Report do not represent the specific beliefs of any given member of the Board. The authors of the Long-Term Legal Strategy Report, Philip Heymann and Juliette Kayyem, are responsible for the final analysis herein.

DIRECTORS

Philip B. Heymann, James Barr Ames Professor of Law at the Harvard Law School; former Deputy U.S. Attorney General; former Associate Prosecutor and Consultant to the Watergate Special Force.

Juliette N. Kayyem, Acting Executive Director for Research and Adjunct Lecturer at the Belfer Center for Science and International Affairs at Harvard University's Kennedy School of Government; former Member of the National Commission on Terrorism; former Legal Adviser to the Attorney General.

Harvard University's Long-Term Legal Strategy Project is supported under Award MIPT-2003D-C-002 from the National Memorial Institute for the Prevention of Terrorism (MIPT) and the Office for Domestic Preparedness, U.S. Department of Homeland Security. Points of view in this document are those of the author(s) and do not necessarily represent the official position of the U.S. Department of Homeland Security or MIPT.

ADVISORS

Joseph R. (Bob) Barnes, Senior Policy Advisor (Department of Defense), The Nature Conservancy; Brigadier General, U.S. Army (retired).

Bob Barr, 21st Century Liberties Chair for Freedom and Privacy, American Conservative Union.

Rand Beers, Former Special Assistant to the President and Senior Director for Combating Terrorism; National Security/Homeland Security Issue Coordinator for John Kerry's Presidential campaign.

Michael Chertoff, Circuit Judge, U.S. Court of Appeals for the Third Circuit; former Assistant Attorney General for the Criminal Division at the U.S Department of Justice (2001–2003). On February 15, 2005, Michael Chertoff was sworn in as the second Secretary of the Department of Homeland Security.

Vicki Divoll, Former General Counsel (2001–2003) to the Senate Select Committee on Intelligence; former Assistant General Counsel to the CIA.

Paul Evans, Director, Police Standards Unit, London; former Police Commissioner, Boston Police Department.

Neil Gallagher, Homeland Security Executive, Bank of America; former Assistant Director of the Federal Bureau of Investigation's (FBI) National Security Division.

Mary Graham, Co-Director, Transparency Policy Project, Harvard University's Kennedy School of Government; Visiting Fellow, Brookings Institution.

Donald R. Hamilton, Coalition Provisional Authority, Baghdad, Iraq and Deputy Director, National Memorial Institute for the Prevention of Terrorism (MIPT), Oklahoma City, Oklahoma.

Eleanor Hill, Partner, King & Spalding, LLP; former Staff Director, House and Senate Intelligence Committees' Joint Inquiry regarding the Terrorist Attacks of September 11, 2001.

Lance Liebman, Director, American Law Institute; William S. Beinecke Professor of Law at Columbia Law School; Director, Parker School of Foreign and Comparative Law.

John MacGaffin, Former Member, Senior Intelligence Service and former Associate Deputy Director for Operations for the CIA; former Senior Advisor to the Director and Deputy Director for the FBI.

Robert McNamara Jr., Former General Counsel to the CIA; former Chief Enforcement Attorney for the U.S. Treasury Department.

Oliver "Buck" Revell, Founder and President, Revell Group International, Inc.; former Special Agent and former Senior Executive to the FBI.

Suzanne Spaulding, Chair of the American Bar Association's Standing Committee on Law and National Security; former Democratic Staff Director for the Permanent Select Committee on Intelligence in the U.S. House of Representatives.

Michael Traynor, Lawyer practicing in San Francisco, California.

Michael Vatis, Independent Consultant on Security and Intelligence Issues and an Attorney; former Official for the Departments of Defense and Justice and the FBI.

PARTICIPANTS FROM THE UNITED KINGDOM

Experts from the United Kingdom served as observers to the proceedings.

Chris Albiston, Consultant to the Director General of the Estonian Police Service in Tallinn; former head of the Police Service of Northern Ireland's (PSNI) Crime Department; former UN Police Commissioner in Kosovo.

Lord Alex Carlile of Berriew Q.C., Independent Reviewer of Terrorism Legislation, appointed by the UK Home Secretary to report to him and to Parliament; Head of Chambers (Chairman) at 9–12 Bell Yard, London WC2.

David Feldman, Rouse Ball Professor of English Law at the University of Cambridge and Fellow of Downing College, Cambridge; Judge of the Court, Constitutional Court of Bosnia and Herzegovina; former Legal Adviser to the Joint Committee on Human Rights, Houses of Parliament.

Sir Ronnie Flanagan, HM Inspector of Constabulary.

Tom Parker, Fellow at Brown University; former Special Adviser on Transitional Justice to the Coalition Provisional Authority (CPA) in Baghdad, Iraq and former Head of the CPA's Crimes against Humanity Investigation Unit.

Peter Smith Q.C., Deputy Judge, High Court, Northern Ireland; Judge of the Court of Appeals of Jersey and Guernsey.

Index

BCSIA Studies in International Security

Published by The MIT Press

Sean M. Lynn-Jones and Steven E. Miller, series editors
Karen Motley, executive editor
Belfer Center for Science and International Affairs (BCSIA)
John F. Kennedy School of Government, Harvard University

Agha, Hussein, Shai Feldman, Ahmad Khalidi, and Zeev Schiff, *Track-II Diplomacy: Lessons from the Middle East* (2003)

Allison, Graham T., Owen R. Coté, Jr., Richard A. Falkenrath, and Steven E. Miller, *Avoiding Nuclear Anarchy: Containing the Threat of Loose Russian Nuclear Weapons and Fissile Material* (1996)

Allison, Graham T., and Kalypso Nicolaïdis, eds., *The Greek Paradox: Promise vs. Performance* (1996)

Arbatov, Alexei, Abram Chayes, Antonia Handler Chayes, and Lara Olson, eds., *Managing Conflict in the Former Soviet Union: Russian and American Perspectives* (1997)

Bennett, Andrew, *Condemned to Repetition? The Rise, Fall, and Reprise of Soviet-Russian Military Interventionism, 1973–1996* (1999)

Blackwill, Robert D., and Michael Stürmer, eds., *Allies Divided: Transatlantic Policies for the Greater Middle East* (1997)

Blackwill, Robert D., and Paul Dibb, eds., *America's Asian Alliances* (2000)

Brom, Shlomo, and Yiftah Shapir, eds., *The Middle East Military Balance, 1999–2000* (1999)

Brom, Shlomo, and Yiftah Shapir, eds., *The Middle East Military Balance, 2001–2002* (2002)

Brown, Michael E., ed., *The International Dimensions of Internal Conflict* (1996)

Brown, Michael E., and Šumit Ganguly, eds., *Government Policies and Ethnic Relations in Asia and the Pacific* (1997)

Brown, Michael E., and Šumit Ganguly, eds., *Fighting Words: Language Policy and Ethnic Relations in Asia* (2003)

Carter, Ashton B., and John P. White, eds., *Keeping the Edge: Managing Defense for the Future* (2001)

de Nevers, Renée, *Comrades No More: The Seeds of Political Change in Eastern Europe* (2003)

Elman, Colin, and Miriam Fendius Elman, eds., *Bridges and Boundaries: Historians, Political Scientists, and the Study of International Relations* (2001)

Elman, Colin, and Miriam Fendius Elman, eds., *Progress in International Relations Theory: Appraising the Field* (2003)

Elman, Miriam Fendius, ed., *Paths to Peace: Is Democracy the Answer?* (1997)

Falkenrath, Richard A., *Shaping Europe's Military Order: The Origins and Consequences of the CFE Treaty* (1994)

Falkenrath, Richard A., Robert D. Newman, and Bradley A. Thayer, *America's Achilles' Heel: Nuclear, Biological, and Chemical Terrorism and Covert Attack* (1998)

Feaver, Peter D., and Richard H. Kohn, eds., *Soldiers and Civilians: The Civil-Military Gap and American National Security* (2001)

Feldman, Shai, *Nuclear Weapons and Arms Control in the Middle East* (1996)

Feldman, Shai, and Yiftah Shapir, eds., *The Middle East Military Balance 2000–2001* (2001)

Forsberg, Randall, ed., *The Arms Production Dilemma: Contraction and Restraint in the World Combat Aircraft Industry* (1994)

George, Alexander L., and Andrew Bennett, *Case Studies and Theory Development in the Social Sciences* (2005)

Hagerty, Devin T., *The Consequences of Nuclear Proliferation: Lessons from South Asia* (1998)

Heymann, Philip B., *Terrorism and America: A Commonsense Strategy for a Democratic Society* (1998)

Heymann, Philip B., *Terrorism, Freedom, and Security: Winning without War* (2003)

Heymann, Philip B., and Juliette N. Kayyem, *Protecting Liberty in an Age of Terror* (2005)

Howitt, Arnold M., and Robyn L. Pangi, eds., *Countering Terrorism: Dimensions of Preparedness* (2003)

Hudson, Valerie M., and Andrea M. den Boer, *Bare Branches: The Security Implications of Asia's Surplus Male Population* (2004)

Kayyem, Juliette N., and Robyn L. Pangi, eds., *First to Arrive: State and Local Responses to Terrorism* (2003)

Kokoshin, Andrei A., *Soviet Strategic Thought, 1917–91* (1998)

Lederberg, Joshua, ed., *Biological Weapons: Limiting the Threat* (1999)

Mansfield, Edward D., and Jack Snyder, *Electing to Fight: Why Emerging Democracies Go to War* (2005)

Martin, Lenore G., and Dimitris Keridis, eds., *The Future of Turkish Foreign Policy* (2004)

Shaffer, Brenda, *Borders and Brethren: Iran and the Challenge of Azerbaijani Identity* (2002)

Shields, John M., and William C. Potter, eds., *Dismantling the Cold War: U.S. and NIS Perspectives on the Nunn-Lugar Cooperative Threat Reduction Program* (1997)

Tucker, Jonathan B., ed., *Toxic Terror: Assessing Terrorist Use of Chemical and Biological Weapons* (2000)

Utgoff, Victor A., ed., *The Coming Crisis: Nuclear Proliferation, U.S. Interests, and World Order* (2000)

Williams, Cindy, ed., *Holding the Line: U.S. Defense Alternatives for the Early 21st Century* (2001)

Williams, Cindy, ed., *Filling the Ranks: Transforming the U.S. Military Personnel System* (2004)

The Robert and Renée Belfer Center for Science and International Affairs

Graham T. Allison, Director
John F. Kennedy School of Government
Harvard University
79 JFK Street, Cambridge MA 02138
Tel: (617) 495–1400; Fax: (617) 495–8963
http://www.ksg.harvard.edu/bcsia   bcsia_ksg@harvard.edu

The Belfer Center for Science and International Affairs (BCSIA) is the hub of research, teaching and training in international security affairs, environmental and resource issues, science and technology policy, human rights, and conflict studies at Harvard's John F. Kennedy School of Government. The Center's mission is to provide leadership in advancing policy-relevant knowledge about the most important challenges of international security and other critical issues where science, technology and international affairs intersect.

BCSIA's leadership begins with the recognition of science and technology as driving forces transforming international affairs. The Center integrates insights of social scientists, natural scientists, technologists, and practitioners with experience in government, diplomacy, the military, and business to address these challenges. The Center pursues its mission in four complementary research programs:

- The **International Security Program** (ISP) addresses the most pressing threats to U.S. national interests and international security.

- The **Environment and Natural Resources Program** (ENRP) is the locus of Harvard's interdisciplinary research on resource and environmental problems and policy responses.

- The **Science, Technology and Public Policy Program** (STPP) analyzes ways in which science and technology policy influence international security, resources, environment, and development, and such cross-cutting issues as technological innovation and information infrastructure.

- The **WPF Program on Intrastate Conflict, Conflict Prevention and Conflict Resolution** analyzes the causes of ethnic, religious, and other conflicts, and seeks to identify practical ways to prevent and limit such conflicts.

The heart of the Center is its resident research community of more than 140 scholars: Harvard faculty, analysts, practitioners, and each year a new, interdisciplinary group of research fellows. BCSIA sponsors frequent seminars, workshops and conferences, maintains a substantial specialized library, and publishes books, monographs, and discussion papers.

The Center's International Security Program, directed by Steven E. Miller, publishes the BCSIA Studies in International Security, and sponsors and edits the quarterly journal *International Security.*

The Center is supported by an endowment established with funds from Robert and Renée Belfer, the Ford Foundation and Harvard University, by foundation grants, by individual gifts, and by occasional government contracts.